AS AMERICA HAS DONE TO ISRAEL

John P. McTernan

As America Has Done to Israel

WHITAKER HOUSE

All Scripture quotations are taken from the King James Version (KJV) of the Holy Bible.

AS AMERICA HAS DONE TO ISRAEL

John P. McTernan
McT911@aol.com
PO Box 444, Liverpool, PA 17045
www.defendproclaimthefaith.org

ISBN: 978-1-60374-038-8
Printed in the United States of America
© 2006, 2008 by John P. McTernan

1030 Hunt Valley Circle
New Kensington, PA 15068
www.whitakerhouse.com

Library of Congress Cataloging-in-Publication Data (pending)

No part of this book may be reproduced or transmitted in any form or by any means, electronic or mechanical—including photocopying, recording, or by any information storage and retrieval system—without permission in writing from the publisher. Please direct your inquiries to permissionseditor@whitakerhouse.com.

1 2 3 4 5 6 7 8 9 10 11 ш 15 14 13 12 11 10 09 08

Contents

Dedication

This book is dedicated to the memory of my grandfather, John J. Kane, Sr. I learned the love of knowledge, reading, and studying from him. He passed away long ago, but not too many days go by without my thinking about him, and all the memories are wonderful.

Introduction

Starting in 1987, I first started noticing the direct correlation between massive natural disasters striking America and national events. These events included Gay Pride Day, Supreme Court decisions protecting abortion, and related events. Starting in 1991 with the Madrid Peace Process, I noticed the correlation between massive disasters and the United States pressuring Israel to surrender land for peace. The disasters always occurred within twenty-four hours of the event.

In 1997 I printed my first book, *God's Final Warning to America*, which documented these correlations of disasters and same day events. The national events and the massive destructive disasters, such as earthquakes, hurricanes, floods, and tornado outbreaks, began to number in the dozens. By 2001, the correlation of events was so compelling that I decided to publish a second book focusing solely on Israel. This book is the third in my series that deals with biblical prophecy and current events.

In November 2001, I published *Israel: The Blessing or the Curse*, which dealt exclusively with the United States pressuring Israel to give away sections of its land for peace. The title of that book came from Genesis 12:3: "*And I will bless them that bless thee, and curse him that curseth thee: and in thee shall all families of the earth be blessed.*" Genesis 12:3

states that there is a blessing or a curse associated with Abraham and his descendants, the Jews. The people who bless Abraham will be blessed, while those who curse Abraham will suffer curses. The Bible says that forcing the Jews to divide the covenant land brings a curse. God will judge nations that interfere with the integrity of Israel's borders.

I felt *Israel: The Blessing or the Curse* did an excellent job of detailing how curses or disasters hit America as the nation pressured Israel to divide the land, but there was also a blessing associated with Genesis 12:3. My book had only covered the curses, not the blessings. Many people questioned me about the blessing part of the verse. I had no examples.

The fact that I had no positive examples of blessings disturbed me. If the negative was true, there should also be blessings for all to see. I pondered this for many years, and finally found the answer in the history of the United States. As I correlated the history of the United States with how the country treated and blessed the Jews, an astounding parallel emerged. God blessed the United States of America at the very time the nation was blessing the Jews! *As America Has Done to Israel* shows this correlation. I go back to 1654, when the Jews first came to America, and work my way forward to today. The blessings are evident.

From its founding, America always blessed the children of Abraham. Unlike in Europe, the Jews never suffered organized persecution in America. For most of American history, the Jews were treated as equal citizens; however, the period from 1920 to 1940 proved an exception. This period was the darkest time in American history for the Jewish people.

This book is also an update to *Israel: The Blessing or the Curse*. In *As America Has Done to Israel*, I fully document the curses or awesome disasters that hit America on the days the nation pressured Israel to divide the land. This book opens in September 1938 with the Great New England Hurricane. It shows how God dealt with America when the nation wronged the Jewish people. I arrived at a balance in this book by showing the blessings and the curses.

I chose the name for the book from a Bible verse. The prophet Obadiah wrote of the time we are now living in. He refers to the time of Israel's restoration to the land as the approaching day of the Lord. The day of the Lord begins at the second coming of Jesus Christ. The prophet states that during this time, God deals with any nation in direct relation to how that nation interacts with Israel. If a nation blesses Israel, God blesses that nation. If a nation curses Israel, He curses that nation. It is that simple.

> *For the day of the Lord is near upon all the heathen:* ***as thou hast done*** **[to Israel]**, *it shall be done unto thee: thy reward shall return upon thine own head.*
>
> (Obadiah 1:15, emphasis added)

As America Has Done to Israel also touches on biblical prophecy. The key to prophecy is understanding God's plan for Israel. Israel becomes God's anvil among the nations. Israel's ancient prophets clearly laid out the future. I believe we are now on the verge of what the prophets call the day of the Lord, when the holy God of Israel judges the nations for rejecting the Gospel of His Son. It is also the time when God once again turns to His people Israel and all Israel will be spiritually saved at the second coming of Jesus Christ.

My hope in writing this book is that the reader will understand God's prophetic plan and how Israel fits into this plan. I hope the book generates faith in God's Word, the Bible, as well as boldness to stand with Israel. My greatest desire is that the reader will understand that the events involving Israel and Middle East are rushing toward a conclusion. This conclusion will be the greatest event of all time: the second coming of Jesus Christ. My prayer is that every reader will be ready for this event.

Through the years, I have spoken with many people about God and the Bible. On a number of occasions, the question was posed, *What proof is there of God?* A similar question asked is, *How do you know the Bible is the Word of God?* There are many ways to answer this question, but I have taken the approach that the authority of the Bible can be proven through the history of the Jewish people and the rebirth of the nation of Israel. The rebirth of Israel is the key.

Understanding why God called the nation of Israel, the history of Israel, and prophecy related to Israel, all show the awesome authority of the Bible as the word of God. If Israel is understood spiritually and not just politically, an entirely new and exciting reality of the time we live in unravels.

We are now living in the time that the ancient Jewish prophets wrote about. The nation of Israel has been reborn and Jerusalem is once again its capital. The reality of God and the Bible then can be proven through the fulfillment of what the Bible states about the nation of Israel. What an awesome concept this is—biblical prophecy is alive before our eyes!

The rebirth of the nation of Israel is unique among all the nations in history. The entire nation was destroyed—not once, but twice. Amazingly, after each devastation it came back into existence. Not only was the nation destroyed twice, but both times the vast majority of the people were taken captive into foreign countries. Yet the Jewish people always returned to the land. All this points to the uniqueness of Israel. This nation is not like other nations.

In 586 BC, the great Babylonian king Nebuchadnezzar totally destroyed the nation, Jerusalem, and the temple. This destruction resulted in nearly all the Jews being taken captive to Babylon. When a people were taken captive as the Jews were, they were usually lost to history. The Jewish people were different. They remained in Babylon for seventy years and then returned to rebuild Jerusalem and their temple. This occurred 2,540 years ago.

The Romans again destroyed the nation, the city of Jerusalem, and the temple some 650 years later in 70 AD. In 136 AD, the Jews again revolted against Rome. They were totally defeated and suffered the final dispersion into all the world. Very few Jews remained on the land after this war with Rome. The devastation was catastrophic. This occurred almost nineteen hundred years ago.

Israel should have ended as a nation and probably as a people in 586 BC, but it survived. Israel definitely should have ceased to be a nation in 70 AD, but as the ancient prophets wrote, the nation was literally reborn.

After ceasing to be a nation for 1878 years, Israel once again became a nation on May 14, 1948. In June 1967, Jerusalem once again became the unified capital of Israel. The Hebrew language was almost extinct, yet it was revived; today, the Israelis speak Hebrew—the same language as their ancestors. They kept the same religion while in exile. There is simply no other nation like Israel.

Several years ago, I took a tour of the biblical sites in Israel. The tour stopped at the museum of the Dead Sea Scrolls. In the center of the building was a large, circular glass cabinet in which the complete Isaiah scroll was on display. The scroll was set in the cabinet and illuminated so it could be read.

I asked the Israeli tour guide if he could read the scroll. He went to the scroll and started to read a two thousand-year-old document written in ancient Hebrew. He said it was somewhat hard to read because the letters were shaped slightly differently in modern

Hebrew. As he started to read the scroll, I realized it was Isaiah chapter 59. I had him read back in the scroll until he found Isaiah 53. (The Bible was not divided into chapters until the 1500s.) This chapter is one of my favorites in the Bible. To my amazement, he read this chapter to me.

A man whose nation was destroyed nineteen hundred years ago read to me a language that was nearly extinct! The English language did not exist two thousand years ago. It is not easy to read English from only two hundred years ago, let alone two thousand years ago.

What other nation is like Israel? What is the explanation for the preservation of the Jews and the rebirth of Israel? The explanation is found in the everlasting covenant God made with Abraham four thousand years ago. That covenant is the reason the Jewish people and the nation of Israel exist today.

Preface

When I was growing up on Long Island, New York, in the 1950s and 60s, I was raised for the most part by my grandparents, John and Elizabeth Kane. My parents named me John after Grandpa Kane. He was born in Ireland and came to the United States around 1912. My grandfather was a big, strong man. Early in his life, he worked in various mines and developed a powerful build. I can still see his huge hands.

Grandpa had no formal education, but he was highly intelligent. He seemed to know everything about everything. As a youngster, I can remember him building our house with his friends. He built the house with his own hands, block by block! Grandpa was always reading in his spare time. He would read magazines, newspapers, journals, and books. He read all the time.

The Irish have a reputation for storytelling and my grandfather was no exception. My earliest memories are sitting near him and listening as he told me about Ireland and his early life in the United States, now about one hundred years ago. I heard about World War I, the Roaring Twenties, the Great Depression, the rise of Hitler, and World War II. I vividly remember him telling me about participating in forming unions in the mines of Colorado and the horrors that followed. Many miners died in a conflict that erupted over the unionizing of the mines.

We always seemed to have company. Our door was always open and my grandparents' friends, neighbors, and relatives would just drop in to visit. We watched very little TV in those days, and soon after the company arrived, the storytelling started. When the men talked, I would just sit and listen. No one ever said I could not ask questions, but it just seemed out of place to ask. They talked about anything and everything. I was getting an education in history, politics, and life, and did not even realize it.

Most of the talk was about world and national events. When the talks would get around to local events, the two hot topics were the Great Hurricane of 1938, which devastated Long Island, and the German–American Alliance. The name for this Alliance was the Bund (pronounced "Bundt"), the Nazi organization in the United States. Its headquarters were in New York City and later at Camp Siegfried on Long Island, less than ten miles from where I grew up.

Grandpa with "Johnny Mac" as he called me

Everyone had harrowing experiences to share about the hurricane, and the stories were vivid with great detail. When I first heard about the hurricane, I was not old enough to fully reason. I can remember being afraid at the beach because a hurricane might come.

My family would go to Jones Beach State Park, which was nothing more than a sandbar off the coast of Long Island. At the beach, I was ever watchful of the ocean and ready to flee should another great hurricane appear. Relaxing was impossible, and I carefully watched the horizon while at the beach. I finally talked my mother in taking me to the other side of the sandbar to a beach called Zach's Bay. I felt comfortable when not facing the ocean. I never told anyone my fears.

I also heard frightening stories about the Bund. The stories detailed Nazi activities on Long Island. There were the candlelight marches at night. The Bundists dressed their children in Nazi uniforms and walked around the towns, "sieg heil-ing" each other. There were huge gatherings at Camp Siegfried where tens of thousands would congregate. This was all very confusing to me because I heard the stories of how terrible the Nazis were and how the United States fought them in World War II.

Photo Credit: Jacob Rader Marcus Center, American Jewish Archives, Hebrew Union College

Nazi youth at Camp Siegfried, 1937

One year my grandparents bought me a Lionel train set for Christmas. I loved that train set, but one day the engine stopped running.

Grandpa called around and finally located a hobby repair shop. He called for directions, and I was standing next to him listening. To my horror, I heard the word "Yaphank." I remembered stories about the Bund in Yaphank, and I was afraid. I thought the Bund was still active.

The time came to go, and I got into Grandpa's 1948 Plymouth. He said nothing about Yaphank, which seemed strange to me. I was concerned because of the Bund, although I still wanted to see youngsters like me dressed as Nazis. I kept ask-ing Grandpa if we were in Yaphank, and finally he told me that we were. With my train engine sitting on my lap, I looked all around for Nazis but did not see one. I stayed very close to him when we left the car and walked into the repair shop. The repair man did fix the engine. I never told Grandpa I was a afraid of the Bund.

In all my years of college and study, I never heard of the Bund activities outside my grandfather's house. After World War II, the Nazi activity in the United States was swept under the rug and scarcely mentioned again. I grew up in the 1950s only ten miles from the Nazi headquarters in America and never heard one word of it mentioned by others. I only heard about it through Grandpa Kane.

As America Has Done to Israel is the sequel to my book, *Israel: The Blessing or the Curse*. When I first wrote *Israel: The Blessing or the Curse*, I made no connection between the Bund and the Great Hurricane of 1938. As you read this book, you will see a truly amazing connection.

I had not thought of the Bund for over forty-five years, but one day in 2004 I was thinking of all the hurricane disasters recorded in *Israel: The Blessing or the Curse*. My mind drifted back to those memories about the Great Hurricane of 1938, and in a flash God quickened my mind to connect it with the Bund. All those stories I heard at

Grandpa Kane's came to life forty-five years later and now are a part of this book.

Writing this book brought back long forgotten but wonderful memories of my grandparents. One of these memories is worth sharing. My grandparents were good people. I grew up without any prejudice. They seemed to love all people.

My grandparents taught me to respect the Jewish people. Before moving to Long Island, New York, we lived in an Irish-Jewish ghetto in the Bronx, New York City. I heard lots of stories about my grandparents' life with the Jewish people in the ghetto. Actually, I was born in the ghetto, but we moved out when I was very young.

My grandmother told me she was good friends with a Jewish seamstress, who made clothes for our family. One day there was a banging on the door, and when my grandmother opened it, the woman was lying, hysterical, on the floor. My grandfather came and carried her into the apartment. The woman was sobbing, saying, "Hitler got them all," over and over again.

She was from Poland and had just learned that the Nazis had eliminated her entire family back home. Grandpa stayed with her until her husband came home. Grandma said the woman lived only a month or so after that day and died of a broken heart.

I hope this book is a blessing to all who read it. The facts reported in this book are irrefutable, but my interpretations of these facts are open to question. I interpret these facts through the Bible. God said of Abraham and the Jewish people in Genesis 12:3, "*I will bless them that bless thee, and curse him that curseth thee: and in thee shall all families of the earth be blessed.*" This book proves the promise is to be taken literally.

You will see from this book that Genesis 12:3 has been applied to the United States. The Bible is to be taken literally. The Jewish people and the nation of Israel are living proof of the authority of the Bible.

I always wanted to be like Grandpa Kane. He had such great knowledge and loved to share with those who would listen. He was always reading. I read a lot and love to talk, so maybe a part of Grandpa rubbed off on me. Grandma often said, "You are just like your grandfather." I sure hope she was right.

–John McTernan

Part One: Israel's Past and Present

CHAPTER ONE

Hitler and the Hurricane: September 1938

For the day of the LORD *is near upon all the heathen: as thou hast done* [to the Jews], *it shall be done unto thee: thy reward shall return upon thine own head.* (Obadiah 1:15)

September 1938 was a critical month in world history. The eyes of the entire world, including the United States, were riveted on Europe. Hitler was on the move and there was talk of imminent war. For the entire month, the headlines in the nation's newspapers followed the events in Europe. As one reads these newspapers, the feeling of desperation still screams from the headlines. Even after seventy years, the tension is still easily felt.

The source of all this tension was Nazi Germany and the Republic of Czechoslovakia. Hitler wanted to annex a section of Czechoslovakia called the Sudetenland, comprised mostly of ethnic Germans, as part of Germany. Hitler made the false claim that the Czechs were mistreating the ethnic Germans, who needed the protection of Germany.

The Nazi propaganda machine began to threaten imminent war unless the Czechs surrendered the Sudetenland to Germany. President Edvard Beneš of Czechoslovakia appealed to Great Britain and France for help, and thus the prospect of war loomed greater and greater each day.

Hitler came to power in January 1933. By September 1938, the Nazi war machine was in high gear. The Nazi army was gaining power, and Hitler was now ready to test the will of Great Britain, France, and the rest of the world.

Hitler had consolidated his power in Germany and was looking beyond its borders. In early March 1938, he forced Austrian Chancellor Kurt Schuschnigg to resign. Dr. Arthur Seyss-Inquart, a Nazi puppet, replaced Schuschnigg. On March 12, 1938, the Nazi army crossed into Austria. Hitler achieved his Anschluss: the union of Austria and Germany.

No nation objected to what Hitler did to Austria. Then, six months later, he wanted the Sudetenland and tested the will of Europe by threatening war. Little did the nations realize that this would be their last opportunity to stop Hitler before total war broke out.

Czechoslovakia was willing to resist the Nazis, but could not do so alone. The nation had a large, well trained 1.5 million-man army and could have defeated Hitler with help. Czechoslovakia's appeal fell on deaf ears; not one Western nation, including the United States, came to its aid. Anyone who stood with Czechoslovakia against Hitler was branded a warmonger. Whoever went along with the division of Czechoslovakia and appeasing Hitler was looked upon as favoring peace.

With the hindsight of history, it is chilling to read the newspapers of September 1938. Day after day, the papers were full of headlines about the Nazis, Czechoslovakia, and war. One could feel the tension as it mounted to a climax on September 29 at the Munich Conference. At this conference, Britain and France betrayed Czechoslovakia and appeased Hitler by agreeing to all his demands. The Munich Conference resulted in the dismantling of Czechoslovakia.

The following are just a few examples of the September 1938 front-page headlines that gripped the United States:

September 15, *New York Times*:

- Chamberlain Off by Plane to See Hitler
- Will Make Personal Plea to Avert War
- Prague Firm as Sudetens Battle the Police

September 19, *New York Times*:

- Britain and France Accept Hitler Demands on Czechs
- Will Ask Beneš Today to Surrender German Areas
- Prague Incredulous, Regards Action as Betrayal
- Roosevelt Urged to Act in Europe

September 21, *New York Times*:

- Britain, France Give Prague Hours to Submit
- On the Peril of Immediate German Attack
- Czechs Are Declared Determined to Resist

September 24, *The Providence, Rhode Island, Evening Bulletin*:

- European Armies Mobilizing
- Hitler Reported Ordering Czechs to Yield in One Week

September 26, *New York Times*:

- Roosevelt Appeals to Hitler and Beneš to Negotiate
- British and French Premiers Also Plea to Reich
- Terms Unacceptable; Hitler Talk to Attack Czechs

September 28, *New York Herald Tribune*:

- Roosevelt Appeals Anew to Hitler Against War
- Proposes Conference of All Involved in Europe
- British Mobilize Navy, Chamberlain's Hope Faint

September 30, *New York Times*:

- Four Powers Reach a Peaceable Agreement
- Germans to Enter Sudeten Area Tomorrow and Will Complete Occupation in Ten Days
- Nazi Demands Met

Great Britain, France, Italy, and Germany sent representatives to the Munich Conference. Czechoslovakia, the subject of this conference, was not represented! The country being divided to appease Hitler had no say in the matter.

Without the support of Great Britain and France, the Czechs had no alternative but to agree to Hitler's demands. At the conclusion of the Munich Conference, the Czech Premier Jan Syrovy stated, "We have been abandoned."[1] By March 15, 1939, whatever remained of Czechoslovakia fell under Hitler's control. In six short months, Hitler gained the rest of the country. It was clear to Hitler that the European nations had no will to stop him. Hitler's road to European and world conquest was now wide open.

Prime Minister Neville Chamberlain represented Great Britain at the Munich Conference. Chamberlain boasted after the Munich Conference that he achieved "Peace in our time," and "Peace with honor."[2] There was even a newsreel of Chamberlain disembarking a plane after returning from the Conference. In the newsreel, he is waving the treaty with Hitler in the air and saying, "Peace in our time." Huge crowds of excited people met Chamberlain when he returned to Great Britain.

Photo Credit: Hulton-Deutsch Collection/Corbis

Neville Chamberlain with Munich Agreement in hand, saying, "Peace in our time."

These crowds lined the route Chamberlain traveled from the airport to London. He made a speech about "Peace with Honor," telling the crowd, "A British Prime Minister has returned from Germany bringing peace with honor." The crowd cheered him wildly all the way back to London.

Looking back to the Munich Conference, it is almost comical from today's standpoint—except that millions soon died. A side issue of the Conference was the "Anti-War Pact" between Hitler and Chamberlain.[3] The Pact called for Germany to demobilize when Hitler was convinced the Czechoslovakian government was carrying out the agreements of the Munich Conference. Chamberlain made a statement about the agreement with Hitler that is truly tragic:

> We regard the agreement signed last night and the Anglo-German naval agreement as symbolic of the

> desire of our two peoples never to go to war with another again.

The world looked to the United States and President Franklin Delano Roosevelt for leadership in this crisis to avert possible war. On September 19, the *New York Times* reported the desperation of nations to prevent war in a front page article titled "Roosevelt Urged to Act in Europe." This article quoted an editorial from the Canadian newspaper, *Toronto Globe*, and several French newspapers. The *Globe* editorial titled the Czechoslovakian crisis, "Europe still waits in the shadow of Armageddon." It went on to state that only President Roosevelt had the leadership to end this crisis. An excerpt from this editorial follows:

> What is needed is not a plan, but fresh leadership.... There is but one man whom the world, if it could speak, would elect for the task. A man universally known for his humanitarianism...President Franklin D. Roosevelt.

The *New York Times* article went on to quote former French Premier Leon Blum. Blum wrote in the French newspaper *Populaire*, openly requesting that President Roosevelt intervene in this crisis. The French wanted Roosevelt to intervene and save France, just as President Woodrow Wilson had done during World War I. A translated quotation from the former French Premier follows:

> Is it not time that he address himself to Europe with the prestige of his person and with all the authority of the State whose moral or material support would be finally decisive in any general war?

Roosevelt did personally intervene and requested a conference addressing the Czechoslovakian problem. President Roosevelt made two direct appeals to Adolf Hitler. The first was on September

26 and the second on September 28. These requests called for negotiations and a peaceful solution to the crisis. Hitler and the other European leaders responded to the second appeal, and the Munich Conference was set for the following day. A part of the President's appeal to Hitler follows:

> Should you agree to a solution in this peaceful manner, I am convinced that hundreds of millions throughout the world would recognize your actions as an outstanding historic service to all humanity.[4]

President Roosevelt was a party to this appeasement of Hitler as he failed to stand with Czechoslovakia. He failed to confront Hitler and instead called for negotiations to end the crisis. Of course, these negotiations meant the dismantling of Czechoslovakia.

The Munich Conference was the idea of President Roosevelt. Afterwards, Roosevelt failed to comment on the results of the Munich Conference. Secretary of State Cordell Hull said there was a "universal sense of relief" over the peace settlement.

By September 1938, Hitler's attacks on the Jewish people were well known. The very core of the Nazi ideology was the destruction of European Jewry. The Nazis were not secretly carrying out this hatred of the Jews. President Roosevelt was well aware of what the Nazis were doing to the Jews. Surrendering the Sudetenland to Hitler would put thousands of Jews in grave danger. But no one seemed to care what the Nazis were doing to Jews. It was as if the Jews did not exist, and what the Nazis were doing to them did not matter.

The Nazis even tried blaming the Jews for the trouble over the Sudetenland. The Nazis created the tension and then shifted blame to the Jews. Hermann Goering, the second-highest ranking Nazi, used this tactic in a vicious speech given on September 10, 1938. In his speech, Goering stated:

> This miserable pygmy race without culture, no one knows where it came from, is oppressing a cultured people [Sudeten Germans] and behind it is Moscow and the eternal mask of the Jew devil.[5]

By appeasing Hitler, the American president was indirectly condoning Hitler's conduct against the Jews. Roosevelt's failure to confront Hitler about the brutality of his regime, paired with appeasement over the Sudetenland, encouraged Hitler to continue his course of destruction.

The nations cared little about the Jews and none came to their aid. They allowed Hitler to attack the Jews with virtually no opposition. On November 8, 1938, just thirty-eight days after the Munich Conference, the Nazis launched what became known as Krystalnacht, or the "night of broken glass." Krystalnacht was the night when the rhetoric against the Jews turned into organized violence and destruction of Jewish businesses throughout Germany. The Munich Conference turned out to be a boost for Hitler's Jew-hating agenda. When World War II started, he then attempted to destroy all European Jewry.

The negotiations at the Munich Conference started the dismantling of the Republic of Czechoslovakia. The nations allowed Germany to annex the Sudetenland. Poland obtained the Teschen district while Hungary received the remaining parts of Slovakia. It is truly ironic that Poland was greedy and aided in the dismantling of Czechoslovakia. In a very short time, Hitler dismantled Poland—not with a conference, but with war. Poland suffered greatly for failing to stand against Hitler.

Thus, to appease Hitler, Great Britain and France dismantled a sovereign nation and divided it into three sections. Now, with the Sudetenland, Hitler solidified Germany and gained a powerful industrial base. He was ready to turn east toward Poland and ignite World War II.

The fuse to spark World War II was lit on September 29, 1938. The Nazi army was becoming more and more powerful by the day. Hitler was honing the German war machine. This war resulted in the death of thirty to forty million people, including over six million Jews.

The countdown from the Munich Conference to the start of World War II was a mere 335 days. Hitler attacked Poland on September 1, 1939, igniting World War II. September 1938 was undoubtedly a critical month in world history.

September 1938: The Long Island Express

> If New York and the rest of the world have been so well informed about the cyclone it is because of an admirably organized meteorological service.
>
> (*New York Times* editorial entitled "Hurricanes," September 21, 1938)

From reading the September 1938 headlines, it is easy to understand why the United States public focused on Europe. The entire nation was caught up in the specter of another world war. People were glued to the radio, trying to get news about a possible war in Europe.

As terrible as Hitler was, an even greater immediate danger was headed directly toward the United States. A powerful category-five hurricane, or as it was called then, a Cape Verde Cyclone, was heading directly toward Florida. Hurricanes were called Cape Verde Cyclones because they developed near the Cape Verde Islands off the west coast of Africa. These storms then moved on a westward course toward the United States.

In early September, a tropical depression formed off the coast of Africa near Cape Verde. By September 10, it was a tropical depression, gaining power by the hour. It was heading west at about ten miles an hour. On September 18, it was near Puerto Rico and had grown to a monster category-five storm.[6]

In 1938, the Weather Bureau did not name hurricanes. If a storm hit land, or fell on a holiday, it was named for the location or date the eye made landfall. An example was the Galveston Hurricane of 1900. It was not until 1951 that the Weather Bureau named hurricanes. This hurricane was named the Great New England Hurricane of 1938 or the Great Hurricane of 1938. Its effect on the Northeast coast is still visible to this day.

Category-five hurricanes are among the most powerful and destructive forces in nature. These hurricanes sustain winds of 155 miles per hour or greater with an enormous wave surge as they come ashore. Since 1851, only three category-five hurricanes have hit the United States mainland. These three were Andrew in 1992, Camille in 1969, and the Florida Keys Hurricane of 1935.

In 1870, the United States created a national weather monitoring agency called the United States Weather Bureau. By 1938, the United States Weather Bureau had developed a hurricane monitoring system. There were hurricane monitoring stations throughout the Caribbean, and ships at sea radioed information about these storms. During September 1938, the Weather Bureau was closely monitoring all information about this extremely powerful hurricane.

On September 19, the storm was four hundred miles in diameter and still heading directly toward Florida. The entire state panicked as the storm grew closer. The storm began weakening to a category-three, then curved away from Florida and headed north. After the storm turned, the media and the nation had little interest and focused back on Europe and Hitler. A category-three is still a very lethal storm. These storms pack winds between 111 and 130 miles per hour, and can do enormous damage.

This curving movement was typical of most Cape Verde Hurricanes. As they approached the United States, the prevailing winds began to curve the hurricane northward. The hurricane then began a looping move, first to the north and then eastward out into the Atlantic Ocean. A hurricane depends on warm water—at least eighty degrees Fahrenheit—to maintain its power. Once over the colder ocean waters, these storms soon lose power and die.

On September 21, as the hurricane turned northward, Charles Pierce, a junior meteorologist with the Weather Bureau in Washington, D.C., tracked the storm. He carefully reviewed the weather charts and immediately recognized the danger this storm posed for Long Island, New York, and southern New England.

There were two powerful high-pressure systems that had the hurricane trapped between them. The hurricane could not curve eastward and out to sea because the Bermuda high pressure over the Atlantic Ocean was far to the north. This blocked the hurricane from making the eastward curve and turning harmlessly out into the Atlantic Ocean. The hurricane could not turn west because there was a powerful high-pressure system over Ohio. There was a strong low system over New England which would draw the hurricane to it like a magnet. The high-pressure systems forced this powerful hurricane on a direct northerly course. Long Island and southern New England were the targets.

Pierce explained all this to his superiors, but they refused to heed his assessment. The last major hurricane to hit New England was in

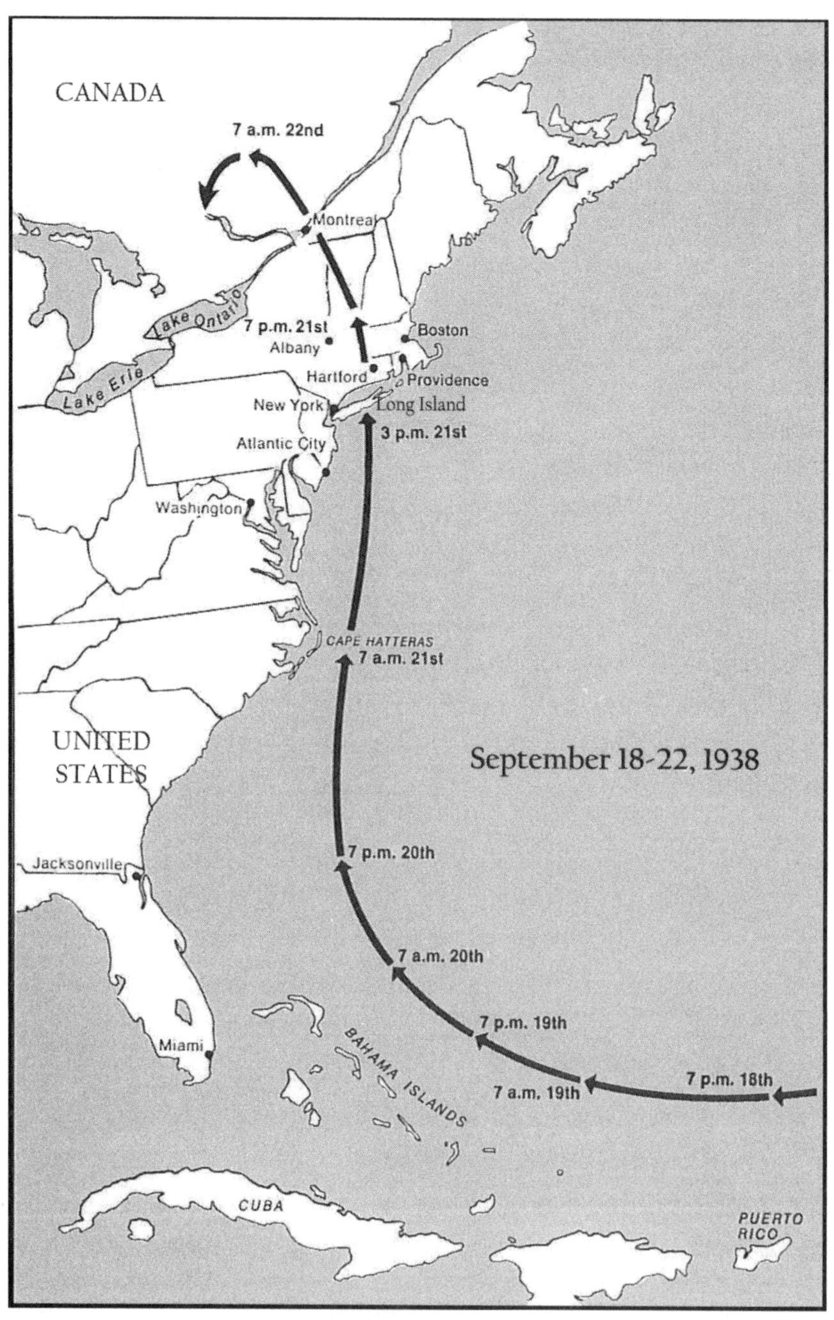

Map of the Great Hurricane

1815, and before that 1635. Category-three hurricanes hitting New England were extremely rare. Pierce was overruled by his superiors, who believed the hurricane would turn out to sea. In desperation, Pierce held a second meeting and was overruled again.

At 7:00 a.m. on September 21, the Great Hurricane was off Cape Hatteras, North Carolina. Hurricanes normally weaken north of this location because of the colder water. But this hurricane accelerated, followed the Gulf Stream, and failed to weaken. The two high-pressure systems squeezed the hurricane, causing it to tighten and accelerate. Both the tightening and accelerating greatly magnified the power of this storm.

Most hurricanes travel at less than twenty miles per hour. The winds within the hurricane can be swirling at great speed, but the storm itself moves less than twenty miles per hour. Picture the way a top spins, and you can understand a hurricane. The top itself spins very fast while it may be moving slowly along the floor. The Great Hurricane of 1938 began to rapidly increase in forward speed and approached seventy miles per hour—a record to this day.

The Weather Bureau advised the Coast Guard that the hurricane was turning out to sea, and to expect strong winds and high seas along the coast. The Coast Guard then notified the news services, who informed the public that the storm was turning away from the coast and out to sea.

The Great Hurricane of 1938 was bearing down on Long Island at seventy miles per hour and no one knew it was approaching. The only person in the entire nation that knew its true course was Charles Pierce, and no one believed him. The nation was watching Hitler in Europe and not the hurricane in the Atlantic Ocean. Everyone believed it had turned out to sea.

The meteorological equivalent of the surprise attack on Pearl Harbor, which occurred three years later, was bearing down on the east coast of the United States. No one was prepared for this storm. The storm would stretch from New Jersey in the west to Boston in the east. The eye of the storm was fifty miles wide; it was a monster.

The summer of 1938 was extremely wet in New England. In the weeks prior to the hurricane, Long Island and New England received record rains. There were torrential rains the week before September 21, and the ground from Long Island to Vermont was soaked, making trees unable to withstand hurricane-force winds.

The weather was also abnormally warm. A hurricane normally weakens quickly upon landfall, but the weeks of rain had resulted in soaked, moist land that actually caused the hurricane to gain strength. This made the Great Hurricane of 1938 incredibly powerful for miles inland. The eye remained intact well into southern Vermont. The storm also approached at the worst possible time. September 21 was the autumnal equinox, which created the highest high tide of the year. The storm surge rode on top of this high tide.

Blue Hill Observatory in Massachusetts, which was miles inland, recorded sustained winds of 121 miles per hour with gusts up to 186 miles per hour. Boston Airport registered winds of one hundred miles per hour. This massive hurricane affected the entire New England region. The hurricane maintained its strength well into Canada and finally dissipated near Montreal.

As the winds began to increase, no one paid attention on Long Island or the New England coast. By 3:00 p.m., something was radically wrong. The wind and waves on the ocean were fierce. To the south of Long Island there appeared to be a fog or mist on the ocean, but this was no fog. It was a 25- to 30-foot wall of water (called a storm surge) hurtling forward at seventy miles per hour and heading straight for the Long Island coast. Because this hurricane was moving so fast, it was nicknamed the Long Island Express.

The hurricane hit Long Island with such force that it registered on seismographs from New York to Alaska.[7] So many waves were hitting the coast that New England was vibrating and ringing like a bell! The coastline was dramatically altered by this collision with the powerful storm surge. Not only was Long Island's coastline altered, but all of southern New England's as well.

The storm killed more than seven hundred people. It is a wonder, when reading the accounts of the storm, that the loss of life was not ten times greater. There were sixty-three thousand people left homeless. The storm destroyed or damaged almost nine thousand buildings and over twenty-six thousand automobiles. The storm surge wiped out entire marinas together with thirty-three hundred boats and ships, and it destroyed most of New England's fishing fleet. Many New England rivers were already at flood stage, and the rains of the hurricane caused record flooding.

The combination of the tremendous velocity of the winds and the soggy ground resulted in the destruction of entire forests throughout New England. Most of the trees that survived the storm died within a few weeks due to the salt spray that had saturated their leaves. Large sections of the beautiful New England forests were gone. The fierce wind destroyed an estimated 750 million to two billion trees!

The Blue Hill Observatory recorded the highest wind gusts of 186 miles per hour. This observatory was 130 miles from the Long Island coast! The states of New York, New Jersey, Connecticut, Rhode Island, Massachusetts, Vermont, New Hampshire, and Maine all felt the effects of this hurricane. Hundreds and hundreds of miles of coast line were damaged. Providence, Rhode Island, was under fourteen feet of water. People drowned as they left work because they had no prior warning that the hurricane was coming upon them.

The floods cut road and rail lines, and bridges washed away. The millions of fallen trees took down most of the power and telephone lines. Cities and towns were isolated and destroyed without warning. The hurricane traveled so fast that it was impossible to send warnings ahead.[8]

This was the first time that an entire region of the nation was devastated by a disaster. The Galveston Hurricane of 1900 killed more people, but only in that city. The San Francisco Earthquake and Fire of 1906 destroyed more buildings, but the massive destruction was limited to that city. This disaster destroyed multiple states. To help these states recover, the federal government rushed in an army of 110,000 workers. This was a massive recovery operation, the likes of which the United States had never witnessed before this hurricane.

The nation's newspapers before September 21 were fixed on Hitler and events in Europe. Now the Great Hurricane of 1938 shared the front page headlines. Some of these headlines follow:

September 22, *New York Times*:

Hurricane Sweeps Coast;
11 Dead, 71 Missing, LI Toll;
80 Die in New England Flood;
Storm Batters All New England;
Providence Hit by Tidal Wave

Czechoslovakia Decides to Give Up
Crowds Protest, Cabinet in Peril
Chamberlain to Demand Guarantees

September 23, *New York Herald Tribune*:

Hurricane Deaths Mount to 439;
Half of Them in Rhode Island;
L.I. South Shore Is Devastated

Berlin Says Czechs Kill 16 at Border
Chamberlain Sees Hitler, Urges Calm

Hitler and the Hurricane

September 24, *The Evening Bulletin*, Providence, Rhode Island:

Toll of Hurricane Reaches 300; European Armies Mobilizing

September 25, *The Providence Sunday Journal*:

251 Dead; State Pushes Recovery; Hitler Gives Czechs 7 Days to Bow

It was impossible to miss these two awesome events when reading the newspapers or listening to the radio. They were linked together on the front page of every newspaper in the nation. Encouraged by the United States, Hitler was allowed to annex part of Czechoslovakia. This happened at the exact time one of the greatest disasters ever to hit the United States occurred.

At first glance, it might appear that these events were not related and that it was all just a coincidence. This was not a coincidence, but the fulfillment of a promise in the Bible. God told Abraham and his descendants in Genesis 12:3 that He would bless those who blessed them and curse those who cursed them.

The United States turned its back on the Jewish people and an awesome tragedy occurred, starting a pattern that continues until this day. There are literally dozens of examples like the Great Hurricane of 1938 where disasters strike America on the very day the United States meddles with God's covenant land of Israel. This concept is fully developed with numerous examples later in the book.

The hurricane was four hundred miles in diameter and the eye was fifty miles wide. The epicenter of the eye of this massive hurricane hit Bellport, Long Island,[9] where the lowest barometric pressure of the storm was recorded—an incredibly low reading of 27.94. This low pressure shows that Bellport was ground zero, where the eye of The Great Hurricane of 1938 made landfall with the greatest force.

The town immediately north of Bellport is Yaphank. This town played a key role in the connection between the disaster and the

Nazis. Located in Yaphank, Long Island, was Camp Siegfried, the direct link to Hitler and the Nazis. Yaphank became a major center for the Nazi movement in the United States.

Camp Siegfried

> Siegfried: a legendary hero in medieval German literature. He killed a dragon and bathed in its blood, which made his body invulnerable.

The 1930s were a turbulent decade in American history. The Great Depression and the tragedy of the Midwest Dust Bowl received most of the attention during these years, but the social and political unrest was just as difficult. The very soul of America was being tested. For most people, life was hard in every way during the 1930s.

Looking over the span of American history, the 1930s were the worst years for the Jews in America. During this turbulent time, the seemingly ingrained European hatred for the children of Israel tried taking root in the United States. A certain segment of America singled out the Jews as a people and blamed them for all the world's problems. Some Americans blamed the Jews for causing the Great Depression and creating communism.

There was a concerted effort to exclude Jews from mainstream America and demonize them. This is exactly what Hitler had done to the Jews in Germany and Europe. Once the Jews were marginalized and demonized, the nation was ready to accept physical attacks against them. This was the fertile ground in which the Holocaust could take place.

During the 1930s, the process of trying to destroy Jews was in high gear in the United States. This had been routinely done in

Europe through the ages, but not in the United States. The Jews did suffer in America during the 1930s, although the hatred directed at them never rose to the level it had in Europe.

The actual foundation for the attacks on the Jews began shortly after World War I. The great industrialist Henry Ford of Ford Motor Company was a catalyst for this hatred. Convinced that the Jews had started World War I and the Russian Revolution, Ford believed that communism was a Jewish plot to destabilize nations and take over the world.[10] This is not well known today, but Ford was at the very center of marginalizing and demonizing the Jews in the early 1920s. His legacy was not continued by his son and grandson, however; they reversed the anti-Semitism of Henry Ford Sr.

In 1920, Ford bought the *Dearborn Independent*, a small newspaper, to act as his propaganda outlet. On May 22, 1920, Ford began his attack on the Jews. The headline of the paper read, "The International Jew: The World's Foremost Problem." This was the greatest and most damaging public attack on the Jewish people in American history. The effect of Ford's anti-Semitism is still felt today.

By 1924 the *Dearborn Independent* had 700,000 subscribers, making it one of the largest papers in the country. Ford was trusted by the majority of Americans and was looked upon as a great American. His attack poisoned the atmosphere in America against the Jewish people. The type of anti-Semitism established in Europe now had a powerful voice in the United States.[11]

Many public figures were alarmed by what Ford was doing and denounced both him and his newspaper. Numerous senators, congressmen, lawyers, and clergy denounced Ford. Presidents William Taft, Woodrow Wilson, and Warren Harding all publically denounced this wave of anti-Semitism. Evangeline Booth, the head of the Salvation Army, also denounced the attacks on the Jewish people.

Perhaps the greatest damage Ford did was achieved by publishing a four-volume book titled *The International Jew: The World's Foremost Problem*. This book sold millions of copies and was translated into sixteen languages. It was translated into German and had a great effect on Hitler and the Nazis, selling millions of copies in Germany. In August 1938, Ford was decorated by the German government for his service to world industrialism.

By 1939, the assault on the Jews had reached its peak. There were dozens of anti-Semitic groups in America verbally attacking the Jews with methods similar to those used by Hitler. One such leader was Father Coughlin, a radio talk show host from Detroit, who had

Photo Credit: Bettmann/Corbis

Henry Ford receives the highest Nazi award given to a foreigner, the Grand Cross of the German Eagle. Karl Kapp, German consul Cleveland, presents the award, while Fritz Heller, German consul Detroit, shakes Ford's hand. July 31, 1938.

a huge audience of listeners. It was estimated that one-third of all radio listeners tuned in to hear him. His weekly magazine, *Social Justice*, followed the agenda of his radio show.

William Dudley Pelley headed the Silver Shirts, a pro-Nazi group. Robert Edmondson published the *American Vigilante Bulletin*, while James True published the *Dope Letter.* All were anti-Jewish and blamed virtually every problem on the Jews. These are just a few of the groups that formed to identify the Jews as the cause of all the world's problems.

Of all the anti-Semitic groups of the 1930s, one stands out above the others. It was officially called the German-American National Alliance, but was more commonly known by its German name, the Bund (pronounced "Bundt"). The core of the Bund was mostly made up of German immigrants. This was the true Nazi party in the United States.

The Bund identified openly with Hitler. The Bundists marched in Nazi uniforms with swastikas. They called for a boycott of Jewish businesses, and followed Henry Ford by blaming all evil on international Judaism. They promoted an extremely anti-Semitic book titled *The Protocols of the Elders of Zion*, which was produced in Russia and espoused fraudulent information. They did everything possible to attack the Jews.

The Bund made its beliefs very clear. They published what was titled *The Bund Declaration of Principles*,[12] an excerpt of which follows:

1. A socially just, white, Gentile-ruled United States.
2. Gentile-controlled labor unions free from Jewish, Moscow-directed domination.
3. Gentiles in all positions of importance in government, national defense, and educational institutions.

4. Immediate cessation of the dumping of all political refugees on the shores of the United States. (This meant no more Jews allowed into the country.)

The Bundists were serious Nazis and focused on the Jews. They went so far as to begin a petition to amend the Constitution of the United States. They wanted Jews excluded from all governmental functions. This petition follows in part:

> A petition for an amendment to the constitution of the United States, to elect and appoint none but Aryans to Public Office and Supreme, Federal, State, and Municipal Courts. The United States of America is a White Gentile Nation. The founders of the republic who gave us our nation were Aryan men.[13]

By the end of 1938, the Bund had sixty-five chapters across America with twenty-eight camps. The chapters were located in cities that included New York City, Cleveland, Detroit, Chicago, Milwaukee, St. Louis, Baltimore, Philadelphia, Pittsburgh, Oakland, and San Diego. The membership was never known, but estimates run as high as two hundred and fifty thousand.[14]

The Bund bought land near cities and established camps. They conducted parades, speeches, events, and marched just like the Nazis did in Germany. The major camps were Nordland in New Jersey, Hindenburg near Milwaukee, and Hindenburg Park near Los Angeles. But the largest and most infamous was Camp Siegfried in Yaphank, New York. This camp was similar to Nuremburg, which was the very heart of the Nazi movement in Germany.

Camp Siegfried was a forty-five-acre compound located about sixty miles east of New York City on Long Island. The Bundists rented entire trains running from Manhattan to the Yaphank station, called the "Camp Siegfried Special." They held torchlight marches at night just as the Nazis did in Germany. At Camp Siegfried, the Nazis initiated thousands of youth into the Bund.

The largest Nazi rallies outside of Germany took place at Camp Siegfried. This camp became the center of the Nazi movement in the United States. Of all the fascists groups in America, the Bund was the most extreme, and Camp Siegfried was the heart of the Bund.

The Bund liked Camp Siegfried so much that they decided to build a little Nazi village. In January 1937, the local township approved a tract of land for development. It was named German Gardens. The township approved names for the streets which included Hindenburg Street, German Street, Goering and Goebbels streets, and, worst of all, Adolf Hitler Street.[15] To this day, "Adolf Hitler" is still the official name for this street. Now it is named "Park Boulevard," but the deed map and town tax records for the homes still reflect "Adolf Hitler Street."

The newspapers reported the first large crowd at Camp Siegfried on September 25, 1935. There were more than five thousand people present, and it ended with a torch procession. On July 21, 1936, the rally centered on attacking the Jews. Italian fascists joined the Bund for a rally on September 1, 1936, and more than twelve thousand people attended. Some of the speakers were Bernhard G. Lippert of the German consul-general and Reverend Kropp of the Evangelical Lutheran church, New York City.

Two huge Nazi rallies were later held at Camp Siegfried. The first was on August 29, 1937, when as many as thirty thousand may have attended. Various fascist groups joined the Bund for this meeting. On August 14, 1938, the largest Nazi rally outside of Germany took place—on American soil! The *New York Times* reported that forty thousand people attended this rally.[16]

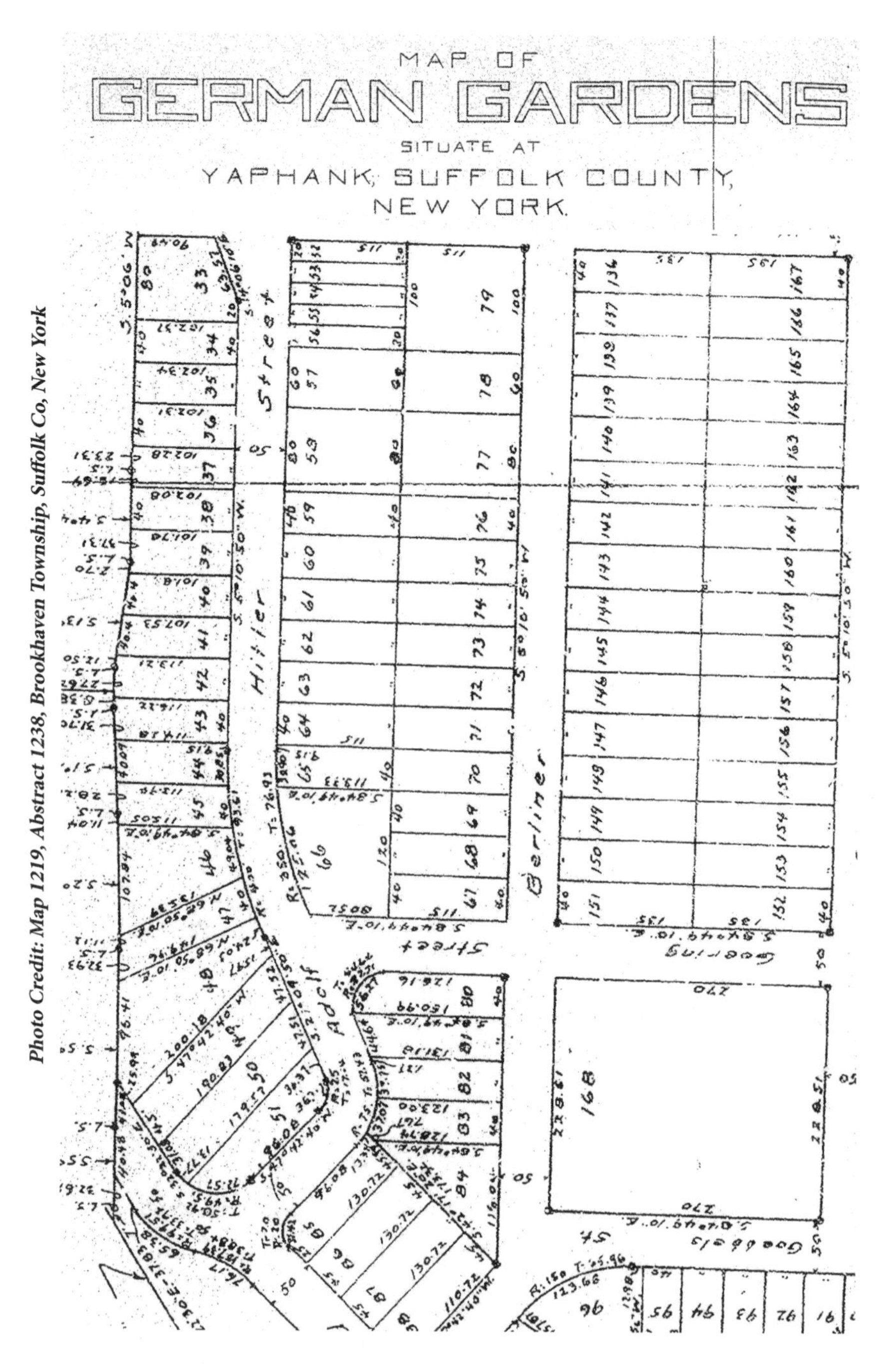

Photo Credit: Map 1219, Abstract 1238, Brookhaven Township, Suffolk Co, New York

Map showing Adolph Hitler Street, Yaphank, New York

Photo Credit: Bettmann/Corbis

Then: Adolf Hitler Street, Camp Siegfried, 1938

Photo Credit: Jesse McTernan

Now: John McTernan at the corner of Hitler St. (Park Blvd.) and Goering St. (Oak St.), Yaphank, New York

The Lord's Tempest

But the Lord *sent out a great wind into the sea, and there was a mighty tempest in the sea.* (Jonah 1:4)

On September 4, 1938, just three weeks after the largest Nazi rally in America, the Great Hurricane of 1938 was born. As mentioned earlier, the epicenter of the storm was Bellport, New York. The epicenter of the eye of the Great Hurricane of 1938 then passed directly over Camp Siegfried, a mere thirty-eight days after it had been the center of the largest Nazi rally outside of Germany.

Since 1635, this was only the third hurricane of this magnitude to hit Long Island and New England. The Great Hurricane of 1938, perhaps the most powerful of the three, went directly over Adolf Hitler Street. This happened during the time the president of the United States turned his back on Czechoslovakia and the Jews. Along with the rest of the world, the president was feeding into Hitler's plan of world domination and annihilating world Jewry. In September 1938, the national headlines were Hitler and the hurricane; this correlation was front page headlines on every newspaper and radio news show in America. It seems that the hurricane was a stern warning.

These events were not a coincidence, but an example of a fulfilled promise from the Bible. There are special promises in the Bible regarding the Jewish people and the land of Israel. For most of the history of the United States, the Jews lived quietly and without persecution; the 1930s were an exception.

You will see later in this book that starting in 1991 with the Madrid Peace Conference and the attempts to divide the land of Israel, incredible disasters like Hurricane Andrew, the Northridge Earthquake, and Hurricane Katrina occurred. These events fell on the very days that the United States was involved in pressuring Israel to divide its land. The parallels that began on September 21, 1938, continue to this day.

CHAPTER TWO

The Apple of God's Eye

For thus saith the L*ORD of hosts; After the glory hath he sent me unto the nations which spoiled you: for he that toucheth you toucheth the apple of his eye.* (Zechariah 2:8)

A direct connection between the Great Hurricane of 1938 and Nazism in the United States is not wild speculation. The Bible is the anchor for this connection. The key to understanding the Jewish people is not political, sociological, or economic; rather, the Bible reveals that the key is spiritual.

The prophet Zechariah stated that whoever touches the Jewish people to harm them touches "the apple," or pupil, of God's eye. The pupil is one of the most sensitive parts of the body. A finger poked in the eye inflicts tremendous pain. This is a picture of what happens when the Jewish people suffer persecution. The suffering gets God's attention, and not as a mere annoyance, but as a painful situation that requires immediate attention. The Bund had God's attention on September 21, 1938.

The everlasting covenant God made with Abraham four thousand years ago is a direct relationship between God and the

Jewish people. God created this covenant for several reasons, one of which was to bless all the families of the earth. Abraham's descendants are the vehicle for this blessing. The complete fulfillment of this blessing associated with Abraham comes through the Lord Jesus Christ.

God issued a universal warning. The people who blessed Abraham and his descendants would receive a blessing from God, but those who cursed them would receive a curse. The Bible presents a clear warning that continues to this day.

> *And I will bless them that bless thee, and curse him that curseth thee: and in thee shall all families of the earth be blessed.* (Genesis 12:3)

The Everlasting Covenant with Abraham

> *Which covenant he made with Abraham, and his oath unto Isaac; and confirmed the same unto Jacob for a law, and to Israel for an everlasting covenant.* (Psalm 105:9–10)

God established an everlasting covenant with Abraham and his descendants as a blessing to all people. This covenant focused on the land that is now called the nation of Israel. God deals with nations according to this covenant, and He never abrogated the everlasting covenant concerning the land of Israel.

> *And I will establish my covenant between me and thee and thy seed after thee in their generations for an* ***everlasting covenant****, to be a God unto thee, and to thy seed after thee. And I will give unto thee, and to thy seed after thee, the land wherein thou art a stranger, all the land of Canaan, for an* ***everlasting possession****; and I will be their God.*
> (Genesis 17:7–8, emphasis added)

The Bible shows that God passed this covenant on to Abraham's son Isaac and his grandson Jacob. God made the same covenant with them over the land of Israel that He instituted with Abraham. Each time the covenant was renewed, it included their descendants, the Jewish people.

The covenant passed to Isaac:

> *I will be with thee, and will bless thee; for unto thee, and unto thy seed, I will give all these countries, and I will perform the oath which I swore unto Abraham thy father...and will give* ***unto thy seed*** *all these countries; and in thy seed shall all the nations of the earth be blessed.*
>
> (Genesis 26:3–4, emphasis added)

The covenant passed to Jacob and his descendants:

> *And the land which I gave Abraham and Isaac, to thee I will give it, and* ***to thy seed after thee*** *will I give the land.*
>
> (Genesis 35:12, emphasis added)

Each time God reinforced the everlasting covenant, He included the descendants ("*thy seed*") of Abraham, Isaac, and Jacob. This means Jewish people are still under the everlasting covenant God made with Abraham; whoever blesses them will be blessed, and whoever curses them will be cursed.

When God makes a covenant, it cannot be broken because He bases it on His holiness. God would cease to be God if He violated a covenant.

> *My covenant will I not break, nor alter the thing that is gone out of my lips. Once have I sworn by my holiness that I will not lie unto David.* (Psalm 89:34–35)

It is impossible for God to break this covenant with Abraham, Isaac, Jacob, and the Jewish people.

God's Chosen People

> *For thou art an holy people unto the LORD thy God: the LORD thy God hath chosen thee to be a special people unto himself, above all people that are upon the face of the earth.*
>
> (Deuteronomy 7:6)

People often say that the Jews are "God's chosen people," yet very few know the reason for this expression. The reason is that God wanted to reveal Himself, and He chose Abraham and his descendants as the vehicle for this revelation.

Actually, God had several reasons for making the covenant. He wanted a people to bring forth the prophets and give the world the Bible. The Bible is part of God's blessing through Abraham to all the families of the earth. Israel became the central location for the prophets to write the Bible.

With the central location of Israel, the Jewish people could maintain the unfolding revelation of the prophets. Think of the impossibility of having a cohesive Bible if one prophet was from Europe, one from Eastern Asia, one from Africa, and so on. The prophets' central location in Israel allowed their message to be codified in the Bible and then disseminated throughout the world.

> *What advantage then hath the Jew? or what profit is there of circumcision? Much every way: chiefly, because that unto them were committed the oracles of God.* (Romans 3:1–2)

God called the nation of Israel as a light and witness to the surrounding pagans, who often committed horrible acts such as child sacrifice.

> *I have declared, and have saved, and I have showed, when there was no strange god among you: therefore ye are my witnesses, saith the LORD, that I am God.* (Isaiah 43:12)

God made the covenant, which included a people, a culture, and a genealogy, in order to bring the Messiah, the Savior of mankind, into the world. The Messiah had to be the son of David, the son of Abraham. Through Him, God blesses all the families of the earth.

The location:

> *But thou, Bethlehem Ephratah, though thou be little among the thousands of Judah, yet out of thee shall he come forth unto me that is to be ruler in Israel; whose goings forth have been from of old, from everlasting.* (Micah 5:2)

The genealogy:

> *The book of the generation of Jesus Christ, the son of David, the son of Abraham. Abraham begat Isaac; and Isaac begat Jacob; and Jacob begat Judas and his brethren.* (Matthew 1:1–2)

This everlasting covenant is a way of testing the Bible's authority as God's word. The fulfillment of the everlasting covenant is a way of witnessing God's mighty power and the authority of His word.

The prophet Ezekiel wrote about a day in the future when a huge confederation of nations will try to destroy the regathered nation of Israel. God supernaturally destroys these nations to defend His covenant land. The prophet then stated what happens after this awesome judgment. God uses the tiny nation of Israel so the entire world can see His faithfulness to His covenant people.

> *Thus will I magnify myself, and sanctify myself; and I will be known in the eyes of many nations, and they shall know that I am the* LORD. (Ezekiel 38:23)

The Bible emphatically reveals in many places that God will deal in judgment with nations that attempt to destroy the covenant people. Tyrants and despots through the centuries have tried to destroy Jews or prevent the rebirth of Israel. All these attempts have failed. The tyrants are gone, but Jews are still here and Israel is once again a nation.

> *For it is the day of the LORD's vengeance, and the year of recompenses for the controversy of Zion.* (Isaiah 34:8)

Notice in Isaiah 34:8 that the Bible uses the word "*Zion*." Zion can have five different applications depending on the context. In the Old Testament the word can mean the people or nation of Israel. It can also mean the city of Jerusalem or the location of the temple within Jerusalem. This location is Mt. Zion. The New Testament refers to Zion as heaven. There is no doubt when studying the Bible that God is a Zionist. He is the one creating the events restoring the nation of Israel or Zion.

God had clearly linked His name with Abraham and his descendants: "*And they shall put my name upon the children of Israel; and I will bless them*" (Numbers 6:27).

CHAPTER THREE

The People Whose God Is Jehovah

> May the Children of the Stock of Abraham, who dwell in this land, continue to merit and enjoy the good will of the other Inhabitants; while everyone shall sit under his own vine and fig tree, and there shall be none to make him afraid.[1]
>
> –President George Washington, 1790

In 2004, the Jewish people celebrated their 350th anniversary in America. Most people are astonished to find out that Jewish colonists first arrived in America in 1654. They arrived thirty years before the Germans and fifty years before the Scots-Irish! The Jewish people experienced a very long and successful history in pre-United States America. This success continued after the creation of the United States, and continues today.

Jews never suffered in America as they did in European nations. The United States has been a great blessing to the Israelites, as Americans called them three hundred years ago. In American history there is no record of even one organized government attack on them, nor have there been any attacks sanctioned by religious organizations.

A large percentage of Israelites supported the American Revolution and joined the army. Many were heroes who gave all they had for America, including their lives. They won the respect of the American people. They fought in great numbers during the Civil War, and at least six won the Medal of Honor. One, from the "Stock of Abraham," as the non-Jews called them, became a major general.

The Jewish people first came to America from Brazil in 1654. To escape persecution, many Portuguese Jews fled to Brazil, which was then a Dutch colony. Holland lost the colony to Portugal, and the Jews fled. One ship with twenty-three Jews arrived in New Amsterdam, now New York City, late in September 1654. This was the beginning of Jewish migration to the United States.[2]

Peter Stuyvesant, governor at that time, objected to the Jews and contacted Holland about their presence in New Amsterdam. His orders allowing the Jews to stay are a hallmark of America to this day. When the Dutch gave Jews religious freedom 350 years ago, they sowed some of the first seeds of religious freedom in this nation. This freedom has endured to the present day. Stuyvesant's superiors ordered him to:

> Shut your eyes, at least do not force people's consciences, but allow everyone his own belief, as long as he behaves quietly and legally, gives no offense to his neighbor and does not oppose the government.[3]

Great Britain renamed the city New York when they defeated the Dutch in 1667, and also guaranteed Jews full rights to worship, trade, and property ownership. Most Jews became merchants and were involved in trade.

By the time of the Revolutionary War, Jews were full citizens who suffered virtually no institutionalized prejudice. There were no laws specifically enacted against the Jewish people, and no Jews were forced to convert to Christianity. History does not report any Jewish businesses or homes destroyed because of their religion. The Jewish community was only about three thousand, but they fully blended into America.

When the Revolution started, almost the entire Jewish community joined the American cause. This was the time the Hebrews began to shine in American history. Jewish merchants rallied to the American Revolution. They supplied the army with clothing, guns, powder, and food. Jewish merchants used their ships as blockade runners bringing supplies from Europe. Aaron Lopez of Newport, Rhode Island, used his 130 ships to supply the American army. Most Jewish merchants had lost everything by the end of the war.[4]

Some of the Hebrews who fought in the war attained high military ranks. For example, the British seriously wounded Solomon Bush in battle and captured him. They soon freed him, and he rose to the rank of lieutenant colonel in the Continental army. Francis Salvador was the first Jewish man elected to a state legislature. South Carolina elected him to the General Assembly. Later the people elected him as a delegate to the state's Revolutionary Congress. In 1776, he was killed in battle.[5]

George Washington's personal physician, Dr. Philip Moses Russell, was a Jew. He was with the General at Valley Forge and suffered through the terrible winter. But the most famous Jewish person of the Revolution was Haym Salomon.

The "Little Jew Broker"

Robert Morris, the first Treasurer of the United States, affectionately called Haym Salomon the "little Jew broker."[6] Salomon was born in Poland in 1740 and traveled throughout Europe. He became fluent in seven languages and an expert in international finances. He came to America in 1772 and immediately joined the Sons of Liberty in New York City. The Sons of Liberty were among the most radical revolutionary groups in America. He also became a very successful businessman in New York City.

When the war broke out, he stayed in New York and worked behind the British lines. The British captured him as a spy and imprisoned him, but he was later freed. He was captured a second time as a spy and sentenced to death. Salomon was able to escape and settle in Philadelphia, but lost all his wealth in the process. In Philadelphia, he started over again and established a very successful brokerage firm. He became the top broker in America due to his fluency in languages, extreme honesty, and knowledge of international finances.

Photo Credit: Jacob Marcus Center, American Jewish Archives, Hebrew Union College

Portrait of Haym Salomon, 1740–1785

In 1781, the American currency collapsed and the treasury was empty. The nation was bankrupt. America had no funds for continuing the war or paying its debts. Robert Morris, Secretary of the Treasury, turned to Salomon for help, and the skill, knowledge, honesty, and generosity of Salomon kept America financially solvent. America at this time had no banking system, but Salomon's own credit backed the finances of the United

States! Later, when Morris established a bank, Salomon was its first and largest depositor.

Salomon personally made large loans with no interest to many of the leading Americans of the Revolution, such as: future Presidents James Madison, Thomas Jefferson, and James Monroe, as well as generals von Steuben and St Clair. Salomon personally supported the Spanish ambassador, which promoted Spanish goodwill toward America.

Morris made seventy-five entries in his diary about turning to the "little Jewish broker" for financial help. Salomon was perhaps the person most responsible for establishing the credit of the United States in Europe. He was backing the loans! The Continental Congress appointed him "The Official Broker to the Office of Finance of the United States."

Salomon died in 1785 of a sickness he contracted while in prison in 1776. He was only forty-five years old and died penniless. The exact amount of money the United States owed Salomon was never determined, but a Congressional investigation produced evidence that it was approximately 656 thousand dollars. The exact amount was never actually determined, however, because all of Salomon's records were destroyed in 1814 when the British burned Washington, D.C.

Haym Salomon was a true American patriot who gave his all to America. He helped financially stabilize America during a critical time when the nation was at its economic worst. During Salomon's lifetime, he never received the recognition due him. In 1975 the United States issued a commemorative stamp in his honor. On the back of the stamp was printed:

> Financial hero-businessman and broker Haym Salomon was responsible for raising most of the money

needed to finance the American Revolution and later saved the new nation from collapse.

George Washington's Letters[7]

When George Washington was elected President in 1789, the Jewish centers around the nation sent him letters of congratulation. His response to these letters set the future tone for Jews in America. At the very beginning of the United States, President Washington manifested the attitude of Americans toward Jewish people.

In his letter addressed to the Hebrews in Savannah, Georgia, the President connected the God of Israel, who delivered the Jews from Egypt, to the same God who established the United States. He asked the God of Israel to bless the Hebrews with the "dews of heaven," and he requested the material and spiritual blessings for the people whose God is Jehovah! This letter in part follows:

> May the same wonder-working Deity, who long since delivered the Hebrews from their Egyptian oppressors, planted them in a promised land, whose providential agency has lately been conspicuous in establishing these United States as an independent nation, still continue to water them with the dews of heaven and make the inhabitants of every denomination participate in the temporal and spiritual blessings of that people whose God is Jehovah.
>
> (See Addendum A for the complete letter.)

President Washington also wrote to the Hebrews in Newport, Rhode Island. His letter to the "Children of the Stock of Abraham" contained the same type of blessings. He wanted Jews to have the goodwill of the nation, and he thought of them as equals. This is truly amazing in the light of the worldwide history of the Jewish people. In 1790, Jews in America were the freest on earth. Part of the letter follows:

> May the Children of the Stock of Abraham, who dwell in this land, continue to merit and enjoy the good will of the other Inhabitants; while everyone shall sit under his own vine and fig tree, and there shall be none to make him afraid....May the father of all mercies scatter light and not darkness in our paths, and make us all in our several vocations useful here, and in his own due time and way everlastingly happy. (See Addendum B for the complete letter)

The President clearly referred to Micah 4:4 when he expressed his desire for the children of Abraham to each sit under his own vine and fig tree. The context is in verse three, where the Messiah is presented as the Judge of all the nations. He will end war and bring universal peace. The President chose these tremendous verses to pronounce a blessing on the Children of Abraham.

> *And he shall judge among many people, and rebuke strong nations afar off; and they shall beat their swords into plowshares, and their spears into pruninghooks: nation shall not lift up a sword against nation, neither shall they learn war any more. But they shall sit every man under his vine and under his fig tree; and none shall make them afraid: for the mouth of the* LORD *of hosts hath spoken it.* (Micah 4:3–4)

The President wanted the United States to be like the time of the Messiah's reign for the Jews. This was a far cry from the tyrants of Europe throughout the ages and the horrors they inflicted on Jewish people. What nation ever exhibited such favor to the Jewish people as America? What other nation started with such a favorable attitude toward the Jewish people? America is certainly unique among the nations in this respect.

"Stand By the Flag"

The attitude of President Washington persisted as America developed. After the Revolution, Jewish immigration from Europe picked up, especially in the 1820s. The immigrants came mostly from Germany and central Europe. By the time of the Civil War, there were approximately two hundred thousand Jews in America. They excelled as merchants, bankers, lawyers, doctors, and educators.

The American acceptance of Jews even reached into foreign policy. In 1840, Arabs were killing and torturing Jews in Damascus. The American Jewish community brought this to the attention of President Martin Van Buren. The Ottoman Empire ruled over Syria at this time. The President directed the American ambassador to ask the Ottoman ruler to stop the killing and torturing of Jews, stating that all of America was against this suffering.

President Van Buren then made statements in his letter to the Ottomans that were very revealing about America's attitude toward Jewish people. The President cited America's institutions and said, "They place upon the same footing the worshipers of God, of every faith and form." He followed by stating this intervention was "on behalf of an oppressed and persecuted race, among whose kindred are found some of the most worthy and patriotic of [American] citizens."[8] The Ottoman Empire responded, and the killing stopped.

Jews reached all levels of American society. David Yulee of Florida and Judah P. Benjamin of Louisiana were elected to the US Senate. During this period, the governor of Georgia and mayors of Richmond, Virginia, and Charleston, South Carolina, were Jewish. There were Jews in the first classes at both West Point and Annapolis. Mordecai Noah served as the United States Consul to Tunis. He was the editor of six newspapers and served as an Associate Judge in the New York Court of Sessions. August Belmont was the chairman of the Democratic National Committee from 1860 to 1872.

Uriah P. Levy was the first Jewish man to reach the rank of commodore in the United States Navy. Commodore would equal today's rank of admiral. Prior to the Civil War, Commodore Levy commanded the Mediterranean squadron. He had a distinguished naval career that spanned fifty years from 1812 to 1862. He was one of the naval giants of his age.

Commodore Levy was born in 1792 as a fifth-generation American. His great-great grandfather was Samuel Nunez, one of the founders of Savannah, Georgia. Levy fought in the War of 1812. During the war, he served on the *USS Argus* and was captured by the British. He spent sixteen months as a prisoner of war. After the war, he rose through the ranks and became a commodore. He was the leading reformer in the movement to stop the flogging of sailors for punishment. In 1850, after years of pressure, Congress finally passed an anti-flogging law. In honor of Levy, both a World War II destroyer (USS *Levy* DE-162) and the Jewish chapel at the US Naval Academy in Annapolis were named after the Commodore.

Photo Credit: Naval Historical Foundation

Portrait of Commodore Uriah Levy (1792–1862) holding a scroll inscribed "Author of the Abolition of Flogging in the Navy of the United States."

The Commodore was a great admirer of Thomas

Jefferson. In 1836, he bought Jefferson's house and estate, Monticello. The house was in decay, and he repaired and restored it before opening Monticello to the public. Today Commodore Levy is considered the first to have restored an historic American site. In a final gesture to President Jefferson, Levy commissioned the creation of a life-sized statue of the President and donated it to Congress. This statue currently stands in the Capitol Rotunda, and is the only privately commissioned piece of artwork in the Capitol building.

The Civil War once again showed how Jewish people acted as patriots and American citizens. At this time, the *Jewish Messenger* was one of the most influential Jewish newspapers in America. This was a national paper published weekly.

On December 28, 1860, as the war approached, Samuel Mayer Isaacs, the editor, wrote an astonishing editorial entitled "A Day of Prayer," a moving account of how blessed Jews had been in America. He recounted the freedoms and equality the Jews had enjoyed as Americans under the Constitution as equal citizens. Isaacs wrote how Judaism was not an impediment to advancement in the United States, and that America was the first republic to recognize Jews as absolute equals.

He then read directly from President George Washington's 1790 letter to the Hebrews in Newport. The quotation is the one taken from Micah 4:4, stating that Jews can sit "*under his vine and under his fig tree; and none shall make them afraid.*" This amazing editorial by Samuel Mayer Isaacs follows in part:

> The Union for whose prosperity we ask Divine aid, has been the source of happiness for our ancestors and ourselves. Under the protection of the freedom guaranteed us by the Constitution, we have lived in the enjoyment of full and perfect equality with our fellow citizens....We are enabled to worship the

> Supreme Being according to the dictates of conscience, we can maintain the position to which our abilities entitle us, without our religious opinions being an impediment to advancement....This Republic was the first to recognize our claims to absolute equality, with men of whatever religious denomination. Here we can sit each under his vine and fig tree, with none to make him afraid.[9]

This war started on April 12, 1861, and for a second time the *Jewish Messenger* ran a remarkable editorial by Samuel Mayer Isaacs. This one, dated April 28, 1861, and titled "Stand By the Flag," called for Jewish people to defend the United States and the Constitution, which guaranteed free exercise of religion and guaranteed liberty, justice, and equality. He called the Constitution the "admiration of the world." Isaacs made a stirring call to stand by the flag and asked Jews to defend it with their lives if necessary.

> And the Constitution, guaranteeing to all, the free exercise of their religious opinions, extending to all, liberty, justice, and equality, the pride of Americans, the admiration of the world, shall that Constitution be subverted, and anarchy usurp the place of a sound, safe and stable government, deriving its authority from the consent of the American People? The voice of millions yet unborn, cried out, "Forbid it, Heaven!" The voice of the American people declares in tones not to be misunderstood: "It shall not be!" Then stand by the Flag! What death can be as glorious as that of the patriot, surrendering his life in defense of his country, pouring forth his blood on the battlefield, to live forever in the hearts of a grateful people.[10]
>
> (See Addendum C for the complete editorial)

During the American Civil War, about nine thousand Jews fought for the North,[11] and seven rose to the level of general:[12]

- Leopold Blumenberg, severely wounded at the Battle of Antietam
- Leopold Newman, who died from wounds received during the battle of Chancellorsville
- Alfred Mordecai, leading expert in explosives and gunnery; in 1865, he was appointed instructor of ordnance at West Point
- William Meyer of New York, who received a letter of thanks from President Lincoln for his efforts during the New York draft riots
- Phineas Horowitz, who became the Union's Surgeon General
- Edward S. Salomon of Illinois
- Frederick Knefler of Indiana

Two of these Jewish generals were particularly interesting. At the Battle of Gettysburg, Edward Salomon was a colonel of the 82nd Illinois Volunteer Infantry. He led his men to withstand the final Confederate assault of the battle against Cemetery Ridge. His regiment took fifty percent casualties. He ended the war as a Brigadier General. In 1869, President Ulysses S. Grant appointed him governor of the Territory of Washington. Later, Salomon settled in San Francisco, where he was the district attorney of San Francisco County. He served twice in the California legislature.

Frederick Knefler became the highest-ranking Jewish general. He was first the regimental colonel of the 79th Indiana Infantry. Knefler took part in most of the famous battles of the Western Theater. He was at the battles of Shiloh, Stones River, Chickamauga, and Missionary Ridge. He fought under General William T. Sherman during the Atlanta campaign. Toward the end of the war, he fought at the battles of Franklin and Nashville.[13]

There were six Jewish Medal of Honor winners. These six, along with their units and the battles for which they were honored, were:

1. Sergeant-Major Abraham Cohn, 6th New Hampshire Volunteers, Battle of the Wilderness and Battle of Petersburg, Virginia
2. Corporal Isaac Gause, 2nd Ohio Cavalry, Berryville, Virginia
3. Sergeant Henry Heller, 66th Ohio Infantry, Chancellorsville, Virgina
4. Sergeant Leopold Karpeles, Company E, Massachusetts Infantry, Battle of the Wilderness, Virgina
5. Sergeant Benjamin B. Levy, 40th New York Regiment, Battle of the Wilderness, Virginia
6. Private David Orbansky, 58th Ohio Infantry, Vicksburg, Mississippi

On March 9, 1862, one of the most famous naval battles in world history took place off the coast of Hampton Roads, Virginia. The Union ironclad *USS Monitor* fought the Confederate ironclad *CSS Virginia* (better known as the *Merrimack*) during a four-hour battle that changed the course of naval warfare.

The *Monitor* featured a completely new and radical design with most of its crew below the waterline. It was closer to a submarine with a revolving turret. Because it was so radical, the US Navy requested volunteers to man the ship. One of the sailors answering the call was William Durst, a Jewish man from Philadelphia. A Jewish man was a member of the *USS Monitor* during one of the most famous naval battles in the history of the United States![14]

Jews fought in the Civil War with great honor just as they did in the American Revolution. They were patriots in every sense of the word, and Americans accepted them. There was always individual prejudice, but the hatred and organized prejudice the Jews experienced in Europe was unknown in America.

During the Revolution, Haym Salomon had played a tremendous part in getting the nation through a difficult financial period. Joseph Seligman, a Jewish American, accomplished the same thing during the Civil War. Seligman was an international American clothier who had vast contacts with European banks. The United States needed large amounts of cash to fund the war. Seligman bought United States bonds, and then used his banking contacts in Europe to cash them. He cashed over two hundred million dollars' worth of bonds through Germany. At the beginning of the war, Seligman lent the American government one million dollars to purchase uniforms.[15]

After the Civil War, President Grant offered Seligman the position of Secretary of the Treasury, which he turned down. Amazingly, Jews were instrumental in getting the United States through two very difficult economic times with their own credit.

Like President Washington, President Abraham Lincoln became a good friend of the Jewish people. There were no Jewish chaplains allowed in the military at that time. Lincoln personally had a law passed that allowed Jewish chaplains. This was the first time in United States history that a federal law was enacted specifically to benefit the Jewish people.

On December 17, 1862, General Ulysses S. Grant issued the infamous General Order 11 that expelled all Jews from Kentucky, Tennessee, and Mississippi. It gave Jewish people twenty-four hours to vacate these states. The order was as follows:

> The Jews, as a class violating every regulation of trade established by the Treasury Department and also department orders, are hereby expelled from the department within twenty-four hours from the receipt of this order. Post commanders will see to it that all of this class of people be furnished passes and

> required to leave, and any one returning after such notification will be arrested and held in confinement until an opportunity occurs of sending them out as prisoners, unless furnished with permit from headquarters. No passes will be given these people to visit headquarters for the purpose of making personal application of trade permits.

There was a serious problem at the time with unscrupulous merchants trading with the South, and some of these merchants were Jewish. General Grant issued this order against the Jews as a class. Cesar J. Kaskel, a Jew from Paducah, Kentucky, with the aid of a congressman, first brought this order to the President's attention. Kaskel immediately went to Washington and met with President Lincoln.

Kaskel later wrote of the meeting and reported that President Lincoln had said, "And so the Children of Israel were driven from the land of Canaan." Kaskel responded, "Yes, and this is why we have come to Father Abraham, to ask his protection." Lincoln followed, "And this protection they shall have at once."

President Lincoln immediately contacted the Union's Commanding General, Henry W. Halleck, and had Grant's General Order 11 revoked. The President issued a short note that General Halleck telegraphed, and General Grant immediately revoked the order. On January 6, 1863, General Order 11 was rescinded. This note from the President follows:

> A paper purporting to be General Orders, No 11, issued by you December 17, has been presented here. By its terms, it expels all Jews from your department. If such an order has been issued, it will be immediately revoked.[16]

Rabbi Isaac M. Wise of Cincinnati, Ohio, led a delegation to visit President Lincoln to thank him for revoking General Order 11. The rabbi reported many statements by President Lincoln. Rabbi Wise said the President drew no distinction between Jew and Gentile, and he would allow no harm to any American because of religious affiliation.[17]

This incident with General Grant failed to cause long-term damage within the Jewish community. There were no lasting repercussions against the General. In fact, when Grant ran for president in 1868, the Jewish vote went heavily for Grant.[18]

On April 15, 1865, President Lincoln died from an assassin's bullet. The entire country went into deep mourning—Jewish people included. All across America, Jews held special services in honor of the President. The service held in the southern city of New Orleans, Louisiana, best summed up the attitude of the Jews toward the President. P. J. Joachimsen spoke on behalf of the congregation. This southern Hebrew congregation held President Lincoln in high esteem for defending Jews against General Order 11. The newspapers throughout America reported this touching eulogy:

> And we, as Jews, had a distinct ground to love, respect and esteem him....When an order was made to banish Jews as a class from a particular Department, and their immediate and indiscriminate departure was being carried out, our deceased President at once revoked the unauthorized command. We can carry the memory of Abraham Lincoln with us as that of a triumphant martyr to humanity, and we can also carry into practice the lessons taught us by the short but eventful life of the great departed: To be true and honest to ourselves and to our neighbors and to stand bravely and fearlessly to the performance of our duties as citizens of this great Republic.[19]

Unquestionably, two of the greatest presidents in the history of the United States were also great friends of the Jewish people. They set the example for the rest of the nation to follow.

The Land of Freedom Beyond the Ocean

At the time of the Civil War, America was the envy of world Jewry. American Jews had complete freedom and equality. The European Jews attributed this freedom to the American Constitution, which had established religious liberty. European Jews were amazed by how quickly their brothers in America prospered and were able to reach all levels of society.

In 1862, the London *Jewish Chronicle* reported this observation:

> We now have a few words of the Jews of the United States in general....The constitution having established perfect religious liberty, Jews were free in America....They, therefore in a comparatively short time, prospered, and throve there in a degree unexampled in Europe. Jews were found in all positions of life filling offices from the highest to the lowest.[20]

By 1862 there were about two hundred thousand Jews in America, which was only a fraction of the number in Europe. Although there was such freedom in America, the report went on to explain why so few Jews had left Europe for the United States. The explanation was made that Jews had grown accustomed to persecution, and traveling to America was difficult. The report said:

> But although their happy condition was known in Europe, and although oppression weighed heavily upon them in the Old World, yet, so few were the facilities for traveling, and so accustomed had the grown up

generations been to persecution, that but few sought asylum in the land of freedom beyond the ocean.

This reluctance of European Jewry to seek asylum in the land of freedom beyond the ocean soon came to an end. In 1881, just sixteen years after the close of the Civil War, events in Russia would send millions of desperate Jews fleeing to the land of freedom. The center of world Jewry was about to shift from Europe to the land beyond the ocean.

Photo Credit: Jacob Marcus Center, *American Jewish Archives, Hebrew Union College*

Statue in Chicago with Robert Morris, George Washington, and Haym Salomon

CHAPTER FOUR

The Modern Moses

But lift thou up thy rod, and stretch out thine hand over the sea, and divide it: and the children of Israel shall go on dry ground through the midst of the sea. (Exodus 14:16)

The European-Jewish resistance to emigration changed abruptly—virtually overnight. A census in 1877 listed the Jewish population in America as 250,000. Just thirty years later this population reached two million. A tidal wave of Jews flooded into America, mostly from Russia. Events in Russia changed the course of world history in a dramatic way.[1] This change affected history down to this day.

On March 1, 1881, Tsar Alexander II of Russia was assassinated. This incident set off a series of events that cascaded down through history to this day. The Russian government blamed the assassination on the Jews and violence broke out immediately. The terrible pogrom of 1881 resulted in the murder of hundreds of Jews with thousands injured, their homes and property destroyed.

The Russian government did nothing to stop the pogroms and actually blamed the destruction of Jews on the Jews! Jewish life was terrible in Russia before the pogrom, but it was about to significantly worsen. On May 3, 1882, the Russian government enacted what became known as the May Laws.[2] Directed at the Jews, these laws made life truly intolerable. The May Laws included the following:

- Jews were forbidden to settle outside of towns or shetls (small towns)
- Jews were not allowed to purchase land or houses
- Jews were not allowed to relocate
- Deeds of sale or leases of real estate to Jews who lived outside the towns were canceled
- Jews were prohibited from conducting business on Sundays and Christian holidays
- Jewish education was strictly limited

The May Laws forced the Jews into ghettos. They could not travel throughout Russia without permits. The police brutally enforced the May Laws. The authorities systematically expelled Jews from their houses and forced them to relocate. Jewish people lived in terror.

The Jewish reaction to the May Laws was a mass exodus from Russia to America. Starting in 1881 and accelerating well into the twentieth century, Jews fled Russia to America, and America took them in. No country in the world wanted the Russian Jews except America.

Tens of thousands of poverty-stricken Jews literally walked out of Russia into Western Europe, trying to get to America. Western Europe refused to accept them. The Jews were terrified and desperate. They heard about the freedoms of America and knew that the people of the United States accepted Jews. They referred to America as "the famous land."

Mary Antin was a Russian Jew who escaped to America. She wrote about leaving Russia and the charged emotional atmosphere as Jews were readying for the mass exodus:

> America was in everybody's mouth. Businessmen talked of it over their accounts; the market women made up their quarrels that they might discuss it from stall to stall; people who had relatives in the famous land went around reading their letters for the enlightenment of less fortunate folks....Children played at emigrating; old folks shook their sage heads over the evening fires and prophesied no good for those who braved the terrors of the sea and the goal beyond it. All talked about it.[3]

In total desperation, the fleeing refugees literally walked west without any idea of how to reach America. They flooded Germany by the tens of thousands. Some local people in Germany helped them. European Jews helped by providing the finances for passage to America. Nothing could stop the Russian Jews from getting to America, and this turned out to be one of the greater migrations in history. When the great Russian emigration finished thirty-five years later, more than two million had come to America. It equaled the previous Irish immigration of the 1840s and 1850s.

The vast majority of Jews entered America through New York City. As they entered the harbor, they saw the Statue of Liberty staring at them, which came to represent the hope that America offered to the desperate people of the world. In 1883, a famous poem, written by Emma Lazarus, a Jew, was inscribed at the base of the statue. Lazarus's poem perfectly described the Russian Jews fleeing to America:

> Give me your tired, your poor,
> Your huddled masses yearning to breathe free,
> The wretched refuse of your teeming shore,
> Send these, the homeless, tempest-tost to me,
> I lift my lamp beside the golden door!

Although the vast majority of the Russian Jews left for America, a small number headed south to what is now Israel. Those considered to be the first Zionists in the modern Zionist movement were Russian Jews fleeing the pogroms.[4] The events occurring in Russia directly influenced the creation of modern Israel.

The world looked upon America as the New Jerusalem for the Russian Jews. In November 1881, a political cartoon published by a weekly American/German newspaper called *Puck* captured this idea. The cartoon showed the Atlantic Ocean splitting and Jews coming through to America. Uncle Sam in the cartoon became the "Modern Moses."

Along with this cartoon, *Puck* ran an article about the Jewish people flooding into America. The article was written as if Uncle Sam, the modern Moses, were speaking. It is difficult to imagine an article like this being written in any other country at any previous time.

> All he [Uncle Sam] says to the persecuted races of Europe, whether Jew or Christian, believer or unbeliever, is: "You are welcome to America. Practice any religion you please....If you wish, cover the land with churches or synagogues....As my ancient servant predecessor, Moses, did with the Red Sea, I do with the Atlantic Ocean. The waters are divided, and you can safely pass through them to the land of liberty, and leave oppression, persecution and brutality behind you."[5]

President Washington had wanted the United States to resemble the future reign of the Messiah for Jews living in America; now the nation became just that for the Russian Jews as they fled the oppression of Tsarist Russia. What a contrast between President

George Washington and the Tsar of Russia! The President's letter to the Hebrews of Newport is worth repeating:

> May the Children of the Stock of Abraham, who dwell in this land, continue to merit and enjoy the good will of the other Inhabitants; while every one shall sit under his own vine and fig tree, and there shall be none to make him afraid.

God used the horrors of Russia to begin the migration of Jews back to Israel. Jews flooded into America and had a profound impact on the church, igniting the modern Zionist movement. God also used the church in America to spearhead the modern return of the Jews to their biblical homeland.

The assassination of Tsar Alexander II on March 1, 1881, was a catalyst for the modern rebirth of the nation of Israel. The pogroms and May Laws that followed started a tiny movement of Jews back to Israel. But, more significantly, they awakened the Evangelical church in America to the Jewish plight and the need for a Jewish state in Palestine. The world is still reverberating from March 1, 1881, and the May Laws of 1882.

Christian Zionism

Prior to the Civil War, America had several powerful spiritual revivals that touched the entire nation. The Great Awakening of the 1740s, sparked by the preaching of Jonathan Edwards, spread throughout the nation and changed the course of society. In the year 1800, a great revival started in Kentucky and spread eastward until it affected the entire nation. The Second Awakening began in 1820 under the preaching of Charles Finney and shook the nation.

Toward the end of the nineteenth century, huge segments of American Christianity began focusing on the second coming of the

Lord Jesus and the rebirth of the nation of Israel. This was a powerful movement that reached the highest levels of society. The focus of this revival was the second coming of the Lord Jesus and the restoration of Jewish people back to Israel. This belief became known as premillennialism, the belief that God will restore the nation of Israel before the second coming of the Lord Jesus Christ.

Israel's restoration will be in unbelief. The Lord Jesus will summon the believing church to be with Him in heaven before He returns to Israel. When Jesus Christ returns to Israel, He will come with His church. After this, He will rule and reign from Jerusalem for one thousand years (millennium), hence the term premillennial.

Powerful evangelists like D. L. Moody and William E. Blackstone were proclaiming this message together with hundreds of lesser-known preachers. Blackstone's book *Jesus Is Coming*, first printed in 1878, sold huge numbers and affected millions of people. A network of new Bible colleges spread across the country, as well as dozens of publications, all promoting the premillennialist doctrine.

In the midst of this revival, the Russian Jews began pouring into America. The horrors of what happened to them in Russia touched the hearts of American Christians, who began to help these Jewish refugees by providing food, clothes, and medical attention. The crisis awakened the church to the need for a Jewish homeland. Blackstone became the leader of this movement and traveled extensively throughout America promoting a Jewish homeland in Palestine.

His efforts reached the highest levels of American society, from church leaders to the halls of Congress. Blackstone chaired a conference in 1890, titled "The Past, Present and Future of Israel." Some of the most influential leaders in both the Jewish and Christian communities attended. One result of the conference was that the leaders sent resolutions to the Russian Tsar on behalf of the Jews.

Blackstone felt the resolutions were not strong enough, and the following year he met with President Benjamin Harrison and Secretary of State James Blaine. During this meeting he presented the President with what is now known as "The Blackstone Memorial."[6]

The Blackstone Memorial

The Blackstone Memorial, titled "What Shall Be Done for the Russian Jews?" was an amazing document that helped spearhead the Zionist movement. Modern Zionism actually sprang from the church in the United States. The church witnessed the terrible conditions of the Russian Jews and believed it was time for Jews to go back to their biblical homeland.

Blackstone presented the Memorial to President Harrison six years before world Jewry initiated the first Zionist Congress for the purpose of creating a Jewish state. The Memorial addressed the plight of the Russian Jews and suggested that Palestine become the Jewish homeland. The idea was that poverty-stricken Turkey owned the land of Palestine, and the combined wealth of world Jewry could purchase from Turkey vast tracts of uninhabited land in Palestine.

Blackstone stated, "According to God's distribution of nations, it is their home, an inalienable possession from which they were expelled by force." The idea of the land being an "inalienable possession" is anchored in the everlasting covenant God made with Abraham, Isaac, Jacob, and their descendants.

The Memorial claimed that it was time for the Christian nations to show kindness to the Jews and help restore them to the land. Blackstone requested that the President call an international conference of nations to consider a Jewish state and alleviate the suffering of Russian Jews. Remember, this was years before the initiation of the Jewish Zionist movement. This Memorial follows in part:

> Why not give Palestine back to them again? According to God's distribution of nations it is their home, an inalienable possession from which they were expelled by force....We believe this is an appropriate time for all nations and especially the Christian nations of Europe to show kindness to Israel. A million of exiles, by their terrible suffering, are piteously appealing to our sympathy, justice, and humanity. Let us now restore to them the land of which they were so cruelly despoiled by our Roman ancestors.... To secure the holding at an early date, of an international conference to consider the condition of the Israelites and their claims to Palestine as their ancient home, and to promote, in all other just and proper ways, the alleviation of their suffering condition.[7] (See Addendum D for the complete Memorial)

More than four hundred leading Americans from all walks of life signed the Memorial. Many religious leaders from various denominations signed. The greatest evangelist of the era, D. L. Moody, signed it, along with the outstanding pastor T. De Witt Talmage. Some of the leading members of Congress and mayors of cities signed. Powerful industrialists and bank presidents signed it, including John D. Rockefeller, J. P. Morgan, Cyrus McCormick, and Charles Scribner. Editors and publishers from ninety-three leading national newspapers and religious periodicals signed it. Most of America was behind protecting Jews and the creation of a Jewish nation. A brief list of the signatories follows:

- Dewitt C. Cregier, Mayor of Chicago
- Robert C. Davidson, Mayor of Baltimore
- Edwin H. Fitler, Mayor of Philadelphia
- Hugh J. Grant, Mayor of New York

- N. Matthews Jr., mayor of Boston
- Wm. E. Russell, governor of Massachusetts
- George Jones, *New York Times*
- Melville W. Fuller, Chief Justice of the US Supreme Court
- T. B. Reed, Speaker House of Representatives
- Robert R. Hitt, Chairman House Committee on Foreign Affairs
- William McKinley, Congressman, future President
- B. F. Jacobs, president of the Security and Stock Exchange Commission
- Cyrus H. McCormick, president of McCormick Harvester Company

Blackstone included a cover letter with the Memorial that revealed the depth of his belief in the Bible as the literal word of God. His faith, with millions of others', was the driving force behind the Memorial. He referred to God as the ever-living God of Abraham, Isaac, and Jacob. Like a prophet, he stated this was the time in history for the Gentiles to help bring Jews back to their land. He even referred to Isaiah 49:22 and Ezekiel 34! This section follows:

> That there seem to be many evidences to show that we have reached the period in the great roll of the centuries, when the ever living God of Abraham, Isaac and Jacob, is lifting up His hand to the Gentiles, (Isa 49:22) to bring His sons and His daughters from far, that he may plant them again in their own land, Ezk 34, &c. Not for twenty-four centuries, since the days of Cyrus, King of Persia, has there been offered to any mortal such a privileged opportunity to further the purposes of God concerning His ancient people.

He then closed the letter with an amazing statement. Blackstone requested that the President and Secretary of State take a personal interest in this matter. By pursuing this issue, they might receive the promise of God, who said to Abraham, "*I will bless them that bless thee,*" in Genesis 12:3. This section follows:

> May it be the high privilege of your Excellency, and the Honorable Secretary to take a personal interest in this great matter, and secure through the Conference, a home for these wandering millions of Israel, and thereby receive to yourselves the promise of Him, who said to Abraham, "*I will bless them that bless thee,*" Genesis 12:3.

President Harrison failed to call an international conference or put diplomatic pressure on Russia to end the persecution of Jews. In Harrison's State of the Union message, he mentioned the plight of the Russian Jews but failed to do anything else.

Photo Credit: AME International

William E. Blackstone (1841–1935), American evangelist and father of modern Zionism

For the first time in world history, a powerful Gentile nation supported the creation of a Jewish state. Jews found favor at all levels of American society. The Blackstone Memorial showed that America was concerned for the welfare of Jews and that their concern went beyond welfare; it went all the way to the creation of a Jewish homeland.

Millions of Americans were now praying for the restoration of the Jewish people to their ancient homeland. The church in the United States, and also to some extent in Great Britain, awakened to the Jewish plight and their need for a homeland. The spiritual force of the church was now engaged in a real way for God's restoration of Israel.

This awakening never died in America and remains alive to this day. The support of Israel by Americans is not a recent phenomenon; its roots go back to 1891 and even to the founding of America. The church in America has a special relationship with Jewish people. Actually, the Blackstone Memorial was just a continuation of the respect Americans had for the Bible and the Jewish people.

Blackstone continued to work for the establishment of a Jewish state. In May 1916, he once again petitioned the United States government to help in the creation of a Jewish state. He presented the Memorial to President Woodrow Wilson, who supported the British in the Balfour Declaration. This declaration became the foundation for the modern Jewish state. Blackstone once again called for an international conference to convene for the creation of a Jewish state.

On June 30, 1922, the United States Congress passed a joint resolution supporting the establishment of a Jewish State in Palestine. This resolution put the American government firmly behind the creation of this state. This resolution, titled "Favoring the establishment in Palestine of a national home for the Jewish people," follows:

> Resolved by the Senate and the House of Representatives of the United States of America in Congress assembled. That the United States of America favors the establishment in Palestine of a national home for the Jewish people, it being clearly understood that

> nothing shall be done which should prejudice the civil and religious rights of Christians and all other non-Jewish communities in Palestine, and that the holy places and religious buildings and sites in Palestine shall be adequately protected.

Blackstone's effort in 1891 proved successful; thirty-one years later, the United States government officially supported a Jewish state. In 1916, Blackstone was not far off in calling for an international conference. Just six years later, in 1922, the League of Nations convened just such a conference. Great Britain assumed the responsibility of overseeing this Jewish state in Palestine. This oversight by Great Britain was called the British Mandate of 1922.

Chapter Five

A Tale of Two Countries: America Blessed, Russia Cursed

And I will bless them that bless thee, and curse him that curseth thee... (Genesis 12:3)

America and Russia provide a good test of the accuracy of the Bible regarding the treatment of Jews. Russia has a long and well-established history of hating Jews. America has a long and well-established history of accepting and blessing Jewish people. The comparison of these two nations is astonishing. It shows the authority of God's word regarding the blessing or cursing of the Jews.

The nations of America and Russia are similar in many respects. They are both huge countries with large populations and expansive areas of farmland. They have abundant natural resources such as coal, iron, lumber, oil, and other minerals; they have tremendous rivers. Both nations also have historically Christian roots.

In 1727, Queen Catherine of Russia banned all Jews from the country. Russia partitioned Poland in 1772, and huge numbers of Jews came under the authority of the Tsar, who forced them to live within the Pale of Settlement, a section of western Russia allotted for the Jews. The Russians prohibited the Jews from traveling beyond "the Pale." Life in the Pale was filled with terrible hardships; however, the pogroms of 1881 became a turning point in Jewish history.

With 1881 as the starting point, the blessings and the curses between these two nations become clear. Starting in 1881, Russian Jews experienced a number of pogroms up to the Russian Revolution of 1917. The May Laws of 1882 catalyzed the massive Jewish exodus from Russia.

After the Civil War, the United States military shrank to almost nothing. By 1880, the American navy was virtually nonexistent. In 1881, Congress began debating the need for a modern navy.[1] After two years of debate, Congress then passed the Navy Act of 1883, which called for the construction of four modern cruisers. This modest act was the beginning of the United States becoming a world naval power.[2]

Congress started this debate the very year the great Jewish exodus began from Russia. The Naval Act of 1883 was enacted while tens of thousands of desperate Jews were pouring into America from Russia. America's major thrust toward a world naval power occurred just seven years later. In 1890, the Navy Act called for the building of four battleships—the act that propelled America toward becoming a world naval power.

In 1890, Christian Zionists and Jews met in Chicago and passed resolutions calling on the Tsar to stop the persecution of the Jews. The following year, this Christian Zionist meeting resulted in the Blackstone Memorial. America's rise to becoming a world power parallels this blessing of the Jews.

On February 15, 1898, the battleship *Maine* exploded in the harbor of Havana, Cuba. Congress declared war on Spain in April 1898. On

July 3, 1898, the American Navy completely destroyed the Spanish Navy at the sea battle of Santiago de Cuba. The war resulted in the complete defeat of Spain. America went from having no navy in 1883 to being a world naval power in just fifteen years.

The first Zionist Congress met in Basel, Switzerland, in 1897, and called for a Jewish state in Palestine. America was thrust forward just one year after the Zionist Congress called for a Jewish homeland. The ascent of America as a world power and the official birth of modern Zionism coincided. This was not an accident. America was part of God's plan to restore the nation of Israel.

Russia continued its brutal treatment of Jews, and early in the twentieth century, additional vicious pogroms broke out. The pogroms started in the spring of 1903 and continued through 1906. In the middle of the pogroms, the Russo-Japanese War of 1904 started. On May 27, 1905, the Japanese totally destroyed the Russian navy at the battle of Tsushima Strait. The Japanese also defeated the Russian army in a series of land battles. During the battle of Mukden, the Russians suffered ninety thousand casualties.

By August 1905, Russia wanted to end the war. President Theodore Roosevelt acted as a mediator and the two sides agreed to the Treaty of Portsmouth on September 5, 1905.[3] Japan got what it wanted from this treaty, and Russia was humiliated. This humiliation of Russia came at the very time a vicious pogrom was taking place against the Jews!

There is irony to all this. Anti-Jewish Russia had to agree to a treaty mediated by an American President who greatly favored the Jews. Russia was driving Jews out; America was taking them in. The Russian emissary came to America to sign the treaty! Russia, the greatest Jew-hating nation of the time, came to the greatest Jew-favoring nation to sign a humiliating treaty.

President Roosevelt won the Nobel Peace Prize for his role in ending the war.[4] He refused to accept the cash award for the Nobel Peace Prize while in office. In 1910, he received $45,482.83 as his cash award, giving the entire amount to charity, including such organizations as the Red Cross and the Salvation Army. Then, with greater irony, he gave $4,000 to the Jewish Welfare Fund! There was no prejudice in the President toward Jews.

In 1914, World War I began. Like the Russo-Japanese war nine years before, this conflict resulted in the defeat of Russia and the complete destruction of the Russian army. Before losing the war, the Germans totally annihilated the Russian army. The Russian

Photo Credit: Underwood&Underwood/Corbis

President Roosevelt and the Portsmouth Treaty delegation

army literally threw their weapons down, left the battlefield, and walked back to Russia. This led directly to the Russian Revolution of 1917 when Communists seized control of the country. Following the Revolution, pogroms again broke out in Russia until 1921. It is estimated that one hundred thousand or more Jews were killed at this time.

From 1917 until today, Russia has been a "living hell." Communist tyrants such as Lenin and Stalin rose to power, killing tens of millions of people. Millions starved to death and millions died in prison camps. The people lived in terror. Looking at Russia post-1917, it appears that God applied the May Laws of 1882 in the form of communism to the entire country.

Jews lived in terror; under communism, the entire Russian population lived in terror. Jews could not own property; nor could the Russian population. The Tsar forced Jews to relocate; the Communists uprooted huge numbers of Russians and forced them to relocate. The Jewish people starved; huge numbers of Russians also starved to death. The Tsar hindered Jewish worship; the entire Soviet Union was forbidden worship under communism.

The Russian Orthodox church played a major part in the persecution of Jews. In fact, it added to the pogroms and encouraged the attacks. Konstantin Pobedonostsev, the head of the governing body of this "church," best summed up their position on the May Laws. He expressed hope that "one-third of Jews will convert, one-third will die, and one-third will flee the country."

The Russian Orthodox church soon suffered as the Jewish people did. The Communists applied their own form of the May Laws to the Russian church. They closed the churches and turned them into museums. The Communists killed huge numbers of ministers and herded the rest into concentration camps. The church had no freedom and was actively persecuted by the Communists. The Russian church suffered under the Communists just as much as the Jews had suffered under the Tsars, if not worse.

Russia remained a living hell until communism fell in 1989. Even after the fall, Russians are still suffering from poverty and disease. Russians have the lowest life expectancy in the Western World. This country paid a fearful price for violating God's word about blessing the Jews.

America to the Rescue

On August 1, 1914, World War I erupted in Europe. Turkey soon aligned with Germany, and then used the cover of the war to exterminate its Armenian Christian population. Every conceivable method was used to kill the Armenians. Many were forced to convert to Islam. Before the extermination was over, approximately two million Armenians were slaughtered.

The Christian population was all but eliminated. This was the first great genocide of the twentieth century, and it was a prelude to what the Nazis were about to unleash on the Jews. The Turks were just as vicious towards the Christians as the Nazis were to the Jews. To this day, Turkey refuses to acknowledge their slaughter of the Armenians.

On April 4, 1917, the United States declared war on Germany, followed by a declaration of war on Germany's ally, the Austro-Hungarian Empire. However, America failed to declare war on Turkey, another ally of Germany. It was highly unusual for a nation not to declare war on all its enemy's allies. This "failure" was not a mistake, however, but a conscious decision of President Woodrow Wilson. His foresight saved the fledgling Zionist movement, which blossomed years later into the modern state of Israel.

The Holy Land was under the control of Turkey. When the Turkish government finished slaughtering the Armenians, it turned toward the Jews. It appeared that the Jews were about to suffer extermination like the Armenians. Turkey resented the Zionist movement and was suspicious of the Russian Jews in Palestine. Turkey took steps against the Jews: Jewish property was confiscated, including weapons, and their banks were closed. Turkey was moving to expel the Russian Jews. The Jews were beginning to starve. It was a dire time for the Jews in the Holy Land.

The United States continued diplomatic relations with Turkey throughout the war, and President Wilson personally came to the aid of the troubled Jews. The State Department told Turkey that "the American people would hold them personally responsible for the lives and property of the Jews and Christians in case of a massacre or looting." Turkey agreed to cooperate and allowed America to send food and medical supplies to the Jews. The British agreed to lift their naval blockade and allow supplies to pass through. United States warships rushed the desperately needed supplies to the beleaguered Jews.[5]

Turkey then ordered the Jews of Palestine to take an oath of allegiance to the Turkish empire. The Jews were given one month to renounce their original citizenship and swear allegiance to Turkey's Ottoman Empire. Many Jews refused or were unable to pay the registration fee, and these Jews once again faced destruction. For the second time, President Wilson came to their aid.

Turkey agreed to allow the United States to rescue the Jews who refused the oath by taking them out of Palestine. United States warships ferried tens of thousands of Jews from Jaffa to safety in Alexandria, Egypt. One ship, the armored cruiser *USS Tennessee*, was reported to have ferried six thousand Jews to safety. Alvion P. Mosier was a sailor aboard the *Tennessee*. He kept a diary of events and recorded his observations of the plight of the Jews. An excerpt follows:

> Across the Mediterranean, we went to Jaffa, Palestine (in biblical times, known as Joppa) situated about thirty miles from Jerusalem. The sight I saw there I will never forget–Syrian refugees from the northern part of Palestine, Armenians and Jews so frightened from the treatment they received from the Turks. And the hunger...those poor people had wasted away to mere shadows. They pleaded with our officers to take them away from their tormentors. At this time, early in 1915, the Turks were so busy in other parts of their country that they paid no attention to us. Accordingly, the *Tennessee* made twenty trips to Alexandria, Egypt taking thousands of those poor people out of the hands of their persecutors. The Turks at this time were overrunning the Holy Lands.[6]

Photo Credit: Benton Decker Collection, Hoover Institution Archives

Jewish refugees boarding the* USS Tennessee*, early 1915

Many of Israel's future leaders, including David Ben-Gurion, were saved by the United States. As the war progressed and Turkey began losing Palestine to the British army, Turkey did not molest the Jewish people. The fear of war with the United States kept Turkey from destroying the Jews of Palestine.

In a very real sense, the early Zionist movement was saved by the direct intervention of the United States. The Jews were about to face the same fate as the Armenian Christians. Without America's intervention, the Zionist movement would have ended around 1917, and Israel as it is known today would not exist. Only the foresight of President Wilson and the power of the United States saved Zionism.

The American army helped drive the Germans out of France and brought about Germany's surrender. The British drove the Turks from Palestine and gained control of Jerusalem in December 1917. A German victory in Europe would have changed the military situation in Palestine. The Germans, teamed with the Turks, would have assured a victory and kept Jerusalem under Turkish control. The American involvement in the war assured an allied victory and set the stage for the future restoration of Israel.

In November 1917, Britain issued the Balfour Declaration, which granted Jews the right to return to Palestine and start the creation of a nation. Prior to issuing this document, Arthur Balfour, Great Britain's Foreign Secretary, visited the United States and discussed Britain's plans for postwar Palestine with President Wilson. The President felt that because the war was still in progress, it was best for the United States to remain behind the scenes.

Because the United States supported Zionism, the British felt secure in issuing the Balfour Declaration. Jewish people throughout the world realized Great Britain needed the support of the United

States. When the declaration was made, a crowd of one hundred thousand Jews danced in gratitude outside the American consulate in Odessa, Russia. Similar demonstrations were held in Greece and Australia.

In summary, God used the power of the United States to protect the fledgling Zionist movement. The man of the hour was President Wilson, whose concern for the Jews kept them from starving. Behind the scenes, he was there to ensure that Great Britain issued the Balfour Declaration. President Wilson belongs in the same league as George Washington and Abraham Lincoln as a friend of Israel. He was instrumental in helping fulfill God's plan for the Jewish people and the restoration of the nation of Israel.

America to the Rescue Again

America was also instrumental during World War II in helping to save the Jews and the fledgling state of Israel. On November 8, 1942, the United States army landed in North Africa in what was code named Operation Torch. The main thrust of the army landed in Morocco.

The United States army landed just in time to save about four hundred thousand Jews from extermination in North Africa.[7] The American army was not sent to save the Jews, but this mission was a by-product of fighting the Nazis. These Jews living in Morocco, Algeria, Tunisia, and Libya, were about to face the same fate as the Jews living in Europe.

North Africa was under the control of the French Vichy government and the Italian fascists. Vichy France was a puppet government established by the Nazis, and it controlled Morocco, Algeria, and Tunisia. Fascist Italy controlled Libya. These governments cooperated with the Nazis in attacking the Jews.[8] By November 1942, the

North African Jews were suffering and moving rapidly down the road to extermination. Nazi methods deprived Jews of property, citizenship, education, livelihood, residence, and free movement, and also forced labor, confiscations, deportations, and executions. The Nazis also herded Jews into the forced labor camps they had set up.

Tunisia was especially vicious towards the Jews. The Nazi army actually occupied Tunisia and began implementing the planned destruction of the Jews. Jews were even forced to wear the Star of David for identification. Tunisia became the training ground for many of the most notorious Nazi killers. SS Colonel Walter Rauff, who had invented the mobile death gas van, was in Tunisia. He left for Russia and led the extermination of the Russian Jews. Rauff's Einsatzgruppen, or "action squads," followed the German army and killed all the Jews they could locate.

The United States army attacked the Nazis and Italian fascists from the west while the British army fought from the east. The two armies crushed the vaunted Nazi Afrika Corps and drove them out of North Africa. With the Nazi defeat, the direct threat to the Jews ended. After the war, a great percentage of these North African Jews went to Israel. Today, only a small percent of Jews live in North Africa.

After the war, Nazi documents were uncovered that revealed German plans to have "action squads" follow the army into Palestine. The Nazis planned to destroy all the Jews in Palestine by the same method they used in Russia.[9] Special SS units were stationed in Greece that were prepared to start the Palestinian holocaust. The defeat of the Afrika Corps thus ended this plan, and Palestine was saved for a second time. During both world wars, plans were made to destroy all the Jews of Palestine. On both occasions the United States was instrumental in thwarting this destruction.

America Seals the Deal

After World War II, the European Jews were in a desperate condition. Many of the survivors wanted to go to Palestine. The British controlled Palestine and refused to allow them entry. They were held in refugee camps in Cyprus. Some Jews managed to get into Palestine, and fighting erupted between the Jews and Arabs.

Great Britain no longer wanted control over Palestine and turned to the newly created United Nations. The United Nations intervened, and on November 29, 1947, the General Assembly passed Resolution 181, which called for the partition of Palestine into two nations: one for the Jews and one for the Arabs. The city of Jerusalem was to come under the authority of the United Nations. The partition was to occur in 1948.[10]

Fighting raged in Palestine between the Jews and Arabs, and many nations began to waiver in their support for the partition. Some took actions to rescind Resolution 181. The United States in general favored the creation of a Jewish state, but there were powerful forces in the government who opposed this state. As the time neared for the partition, many feared that the Arab armies would destroy Israel and kill all the Jews.

On May 12, 1948, President Harry S. Truman called for a meeting of his top advisers, the State Department, and his military leaders. The meeting was about the diplomatic recognition of the coming Jewish state. (At this time in history no one knew the state was going to be called Israel.) Most attending the meeting were against recognizing a Jewish state, as they thought the Arab armies would destroy it, and the Arab nations would turn against the United States. The President listened to the advice and made no comment about the position of the United States.[11]

At 6:00 p.m. on May 14, 1948, in Washington, D.C., the President was notified that the nation of Israel had been born. At that very moment the Arab armies were mobilizing for war and Egyptian planes attacked Tel Aviv. President Truman was alone in the White House without any advisers. At 6:11 p.m., a White House spokesman addressed the reporters. President Harry S. Truman's statement was as follows:

> This government has been informed that a Jewish state has been proclaimed in Palestine and that recognition has been requested by the provisional government thereof, the United States recognizes the provisional government as the de facto authority of the State of Israel.[12]

The United States was the first country to recognize the new nation of Israel. The forces in the United Nations working to rescind

Credit: Harry S. Truman Library

This Government has been informed that a Jewish state has been proclaimed in Palestine, and recognition has been requested by the provisional Government thereof.

The United States recognizes the provisional government as the de facto authority of the new ~~Jewish~~ State of ~~state.~~ Israel.

Harry Truman

Approved
May 14, 1948.

Truman's Memo: the document that sealed the recognition of Israel

Photo Credit: Bettmann/Corbis

President Truman holds the Torah he received from Dr. Chaim Weizmann, first President of the New State of Israel, May 25, 1948.

Resolution 181 were now stopped by this recognition. The nation of Israel was officially born—President Truman's action sealed it. Once again at a critical time in history, the United States of America was there for the Jewish people and Zionism.

Harry Truman's action places him among the other great presidents who befriended the Jews and aided in the creation of the modern state of Israel. He ranks with George Washington, Abraham Lincoln, and Woodrow Wilson.

An American Saves the Day

As the time neared for the creation of the State of Israel, it was clear to David Ben-Gurion, soon to be Prime Minister, that the Jewish state needed military leadership to survive. The Arab nations pledged to destroy the new Jewish state and were marshalling armies. Ben-

Gurion went to the United States and approached Colonel David "Mickey" Marcus to head up the Jewish state's army. Marcus had the background and the qualifications needed to become a great general, and he accepted the offer. Because Marcus was in the army reserves at the time, he needed permission from the United States army to join the Israeli army. He applied and received the permission, but he was not allowed to join the Israeli army under his real name or military rank. He went to Israel under the name David Stone.[13]

Marcus was the son of Romanian Jews. As a youngster, he had excelled in athletics and academics, and was admitted at West Point, where he graduated in 1924. He also obtained a doctorate from Brooklyn Law School. He left the army and went on to become an assistant United States attorney and then the Commissioner of Corrections for New York City. As World War II approached he reenlisted in the army and reached the rank of full colonel.

Marcus had a distinguished military career. He organized and commanded the Army Ranger School for jungle fighting. This experience would later prove invaluable to the State of Israel. On June 6, 1944, together with the 101st Airborne Division, he jumped into France. Marcus acted as a legal and military adviser during the war's most important conferences, including Teheran, Yalta, and Potsdam. He played a vital part in drafting the documents for both the Italian and German surrenders, and was awarded the Distinguished Service Medal. After the war, Marcus headed the War Crimes Division, where he was responsible for selecting the judges, prosecutors, and lawyers for trying the Nazi war criminals. In 1947, he retired from the army just before he was to be appointed a brigadier general.

In January 1948, Marcus flew to Palestine to help train and organize the army for the emerging Jewish state. From his familiarity with the United States army field manuals, he compiled the military doctrine for the Jewish army, modeling the army after the United

States Rangers. Israel's army fought under United States army tactics and doctrine, and was even command by an American officer! The Israeli army succeeded and won against incredible odds.

Marcus's tactics worked as the Israelis stopped the Egyptian army and saved Israel from destruction. Next, he was assigned the defense of Jerusalem. The city was cut off and the situation seemed hopeless. He organized the relief of Jerusalem by cutting a new road through impossible terrain. For a second time he succeeded against all odds, and Jerusalem was saved. David Ben-Gurion promoted Marcus to the rank of an Aluf, which is the Hebrew title equivalent to brigadier general. Marcus, an American, was the first Aluf since the days of the Bible!

On June 11, 1948, while defending Jerusalem, Marcus was mistakenly shot and killed by one of his own men. On July 2, he was buried with full military honors at West Point. Marcus was the only soldier buried at West Point who died fighting for another nation. His gravestone reads: "Colonel David Marcus—A Soldier for All Humanity."[14]

The prayers of the American Christian Zionists were now fulfilled. Some fifty-seven years after the Blackstone Memorial, the State of Israel came into existence. Modern Zionism was birthed in America after the Civil War, and America was now God's agent to seal and protect the physical nation of Israel. America was at the very center of His prophetic plan.

From 1948 onward, the United States became the new nation's best friend. America continues to vote with Israel in the United Nations. The United States supplies Israel with its latest military equipment. Russia continues to curse Israel. The Russians always vote against Israel in the United Nations, and Russia continues to supply Israel's enemies with weapons to attack the Jewish state. These nations include Iraq, Syria, Egypt, and now Iran.

The United States became the leader of the free world—the nation with both the greatest military power and the greatest economic power. The nation had the finest universities and medical centers. God blessed America as he blessed no other nation.

The contrast between America and Russia is clear: Russia was cursed in every area while America was blessed. Freedom abounded in America while the entire nation of Russia came under the "May Laws" of communism. It is no accident the United States became a world power in a few years after the country welcomed the Russian Jews. God prepared America as protection for the fledgling nation of Israel, and America did its job well.

Right: Monument in Israel to General Mickey Marcus, located on the spot where he was killed. Inscription on the monument reads: "Aluf D. Marcus. In Memory of Major General David (Mickey) Marcus who fell in the war of Independence on Wednesday in Sivan 1948 (11.6.48). He was faithful to his Jewish people and to his country America."

CHAPTER SIX

The Valley of Dry Bones Shall Live

The hand of the LORD was upon me, and carried me out in the spirit of the LORD, and set me down in the midst of the valley which was full of bones...there were very many in the open valley; and, lo, they were very dry....Son of man, can these bones live? And I answered, O Lord GOD, thou knowest.

(Ezekiel 37:1–3)

About five hundred years after Abraham, God created a second covenant. God gave the law of Moses to the children of Israel as a covenant that reflected His holiness. This time the covenant was conditional, based upon the Jewish people keeping the requirements of the law. The law did not replace the everlasting covenant with Abraham. Here is what God said:

*Now therefore, **if ye** will obey my voice indeed, and keep my covenant, then ye shall be a peculiar treasure unto me above all people: for all the earth is mine.*

(Exodus 19:5, emphasis added)

If the Jewish people obeyed the laws, God would bless them above all people; however, if they disobeyed the laws, He would punish them. One of the punishments was the destruction of the nation and the dispersion of the people into all the world. Either way, the authority of God's word was witnessed through Israel being blessed above all nations or cursed and dispersed into the world. Israel reflected God's holy name, and the entire world could witness God's awesome power working through His people.

God sent prophet after prophet to warn Israel of the coming judgment. Ancient Israel rejected the prophets' warnings and, based on the second covenant, the nation was destroyed. God kept His word. The nation was actually destroyed twice. The first destruction, by the Babylonians, began in 586 BC and lasted seventy years. The second began in 70 AD and lasted until 1967 when Jerusalem was once again the unified capital of Israel.

The following are some of the Scriptures that warned Israel of the dispersion into the nations:

> *I will bring the land into desolation: and your enemies which dwell therein shall be astonished at it. And I will scatter you among the heathen, and will draw out a sword after you: and your land shall be desolate, and your cities waste.*
>
> (Leviticus 26:32–33)

> *The LORD shall scatter thee among all people, from the one end of the earth even unto the other; and there thou shalt serve other gods, which neither thou nor thy fathers have known, even wood and stone.* (Deuteronomy 28:64)

> *It shall come to pass, when all these things are come upon thee, the blessing and the curse, which I have set before thee, and thou shalt call them to mind among all the nations, whither the LORD thy God hath driven thee.* (Deuteronomy 30:1)

In 70 AD the Roman army destroyed Israel, Jerusalem, and the temple. This began the second dispersion; however, this time it was into all the world. God fulfilled His covenant under the law of

Moses to the very letter. Remember, the dispersion was not according to the everlasting covenant with Abraham but according to the covenant with Moses. The covenant with Abraham never changed. The dispersion of the Jews was an awesome witness to the authority of God's word.

The dispersion was only half the equation; the second part involved God's promise to restore the people back to the land and have the nation of Israel literally reborn. The history of the nation of Israel shows the awesome power of God ruling over the affairs of the nations.

When studying the history of Israel, one must understand that Jews are no different from others when it comes to sin. Without understanding the human heart, it could be very easy to condemn Israel for failing God and rebelling against Him. If God had chosen any other people to work through, the result would have been the same. The prophet Jeremiah speaks about the sin nature and states, "*The heart is deceitful above all things, and desperately wicked: who can know it?*" (Jeremiah 17:9).

Although Israel broke the second covenant of the law, God said that He would never completely reject the nation. He would always honor the everlasting covenant with Abraham, Isaac, Jacob, and their descendants. Because of this everlasting covenant, He would one day restore the nation of Israel and bring the people back into the land.

Modern Israel exists because of the everlasting covenant. The destruction of Israel and the restoration of the nation, nineteen hundred years later, is an awesome witness to the authority of the Bible as the Word of God. The Bible states with great clarity that Israel would one day be reborn, and that this would happen because of the everlasting covenant with Abraham. Let us look at some of these verses:

> *Then will I remember my covenant with Jacob, and also my covenant with Isaac, and also my covenant with Abraham will I remember; and I will remember the land. The land also shall be left of them, and shall enjoy her sabbaths, while she lieth desolate without them: and they shall accept of the punishment of their iniquity: because, even because they despised my judgments, and because their soul abhorred my statutes. And yet for all that, when they be in the land of their enemies, I will not cast them away, neither will I abhor them, to destroy them utterly, and to break my covenant with them: for I am the Lord their God. But I will for their sakes remember the covenant of their ancestors, whom I brought forth out of the land of Egypt in the sight of the heathen, that I might be their God: I am the Lord.* (Leviticus 26:42–45)

The Ancient Prophets Speak to Us Today

Prophet after prophet in the Bible told of the restoration of Israel after the dispersion into all the world. The prophecy about the rebirth of Israel from a worldwide dispersion is not a footnote in the Bible; it is written on page after page by prophet after prophet for all to see. God sent prophets to Israel to warn them of the coming judgment on the nation. But these same prophets also comforted the Jewish people by telling them of the restoration. The prophets spoke of the coming Messiah and the golden age of His rule on earth; yet before the rule of the Messiah, God had to restore the nation.

The theme of the dispersion and restoration of Israel is one of the major focuses of the Bible. Verse after verse in the Bible tells about the rebirth of Israel. The prophets Ezekiel and Zechariah devote entire chapters to this theme. When the prophets spoke about the rebirth of Israel, the everlasting covenant with Abraham was their foundation. This covenant was everlasting and did not depend on the performance of the Jewish people. Let us look at what some of these ancient prophets wrote that has such a clear message for today.

Isaiah

About 750 BC, the prophet Isaiah wrote about the rebirth of Israel after a second worldwide dispersion. The first dispersion occurred when King Nebuchadnezzar of Babylon took Israel captive around 600 BC. This captivity was limited to Babylon, and the Jews returned to their land seventy years later.

Isaiah prophesied that their return from a worldwide dispersion would be far greater than the one from Babylon. This restoration would bring Jews back from the ends of the earth, and this has happened in our lifetime. The Jewish people have now returned to Israel literally from the east, west, north, and south. They have returned from the ends of the earth, or as Isaiah called it, the "*islands of the sea.*"

> *And it shall come to pass in that day, that the Lord shall set his hand again the second time to recover the remnant of his people, which shall be left, from Assyria, and from Egypt, and from Pathros, and from Cush, and from Elam, and from Shinar, and from Hamath, and from the islands of the sea.*
>
> (Isaiah 11:11)

> *Fear not: for I am with thee: I will bring thy seed from the east, and gather thee from the west; I will say to the north, Give up; and to the south, Keep not back: bring my sons from far, and my daughters from the ends of the earth.* (Isaiah 43:5–6)

Jeremiah

Jeremiah also prophesied at the time of this first dispersion, around 600 BC. He warned the people not only of the coming

Babylonian captivity but of a greater dispersion into all the world. He prophesied that the people would return from both captivities.

Like all the prophets, Jeremiah told of the rebirth of the nation. Jeremiah stated that God scattered the Jews, and would one day restore them to the land. This regathering of the people was a warning to the nations. Remember, the prophet wrote these verses twenty-six hundred years ago.

> *Behold, I will bring them from the north country, and gather them from the coasts of the earth, and with them the blind and the lame, the woman with child and her that travaileth with child together: a great company shall return thither. They shall come with weeping, and with supplications will I lead them: I will cause them to walk by the rivers of waters in a straight way, wherein they shall not stumble: for I am a father to Israel, and Ephraim is my firstborn. Hear the word of the* LORD, *O ye nations, and declare it in the isles afar off, and say, He that scattered Israel will gather him, and keep him, as a shepherd doth his flock.* (Jeremiah 31:8–10)

Ezekiel

The prophet Ezekiel lived and wrote during the first exile, about 570 BC. King Nebuchadnezzar took him captive to Babylon, where Ezekiel wrote incredibly detailed prophecies about the worldwide dispersion and rebirth of the nation of Israel. In beautifully written language with vivid imagery, the prophet gave a detailed look at God's plan for Israel and the nations. Entire chapters of Ezekiel are devoted to the dispersion, restoration, and events that happen after the restoration.

Chapter 36 gives a panoramic view of what was going to happen to Israel. The prophet first mentioned the destruction of the nation and the wasting of the land, followed with the promise that the land will once again be fruitful and inhabited. Ezekiel promised that Jewish people would again dwell in the land that God promised to their fathers. Ezekiel linked the regathering of Jews from all the nations with the everlasting covenant. Let us look at some of these Scriptures from Ezekiel:

> *I scattered them among the heathen, and they were dispersed through the countries: according to their way and according to their doings I judged them....For I will take you from among the heathen, and gather you out of all countries, and will bring you into your own land....And ye shall dwell in the land that I gave to your fathers; and ye shall be my people, and I will be your God.* (Ezekiel 36:19, 24, 28)

Ezekiel followed the general statements in chapter 36 about the regathering of the nation with a vivid picture in chapter 37. He described the nation as being a huge pile of dead dried bones lying in a valley. These bones represent the nation of Israel. God gave this picture to show the utter hopelessness of the nation.

To the natural eye, Israel had no hope. The nation was destroyed and the people had been dispersed into all the world. The Romans destroyed the temple, their center of worship, and the Hebrew language was gone. The nations persecuted and rejected them from country to country. The vision of the valley of dead bones was a perfect picture of the nation of Israel after its destruction in 70 AD. There was no hope.

Ezekiel does not end with the hopelessness, however; it shows that by a sovereign act of God, the nation was to be reborn. The prophet watched as the nation came together in a piecemeal method. The first step was the bones coming together, followed by sinews holding the bones. Finally, flesh covered the bones. At the very end of this process, God put life in the body, and that life will happen at the second coming of the Lord Jesus.

God is working in the affairs of men and governments to resurrect the valley of dried bones into an exceedingly great army. This will happen according to the will of God in order to fulfill His covenant with Abraham, Isaac, and Jacob. Let us look at the picture Ezekiel gives of the hopelessness of the nation of Israel ever being reborn:

> *The hand of the LORD was upon me, and carried me out in the spirit of the LORD, and set me down in the midst of the valley which was full of bones, And caused me to pass by them round about: and, behold, there were very many in the open valley; and, lo, they were very dry. And he said unto me, Son of man, can these bones live? And I answered, O LORD GOD, thou knowest. Again he said unto me, Prophesy upon these bones, and say unto them, O ye dry bones, hear the word of the LORD. Thus saith the LORD GOD unto these bones; Behold, I will cause breath to enter into you, and ye shall live: And I will lay sinews upon you, and will bring up flesh upon you, and cover you with skin, and put breath in you, and ye shall live; and ye shall know that I am the LORD...there was a noise, and behold a shaking, and the bones came together, bone to his bone. And when I beheld, lo, the sinews and the flesh came up upon them, and the skin covered them above: but there was no breath in them. Then said he unto me, Prophesy unto the wind, prophesy, son of man, and say to the wind, Thus saith the LORD GOD; Come from the four winds, O breath, and breathe upon these slain, that they may live. So I prophesied as he commanded me, and the breath came into them, and they lived, and stood up upon their feet, an exceeding great army.* (Ezekiel 37:1–10)

Immediately after this powerful image, Ezekiel went on to explain the vision. There can be no doubt whatsoever as to the theme of this vision. The bones are the people of Israel without hope, and they are dead in the nations. The prophet calls the nations of the world Israel's graves. The coming together of the bones into a body is the nation being reborn:

> *Then he said unto me, Son of man, these bones are the whole house of Israel: behold, they say, Our bones are dried, and our hope is lost: we are cut off for our parts. Therefore prophesy and say unto them, Thus saith the Lord God; Behold, O my people, I will open your graves, and cause you to come up out of your graves, and bring you into the land of Israel....And say unto them, Thus saith the Lord God; Behold, I will take the children of Israel from among the heathen, whither they be gone, and will gather them on every side, and bring them into their own land....* ***And they shall dwell in the land that I have given unto Jacob my servant****, wherein your fathers have dwelt; and they shall dwell therein, even they, and their children, and their children's children for ever.*
>
> (Ezekiel 37:11–12, 21, 25, emphasis added)

Ezekiel connected the resurrection of the dead nation with God granting the land to Jacob. This is another reference to the everlasting covenant. Over and over again the Bible connects the dispersion and rebirth of Israel to the everlasting covenant. The Bible is crystal clear that when the nation is reborn, it is because God has honored His covenant. God is working in the affairs of men and nations to fulfill His ancient promise.

Zechariah

Zechariah was one of the prophets after the Jews returned to Israel from the Babylonian captivity. He wrote about 520 BC.

Zechariah was unique in that so much of his focus was on the city of Jerusalem. The other prophets talked about the land and some touched on Jerusalem, but Zechariah gave many details about the city.

The prophet said that God chose Jerusalem for His purpose. Of all the cities of the world, God chose this city to work out His redemptive plan for man: "*And the Lord shall inherit Judah his portion in the holy land, **and shall choose Jerusalem again***" (Zechariah 2:12, emphasis added). The prophet Zechariah showed that Jerusalem would be inhabited and restored, just like Israel. The people would come back to Jerusalem from all over the world.

> *Thus saith the Lord of hosts; Behold, I will save my people from the east country, and from the west country; and I will bring them, and they shall dwell in the midst of Jerusalem: and they shall be my people, and I will be their God, in truth and in righteousness.* (Zechariah 8:7–8)

The city will be the center for the worship of God. All the peoples from the nations of the world come to Jerusalem, the city that will be the center of the world's attention. Jerusalem is unlike any city in the world because it is the city God chose. This city will once again be the capital of the reborn nation of Israel.

> *Yea, many people and strong nations shall come to seek the Lord of hosts in Jerusalem, and to pray before the Lord.*
> (Zechariah 8:22)

> *Jerusalem shall be inhabited again in her own place, even in Jerusalem.* (Zechariah 12:6)

When Jews return from their worldwide dispersion and the nation is reborn, this will be the final return. There will be no subsequent third or fourth dispersion into all the world. For this reason, the events that are unfolding before our very eyes are quite significant. God is working in the affairs of the nations, bringing biblical prophecy to a fulfillment. The prophetic plan centers on the day of the Lord, which will be examined later in this book. The prophets have already written the entire script. It is there for everyone to read, understand and believe.

> *I will plant them upon their land, and they shall no more be pulled up out of their land which I have given them, saith the* LORD *thy God.* (Amos 9:15)

CHAPTER SEVEN

The Modern Building of Zion

When the L*ORD shall build up Zion, he shall appear in his glory.* (Psalm 102:16)

The foundation of the Zionist movement began in the 1880s when the church in America started crying out to God for the persecuted Jews. In 1891, William Blackstone petitioned the world governments to create a Jewish homeland in Palestine. God responded with amazing speed. Just six years later, in 1897, the first Zionist Congress met and launched the modern Zionist movement. The existence of modern Israel can be traced back to 1897 and this congress. It took just fifty-one more years to reach the rebirth of Israel in 1948.

During 1894, a sensational trial in France was the catalyst that triggered the Zionist Congress. This incident shook Jewry and sparked the return of Jews in an organized manner back to Israel. The trial revolved around Captain Alfred Dreyfus, an intelligence officer on the French general staff. The French government charged and convicted him of spying for Germany. Dreyfus was the only Jew on the general staff, and it became apparent that because he was Jewish, they framed him. The trial had the world's attention and the media followed it very closely. It caused a tremendous wave of anti-Semitism in France.

Theodor Herzl, a Jewish journalist from Switzerland, covered this trial. Dreyfus was Jewish, and Herzl observed the hatred of Jews that this trial caused in France. He realized it was only a matter of time before all of Europe exploded with a hatred of Jews. The pogroms against Jews were already raging in Russia. This prompted Herzl to take action.

In 1896, Herzl published his book, *The Jewish State: A Modern Solution to the Jewish Question*. The content of this book was almost identical to the ideas found in the Blackstone Memorial. It called for the creation of a Jewish state and had an enormous impact. It led directly to the founding of the Zionist Organization, which spearheaded the return of Jews back to Palestine. The first Zionist Congress met in August 1897, setting the economic foundation for the modern state of Israel.

Thus, the hatred for Jews in France and Russia set the stage for the rebirth of Israel. The pogroms in Russia started a small trickle of Jews heading to Israel, while the hatred in France set the ideological framework. God was using this hatred to put in the hearts of Jewish people a desire for Israel. It was the Roman sword that drove them into all the nations and European hatred that started the drive back.

At one point, Herzl had severe doubts about the restoration of Israel in Palestine. Blackstone heard of this and sent Herzl a Bible in which all the verses about the Jews returning to Israel were underlined. This Bible is on display at the Herzl Museum in Jerusalem.

The early Zionists recognized the importance of William Blackstone in the creation of Israel. Louis Brandeis, an Associate Justice of the United States Supreme Court and one of the leading

Jewish Zionists, stated that Blackstone was the "father of modern Zionism." Justice Brandeis, perhaps the leading Zionist of his era, credited Blackstone, not Herzl, as being the "father of modern Zionism." This shows the powerful connection between the American evangelical church and the formation of modern Israel.[1]

Blackstone addressed the Convention of the Federation of American Zionists in 1916. Brandeis attended this meeting and heard Blackstone speak. He was extremely impressed and realized the significance of the Blackstone Memorial, reacting with this statement:

> Those of you who have read with care the petition presented twenty-five years ago by the Rev. Wm. Blackstone and others, asking that the President of the United States use his influence in the calling together of a Congress of the Nations of the world to consider the Jewish problem with a view to the giving of Palestine to the Jews, must have been struck with the extraordinary coincidence that the arguments which Rev. Blackstone used in that petition were, in large part, the arguments which the great Herzl presented five years later, in setting forth to the world the needs and the hopes of the Jewish people. That coincidence alone, the sameness of the arguments presented in America and later by Herzl, shows how clearly and strongly founded they are.[2]

Zionism and the End of the Times of the Gentiles

They shall fall by the edge of the sword, and shall be led away captive into all nations: and Jerusalem shall be trodden down of the Gentiles, until the times of the Gentiles be fulfilled.

(Luke 21:24)

The expression "*the times of the Gentiles be fulfilled*" by the Lord Jesus means that at some point in history, non-Jewish control of Israel, and especially Jerusalem, will cease. The non-Jewish control of Jerusalem had a finite time period set by God. With the completion of this time period, God would once again restore the nation of Israel.

The time of the Gentiles began in 606 BC when King Nebuchadnezzar first conquered Jerusalem. In 586 BC, he destroyed Jerusalem and led the captive Jews to Babylon. He ended the rule of the Kings of Israel. From 586 BC onward, Israel never had another earthly king. The nation was at the mercy of one empire after another. The Babylonian, Persian, Greek, and Roman empires all ruled over Jerusalem. But this captivity did not destroy the priesthood. During this entire time, the Jews remained under the everlasting covenant with God. This covenant never ceased.

In 66 AD, the Jews revolted against Rome. In 70 AD, the Roman general Titus destroyed Israel and Jerusalem. The temple was destroyed and never rebuilt. This ended the priesthood and the sacrificial system, resulting in the total destruction of Jerusalem, with the Romans killing over one million Jews. The Roman army captured many of the survivors of this war and sold them as slaves. In 136, the Romans crushed a second Jewish revolt before literally plowing up Jerusalem and salting the soil to poison it. The Roman Emperor Hadrian renamed Jerusalem, calling it Aelia Capitolina. Very few Jews remained on the covenant land. From this time until 1948, the nation of Israel was literally dead.

God fulfilled His covenant with Israel by using the Babylonians and Romans. These pagan nations only had authority over God's covenant people because the Jews failed to keep the law. As God's instruments of judgment, the Babylonians took away the kingdom and the Romans took away the priesthood. Yet the everlasting covenant with Abraham still stood through these judgments. The Bible did not mention the duration of the dispersion, but the promise of the restoration remained.

The prophet Hosea, writing about 750 BC, said that Israel would suffer a long time without a king and priesthood. In the latter days they would return to the land. At the end of the age, Jews would return to the land, and the coming of the Messiah would follow. They have returned in our lifetime.

> *The children of Israel shall abide many days without a king, and without a prince, and without a sacrifice....Afterward shall the children of Israel return, and seek the* Lord *their God, and David their king; and shall fear the* Lord *and his goodness in the latter days.* (Hosea 3:4–5)

The expression "*seek...David their king*" means seeking the Messiah. David had been dead for two hundred years when Hosea wrote this. The Messiah was to be a direct descendant of David. He was the son of David, and King over all the earth. The prophet Jeremiah told of a captivity into Babylon that was to last for seventy years, but captivity did not destroy the priesthood.

When the Jews returned after seventy years, they immediately restored the sacrificial system and rebuilt the temple. The captivity Hosea wrote about lasted a long time, during which there was no sacrificial system. This destruction of the priesthood began in the year 70 AD, and continues to this day.

The Roman destruction of the Jewish temple in Jerusalem bears a remarkable similarity to the Babylonian destruction of the temple. Both temples were destroyed on the very same day, 655 years apart. In 586 BC, King Nebuchadnezzar's Babylonian army broke through the defenses of Jerusalem and stopped the sacrifices in the temple on the ninth day of Av.

The Jewish calendar is lunar, and the month of Av would correspond with the months of July and August. More than six hundred years later, the Roman army under General Titus broke through the defenses of Jerusalem, destroyed the temple, and ended the sacrifices on the same day, the ninth of Av! Both destructions marked the beginning of the Jewish captivity into the nations. To this day, the ninth of Av is a day of mourning for the Jews.

With the nation of Israel reborn, the time of the Gentile rule over Jerusalem is drawing to a close. The events now transpiring are leading to the final climax between the God of Israel and the nations of the world who have rejected His word. The final world battle recorded in the Bible will take place over Jerusalem and the land of Israel. All the nations of the world will be involved in this final conflict.

This Land That Was Desolate

> *They shall say, This land that was desolate is become like the garden of Eden; and the waste and desolate and ruined cities are become fenced, and are inhabited.* (Ezekiel 36:35)

The prophet Ezekiel said Jews would go into all the nations and the land would be desolate. The destruction of the temple in 70 AD began the worldwide dispersion. In 136 AD, the Roman army crushed the second revolt. This time they also destroyed Jerusalem. The Romans even changed the name of the area to Philistine. This is where the modern name Palestine originated.

The death of the physical nation continued century after century with no end in sight. Empire after empire ruled the area. There was always a small remnant of Jews living on the land, especially in Jerusalem. Jerusalem was never the capital of another nation. The nations that ruled over Jerusalem from the year 70 AD to present were:

1. Romans and Byzantines ruled until 638. Romans first called the land Palestine.
2. Muslims captured Israel and Jerusalem in 638. This began the rule over the area by the Muslim Caliphs and the religion of Islam. They ruled until 1072.
3. Seljukes ruled from 1072 until 1096.
4. Crusaders ruled from 1096 until 1291.
5. Mamelukes ruled from 1291 until 1516.
6. Ottoman Turks ruled from 1516 until 1918. This ended the rule of Islam over the area of Israel.
7. British were given mandate to rule after WWI from 1918 until May 14, 1948.
8. From May 14, 1948 to the present, the nation has once again been under Jewish control.

In June 1967, all of Jerusalem came under the authority of the nation of Israel. In July 1980, Jerusalem officially became the capital of Israel, as it was nearly three thousand years ago under King David. The Romans, Byzantines, Persians, Arabs, Kurds, Mamelukes, Mongols, Crusaders, Turks, French, and British invaded the land. Through all of this war and conquest, there was a continual Jewish presence on the land. There was never an independent sovereign nation ruling over the land of Israel with Jerusalem as the capital. Even under the rule of the Ottoman Turks, Jerusalem was a desolate city with Damascus as the provincial capital over it.

God seems to have preserved the land for His covenant people with Jerusalem as the capital. All of these empires came and went, but the Jews still returned as an independent nation. Nothing in history prevented the rebirth of the nation.

Jews trickled back into Israel through the early part of the twentieth century. The Turks owned the land and Jews bought whatever land they could. In 1914, World War I started. By November 1917, it was apparent that the British were going to defeat the Turks in the Middle East. The Ottoman Empire was coming to an end. In anticipation of this defeat, and with the Turks losing control over the covenant land, British Foreign Secretary Arthur James Balfour issued the famous Balfour Declaration.

This rather short document recognized the right of the Jewish people to return to Israel as a homeland. It seems that World War I prepared *the land* for the return of the Jewish people. The Balfour Declaration follows:

> His Majesty's Government view with favor the establishment in Palestine of a national home for the Jewish people, and will use their best endeavors to facilitate the achievement of this object, it being clearly understood that nothing shall be done which may prejudice the civil and religious rights of existing non-Jewish communities in Palestine, or the rights and political status enjoyed by Jews in any other country.[3]

On December 9, 1917, British General Edmund Allenby captured Jerusalem. Allenby understood the significance of capturing this city. He gave orders that Jerusalem was not to be taken by force, and the army was not to shell or fight in Jerusalem. The Turks retreated without firing a shot. Jerusalem and the covenant land fell to the British. For the first time in more than six hundred years the land was no longer under the control of an Islamic nation. In 1922, the League of Nations placed Britain in charge of a future Jewish state.

The Arabs put pressure on the British government to restrict Jewish emigration. There were Arab riots throughout the 1920s and 1930s. In 1929, for example, they massacred all the Jews in the city of Hebron. The riots pressured the British to reduce the original land grant planned for the nation of Israel. The Muslim resistance that started in the 1920s continues to this day.

World War II was the next big step in the rebirth of Israel. Following the horrors of the war and the defeat of Germany, the United Nations was created. In 1947, the UN voted to partition Palestine into two sections. One partition designated a small section of land for Jews. The Nazi Holocaust of Jews drove many of the survivors out of Europe. They wanted to go to Israel. By 1948, there were approximately six hundred thousand Jews in Israel. It seems that World War II prepared *the Jewish people* for the land.

The two world wars of the twentieth century had an enormous impact on the rebirth of Israel. World War I broke the hold of Islam over the area and prepared the land for the rebirth. World War II prepared the heart of the people, awakening their desire to go back to the land. The sword drove the Jews from the land, and in many respects it was the sword that drove them back home. Remember, God works in the affairs of the nations to fulfill His covenant with Abraham, Isaac, and Jacob.

The Nazis failed to stop the rebirth of Israel. In fact, their atrocities seemed to accelerate the establishment of the nation. Hitler tried to destroy world Jewry. Yet, just three years after the defeat of the Nazis, Israel was reborn. God told Ezekiel that He would cause the Jewish people to leave the nations and come back to Israel. The horror of World War II was one of the main forces that drove Jews back to Israel.

On May 14, 1948, five Arab nations attacked Israel in an attempt to destroy the newly formed nation. Israel took no aggressive action against the Arabs, but the mere existence of the Jewish state was enough for the Arabs to attack. The Arab nations of Egypt, Syria, Iraq, Jordan, and Saudi Arabia were defeated, and the nation survived its difficult rebirth. When the war ended, Israel was a land area of about 8,000 square miles—approximately the size of New Jersey. The war ended with Jews in control of about two-thirds of Jerusalem. Jordan controlled the rest of the city, including the Temple Mount.

Much of the land for the new nation of Israel came from two sources. Jews bought some of the land from the Turks, and when Turkey was defeated, it turned over to the British large tracts of state owned land. Britain then turned this land over to the newly formed state of Israel.

In 1967, war broke out again. This war became known as the Six-Day War. Egypt and Syria mobilized their armies and threatened to attack Israel. The Egyptian army crossed the Suez Canal and headed toward Israel. Egypt demanded that the United Nations peacekeepers in the Sinai leave, and Egypt closed the Gulf of Aqaba to Israeli shipping. This action by Egypt was an act of war.

On June 5, the Israeli army attacked Egypt and Syria, and crushed the Egyptian and Syrian armies. On the last day of the war, Jordan attacked Israel. In one day, Jordan lost Jerusalem and all the land west of the Jordan River. The tiny nation of Israel became a world military power in only twenty years of existence.

As the ancient prophets stated, Israel was reborn with Jerusalem as the capital. For the first time since 606 BC, Jerusalem was once again the capital of an independent Israel. Jesus Christ said that Jerusalem was God's prophetic timepiece. Just as the Lord Jesus had said in Luke 21:24, all of Jerusalem was again under complete Jewish control. God's unseen hand was working in the affairs of men to fulfill the everlasting covenant.

The fighting over the land continued. In 1973, Syria and Egypt again attacked Israel. This resulted in the Yom Kippur War. The attack was a complete surprise. The nation was nearly defeated but survived the initial surprise attack and began a powerful counterattack. When a truce was declared, the Israeli army was advancing on both Cairo and Damascus.

The land continues to be a source of turmoil. The attacks on Israel from Lebanon caused war in the 1980s and again in 2006. There have been many riots and terrorist attacks throughout the 1980s and 1990s. On September 28, 2000, fighting broke out in Jerusalem over the Temple Mount. This conflict expanded into a low grade war between Israel and the Palestinians, threatening to escalate into a regional war using weapons of mass destruction that could destroy entire nations. The covenant land of Israel has become the source of world attention just as the Bible said it would. God's prophetic word is right on target.

The Latter Day Is Today

> *Afterward shall the children of Israel return, and seek the LORD their God, and David their king; and shall fear the LORD and his goodness in the latter days.* (Hosea 3:5)

The prophet Hosea said that the Jews would return to Israel "*in the latter days.*" Ezekiel put the latter days in the context of Jews returning after a worldwide dispersion. He described a huge army that is going to attack Israel. He then identified the time when this tremendous confederation of nations will attack. This event occurs in the latter years, when the Jewish people return from the dispersion.

> *After many days thou* [invading army] *shalt be visited* [mustered]: *in the* ***latter years*** *thou shalt come into the land that is brought back from the sword, and is gathered out of many people, against the mountains of Israel, which have been always waste: but it is brought forth out of the nations, and they shall dwell safely all of them.*
>
> (Ezekiel 38:8, emphasis added)

The Jews are back and the nation of Israel is a reality. For centuries, the land was a true wasteland, defoliated of trees and full of malarial swamps. The area was poor and supported little agriculture. When the Jews left, a curse seemed to have settled on the land. Now, with the Jewish people back on the land, it is flourishing again. They planted millions of trees and drained the swamps. Israel has developed a wonderful agricultural industry that supplies Europe with much of its fruit.

In the past fifty years, Israel has become a world military power with nuclear weapons. Viewing Israel as just another nation is a huge mistake; Israel is the fulfillment of the everlasting covenant God made with Abraham four thousand years ago. One hundred years ago, no one would have believed that Jews would return to Israel from all over the world, that Jerusalem would again be the capital, that the land would produce incredible agriculture, or that the nation would be a world military power. Yet this is exactly what has happened! The modern nation of Israel is truly supernatural.

No nation in history has been destroyed as Israel was. The capital and religious center was destroyed twice, and the people were twice taken captive; the second captivity lasted nineteen hundred years. For this nation to be reborn and have the same capital is a supernatural event. The people even speak the same language and have the same religion.

What force kept this people together as a nation even though they were scattered throughout the world for nineteen hundred years? What force kept the language and religion intact? What force kept the Jews from complete destruction through pogroms, crusades, holocausts, intifadas, and all the other attempts to destroy them? The Jewish people and the nation of Israel are an enigma unless you understand the Bible.

The rebirth of the nation shows the authority of the Bible as the word of God, and the invisible hand of God working to fulfill His word. The everlasting covenant that God made with Abraham, Isaac, and Jacob cannot fail. God's covenant is the force which has kept Israel through the centuries.

According to the Bible, the return of the Jews makes this time the "*latter day.*" The nation of Israel was reborn just as the Bible said would happen. We are now living in the times the ancient Jewish prophets wrote about. The prophecy about Israel does not stop with the rebirth of the nation; the Bible has laid out the future. As time goes on, God's prophetic plan as outlined in the Bible has become clearer and clearer.

The nation of Israel, and Jerusalem in particular, are God's timepieces. By watching events involving Israel and Jerusalem the prophetic time can be determined. Jesus said that non-Jews (Gentiles) would tread down Jerusalem until a certain fixed period of time. This fixed period of time had to do with the end of the age and His second coming.

> *They shall fall by the edge of the sword, and shall be led away captive into all nations: and Jerusalem shall be trodden down of the Gentiles, until the times of the Gentiles be fulfilled.*
>
> (Luke 21:24)

CHAPTER EIGHT

Jerusalem, God's Anvil

Anvil: an iron or steel block on which objects are hammered into shape

In that day will I make Jerusalem a burdensome stone for all people: all that burden themselves with it shall be cut in pieces, though all the people of the earth be gathered together against it. (Zechariah 12:3)

The rebirth of the nation of Israel has been a very slow process, starting in the 1880s and continuing until today. At times, this process has seemed to stop, only to be suddenly accelerated again by a world-shaking event.

Jews leaving Russia and trickling back to Israel did not seem significant at first. Then came World War I and the Balfour Declaration in 1917. Like an explosion, World War I prepared the land for the return. The period between world wars was one of tension and terrorism. There was no apparent move of God toward fulfilling the covenant, but then came World War II and the Nazi Holocaust. These events set the stage for hundreds of thousands of Jews to flee back to Israel. World War II prepared the people for the land.

Then came the rebirth of the nation on May 14, 1948, and the immediate war that followed. The war ended with Israeli independence, but Jerusalem a divided city. Once again there was a period of tension and terrorism. For twenty years, there seemed to be no end to the fighting. Next came the Six Day War of 1967 and like a bolt of lightning, Jerusalem was the united capital of Israel. Since 1967, there has been a major war, fighting in Lebanon, continuing terrorist attacks, and several intifadas against Israel.

Starting in September 2000, a low-grade war started over Jerusalem. This war was a continuation of the fighting that started in the 1920s. Although the fighting and terrorism appear endless, there will be an end. Terrorism and fighting seem to occur between all the major moves of God to restore Israel. The terrorism and fighting against Israel will continue up to the next major event, which may be the rebuilding of the temple in Jerusalem.

Jerusalem was united nearly forty years ago. Now, the focus of tension is over Jerusalem and the Temple Mount area. The Bible states that the possession of Jerusalem will be the cause of the last great world war. The issues involving Jerusalem will draw all the nations of the world into battle. God is going to use Jerusalem as an anvil against the nations of the world. In September 2000, the Temple Mount became the scene of bloody combat. This could be the fuse that ignites the last world war.

God is moving to fulfill the promises of His everlasting covenant, but human observers need patience. God moved very slowly in fulfilling the promise. Looking back to 1917, it is clear that the Israelis have made tremendous progress as a people and nation. Millions of Jews have returned home. Israel is a nation, and Jerusalem is its capital. Israel is a mighty military power with a powerful economy. Hebrew is the national language. In God's time, He will fulfill the rest of the covenant promises. Israel will rebuild a temple in Jerusalem in the near future. It is just a matter of time.

No group or country has been able to stop the rebirth and development of the nation. Israel is truly like an anvil, and nations are broken that try to destroy God's everlasting covenant. In watching God at work, great patience is required.

The restoration has taken over a century to get this far, but God has His own agenda and timetable. Watching Jerusalem and the intifada that started in September 2000 over the Temple Mount, one sees that God's timetable may be accelerating. Remember, Jesus Christ said that Jerusalem was the key to the timetable.

> *And they shall fall by the edge of the sword, and shall be led away captive into all nations: and Jerusalem shall be trodden down of the Gentiles, until the times of the Gentiles be fulfilled.* (Luke 21:24)

With the rebirth of Israel and Jerusalem as the capital, this nation becomes an anvil for false views of God and Bible doctrine. Most religions of the world do not recognize God's everlasting covenant with Israel. Some believe the Jews had a covenant, but they believe it is no longer in effect.

God is using the restoration of Israel to show that His word is literal. The rebirth of Israel confronts false teaching, false doctrine, and false prophets. Israel becomes an anvil, breaking many false doctrines and misunderstandings about the Bible.

Islam

The Islamic religion does not recognize the covenant with Isaac and Jacob but instead believes God made the covenant with Abraham and Ishmael. The Bible actually states that the everlasting covenant was not with Ishmael but with Isaac; however, Islam refuses to accept the authority of the Bible and insists the covenant was with Ishmael. The Bible verses to show this follow:

> *God said, Sarah thy wife shall bear thee a son indeed; and thou shalt call his name Isaac: and I will establish my covenant with him for an* ***everlasting covenant****, and with his seed after him. And as for Ishmael, I have heard thee: Behold, I have blessed him, and will make him fruitful, and will multiply him exceedingly; twelve princes shall he beget, and I will make him a great nation. But* ***my covenant*** *will I establish with Isaac, which Sarah shall bear unto thee at this set time in the next year.*
>
> (Genesis 17:19–21, emphasis added)

Muslims controlled Palestine for most of the time since 638 yet could not prevent the restoration of Israel. Muslims fought Israel in 1948, 1967, and 1973, followed by continual strife right up to our present day. Yet the Muslim nations failed to destroy Israel. This tension between Israel and the Koran can never be peacefully resolved. For Muslims to recognize the nation of Israel would be an admission that their beliefs are wrong.

The Koran does not mention Jerusalem, and it does not mention the rebirth of the nation of Israel. The Bible mentions Jerusalem 811 times. The rebirth of Israel is on page after page in the Bible, while the Koran is silent. The rebirth of Israel shows the authority of the Bible as the Word of God, and is proof that the Koran and Mohammed are incorrect. For this reason, there will always be tension between Israel and Islam. This tension will not last forever, however.

There is a huge confrontation on the horizon between the Holy God of the Bible and Islam. The heart of the confrontation is Jewish control of Jerusalem. God is using Israel as an anvil against Islam. When the Islamic nations come against Israel and Jerusalem, God will judge them. This destruction will lead them to realize the Bible is the word of God, and the holy God of Israel is the true God.

> *Thus will I magnify myself, and sanctify myself; and I will be known in the eyes of many nations, and they shall know that I am the* LORD. (Ezekiel 38:23)

Christian Replacement Theology

God is also using Israel as an anvil against false teachings within the Christian church. There are false doctrines called dominion theology, covenant theology, and preterism. These doctrines are fluid and have many branches, but there is one basic tenet they all hold: the Christian church has now replaced Israel in the everlasting covenant with Abraham.

These doctrines hold that God has no future plan for the nation of Israel, and that when the Roman armies destroyed Jerusalem and the temple in 70 AD, it ended the everlasting covenant. Israel then fell under the curse of the law, and all the blessings in the Bible now belong to the church. The church now is the seed of Abraham.

These doctrines are in stark contrast to what prophet after prophet stated in the Bible. Jeremiah, for example, stated that the Lord will never cast off all Israel for sin. Jeremiah claimed that the nation of Israel will remain forever, and God will never cast them all away.

> *Thus saith the* LORD, *which giveth the sun for a light by day, and the ordinances of the moon and of the stars for a light by night, which divideth the sea when the waves thereof roar; the* LORD *of hosts is his name: If those ordinances depart from before me, saith the* LORD, *then the seed of Israel also shall cease from being a nation before me for ever. Thus saith the* LORD; *If heaven above can be measured, and the foundations of the*

> *earth searched out beneath, I will also cast off all the seed of Israel for all that they have done, saith the Lord.*
>
> (Jeremiah 31:35–37)

The book of Ezekiel records that God dispersed Israel into all nations because of sin, but God would one day bring them back because of His holy name—not because of their righteousness. The nation of Israel exists today only because of the holy name of the God of Israel.

> *I scattered them among the heathen, and they were dispersed through the countries: according to their way and according to their doings I judged them.... But I had pity for mine holy name, which the house of Israel had profaned among the heathen, whither they went.... Thus saith the Lord God; I do not this for your sakes, O house of Israel, but for mine holy name's sake, which ye have profaned among the heathen, whither ye went. And I will sanctify my great name, which was profaned among the heathen.... For I will take you from among the heathen, and gather you out of all countries, and will bring you into your own land.... And ye shall dwell in the land that I gave to your fathers; and ye shall be my people, and I will be your God.*
>
> (Ezekiel 36:19, 21–24, 28)

Zechariah prophesied the restoration of Israel, but said that when the people return, it will be in unbelief toward God and the Messiah, the Lord Jesus Christ. The prophet showed that God will restore Jerusalem, and that He will judge the nations for trying to destroy Jerusalem. At the time of this judgment, Israel then turns to belief in the Lord Jesus: "*...and they shall look upon me whom they have pierced, and they shall mourn for him*" (Zechariah 12:10). Israel is in unbelief today, just as Zechariah stated would happen. The day of their restoration to the Lord God of Israel remains yet in the future:

> *It shall come to pass in that day, that I will seek to destroy all the nations that come against Jerusalem. And I will pour upon the house of David, and upon the inhabitants of Jerusalem, the spirit of grace and of supplications: and they shall look upon me whom they have pierced, and they shall mourn for him, as one mourneth for his only son, and shall be in bitterness for him, as one that is in bitterness for his firstborn.* (Zechariah 12:9–10)

God is using the rebirth of Israel to prove the replacement doctrines incorrect. Just as Moses and the prophets wrote, the physical descendants of Abraham have returned and restored the nation. In the Bible, Jerusalem literally means the city of Jerusalem, and Israel means Israel; one cannot spiritualize it to mean the church. Islam and replacement theology both refuse to believe the Bible about the restoration of Israel and Jerusalem. These combined false beliefs failed to prevent the restoration of Israel.

If this restoration of Israel is not of God, then what is it? The restoration of modern Israel fulfills the prophecies of the Bible. It comes down to the final authority: is the final authority a man-made doctrine like replacement theology or Islam, or the Bible with its clear verses that establish the restoration of Israel? The restoration of Israel smashes replacement theology. The foundation of replacement theology rests upon unbelief in God's word. This is a serious error that leads to consequences with God, including spiritual blindness.

To try and get around the error of the replacement and covenant theology, some believers in these doctrines have gone so far as to say that the Jews in Israel are not real Jews. When the Tsar was killing "Jews" in the Russian pogroms, no one said, "Stop! They are not real Jews." When the Nazis were killing the Jews, no one said to Hitler,

"Stop! They are not real Jews." Now, when these same Jews go back to Israel, they are accused of not being real Jews.

God is using the rebirth of Israel to cut through false and incorrect views of His word. The promise of God in the Bible is crystal clear on page after page. Man-made doctrines and false prophets have tried to alter this covenant, but in the latter day God has made the truth clear for all to see. God is very serious about His word. "*Then said the LORD unto me, Thou hast well seen: for I will hasten my word to perform it*" (Jeremiah 1:12).

Belief in false doctrines concerning the literalness of the rebirth of Israel blinds people to the work of God that is occurring right before their eyes. God is moving to fulfill His word, and millions cannot see it. It is sad that believers in Jesus Christ, because of false doctrine, are actually against the work of God. Replacement theology and Islamic theology are in agreement against Israel. They both refuse to recognize that Israel exists because of the everlasting covenant.

It is a grave thing to be on the wrong side of God when He is defending His everlasting covenant. The wrong doctrine can cause apathy toward Israel and the Jews, leading to failure to pray for and support Israel in a time of crisis. This incorrect doctrine blinds a person's ability to recognize God's judgment falling on America for forcing Israel to divide the covenant land. Therefore, this person is spiritually unable to intercede for America as it faces judgment.

God is very serious about the land and covenant. The Lord God of Israel will literally use Jerusalem as an anvil to destroy the nations that come against it. Jerusalem will draw the nations like a moth to a light. Multitudes of people have rejected God and the Bible, and this rebellion will cause the nations to come against God's anvil. God has warned beforehand about what will happen when armies try to destroy Israel and take Jerusalem. The entire world will see the mighty power of God as He uses Israel as His anvil.

God is using the rebirth of Israel to expose false prophets and false doctrines and to have a literal witness on the earth to the authority of His Word. It is important that one's faith be in accord with the truth of the Bible. God's Word has been tested in the furnace of the earth, and the Bible has proven itself to be like pure gold and silver. The everlasting covenant has been tested now for four thousand years of history. It is in effect for all to see. God is faithful to His Word and promises.

Credit: National Archives and Record Administration

German American Bund

ADDRESS: GERMAN AMERICAN BUND, P. O BOX 1, STATION "K", NEW YORK, N. Y.

DISTRICT: ....
SECTION: ....
UNIT: ....
ADDRESS: ....
....

Application for Membership

*) Payable when applying

Initiation Fee $1.00
Monthly Dues $0.75
Voluntary Donation $0.50 up

I hereby apply for admission to membership in the „German American Bund". The purposes and aims of the Band are known to me, and I obligate myself to support them to the best of my ability. I recognize the leadership principle, in accordance to which the Band is being directed. I am of Aryan descent, free from Jewish or colored blood.
Please write distinctly.

Full Name: .... Occupation: ....

Exact Address: .... Telephone: ....

Born: .... Place of Birth: .... Single/Married/Widowed: ....
Day Month Year

First Papers. No.: .... What Court and when obtained: ....
....

Final Papers. No.: .... What Court and when obtained: ....
....

When and where immigrated: .... Passport No.: ....

Two References: (1) ....
(2) ....

To what Organizations do you belong? ....

Only U. S. Citizens are eligible for office. First Papers suffice for Membership in "Prospective Citizens' League"

Paid Dues
Initiation Fee .... $:..........
Monthly Dues .... $:..........
Vol. Donation .... $:..........

Date: ....

....
Applicant's Personal Signature

....
Unit Leader

Please do not use this space
No. ....

Application to join the Bund, the American Nazi Party

The application reads: I hereby apply for the admission to the membership in the "German American Bund." The purpose and aims of the Bund are known to me, and I obligate myself to support them to the best of my ability. I recognize the leadership principle, in accordance to which the Bund is being directed. I am of Aryan descent, free from Jewish or colored blood.

Credit: National Archives and Record Administration

Anschriften der Ortsgruppen von Gross New York

ASTORIA

Amerikadeutscher Volksbund, c o Turnhalle, 44-01 Broadway, Astoria, L. I.

BERGEN COUNTY

Amerikadeutscher Volksbund. P. O. Box 128, Hackensack, N. J.

BROOKLYN

Amerikadeutscher Volksbund, 267 St. Nicholas Avenue, Brooklyn, N. Y.

BROOKLYN SOUTH

Amerikadeutscher Volksbund, Prospect Hall, Prospect Ave., Brooklyn, N. Y.

BRONX

Amerikadeutscher Volksbund, New Holbrau, 222½ St. Anns Ave., Bronx, N. Y.

HUDSON COUNTY

Amerikadeutscher Volksbund, 754 Palisade Avenue, Union City, N. J.

JAMAICA

Amerikadeutscher Volksbund. 168-15 91. Avenue, Jamaica, L. I.

LINDENHURST

Amerikadeutscher Volksbund, P. O. Box 555, Lindenhurst, L. I.

NASSAU COUNTY

Amerikadeutscher Volksbund, Brauhof, 3rd Street and Jericho Turnpike. New Hyde Park, L. I.

NEWARK

Amerikadeutscher Volksbund, P. O. Box 65, Irvington, N. J.

NEW ROCHELLE

Amerikadeutscher Volksbund, P. O. Box 724, New Rochelle, N. Y.

NEW YORK

Amerikadeutscher Volksbund, P. O. Box 75, Station K, New York, N. Y.

PASSAIC COUNTY

Amerikadeutscher Volksbund, 269 Passaic Street, Passaic, N. J.

STATEN ISLAND

Amerikadeutscher Volksbund, Atlantic Rotisserie. 191 Canal Street, Stapleton, St. Isl.

WHITE PLAINS

Amerikadeutscher Volksbund, Odd Fellows Home, Main Street, White Plains, N. Y.

YONKERS

Amerikadeutscher Volksbund, Polish Community Center, 92 Waverley Street, Yonkers, N. Y.

Bund chapter locations in New York City area

DEUTSCHER TAG

von

LONG ISLAND

AUF

Camp Siegfried

AM SONNTAG, 14. AUGUST 1938

UNTER DER PAROLE

„Allen Gewalten zum Trotz sich erhalten"

Für Ehre, Recht und Freiheit,

Für ein starkes, nationalbewusstes und sozialgerechtes Amerika

PROGRAMM

Feldgottesdienst: Pastor Kropp

Fahnenaufmarsch - Der grosse Festakt - Militär-Konzert - Sportliche Wettkämpfe

Volksbelustigungen aller Art - Luna Park-Betrieb - Abends Tanz

RIESEN-FEUERWERK

Kommt in Scharen und beweist, dass wir DOCH zusammenhalten können!

Kinder frei! — EINTRITT 25 CENTS — Parken 25 Cents

3 special trains leave Penn. Station New York and Flatbush Station Brooklyn

first train		second train		third train	
Lv. New York	8.51 AM	Lv. New York	10.30 AM	Lv. New York	11.45 AM
Lv. Woodside	8.59 AM	Lv. Woodside	10.39 AM	Lv. Woodside	11.54 AM
Lv. Flatbush	8.45 AM	Lv. Flatbush	10.21 AM	Lv. Flatbush	11.35 AM
Lv. Jamaica	9.11 AM	Lv. Jamaica	10.52 AM	Lv. Jamaica	12.07 PM
Ar. Yaphank	10.30 AM	Ar. Yaphank	11.55 AM	Ar. Yaphank	1.10 PM

Trains leave Yaphank 9.58 PM; 10.58 PM and 11.58 PM.

Roundtrip $1.25; Children 6-12 years 65 cents; under 6 years free.

UNTER DEN AUSPIZIEN DES

Amerikadeutscher Volksbund

Credit: National Archives and Record Administration

Advertisement for largest Nazi meeting outside of Germany, August 14, 1938. (Notice train schedules—this was the Siegfried Special to Yaphank, New York.)

Photo Credit: Town of Brookhaven Historical Collection

Siegfried Special arriving at Yaphank station

Photo Credit: Jacob Rader Marcus Center, American Jewish Archives, Hebrew Union College

Nazi Headquarters at Camp Siegfried, ground zero for the Bund

Photo Credit: Bettmann/Corbis

Main entrance to Camp Siegfried

Photo Credit: National Archives and Record Administration

Nazi youth parade entering through main gate of Camp Siegfried, 1937

Photo Credit: Bettmann/Corbis

Fritz Kuhn, Bund Fuehrer, leading Nazi salute, August 29, 1937, Camp Siegfried

Photo Credit: Bettmann/Corbis

Mass group of Bundists with Nazi salute at Camp Siegfried

Photo Credit: Bettmann/Corbis

Meeting at Camp Siegfried

Photo Credit: Bettmann/Corbis

Bundists marching in New York City, October 30, 1937

Photo Credit: Bettmann/Corbis

Destructive power of the Great Hurricane, Westhampton, Long Island, nearby Camp Siegfried, September 21, 1938

Photo Credit: Bettmann/Corbis

Awesome destruction of New London, Connecticut, by the Great Hurricane

Photo Credit: National Archives and Record Administration

Power of the Great Hurricane's storm surge, Connecticut

Photo Credit: National Archives and Record Administration

Some of the 110,000 WPA workers sent to New England after the Great Hurricane

Photo Credit: National Archives and Record Administration

Millions of trees fell like this all over the path of the Great Hurricane. The trees that survived soon died from the salt.

Photo Credit: National Archives and Record Administration

Thousands of homes were destroyed by the storm surge.

Photo Credit: National Archives and Record Administration

The Great Hurricane even took a train off its tracks in Massachusetts! The wind reached 186 miles per hour.

Photo Credit: National Archives and Record Administration

The Great Hurricane destroyed the forests of New England.

Chapter Nine

America on a Collision Course with God

For, behold, in those days, and in that time, when I shall bring again the captivity of Judah and Jerusalem, I will also gather all nations, and will bring them down into the valley of Jehoshaphat, and will plead [punish, judge] *with them there for my people and for my heritage Israel, whom they have scattered among the nations, and parted* [divided] *my land.*

(Joel 3:1–2)

God greatly used America in His plan for the Jewish people and the nation of Israel. As discussed earlier, the United States was a source of protection and blessing to Jews from the very beginning. Millions of Jews escaped the tyrants of Europe and found safety in America. God used the church in the United States during the late 1880s as the spiritual catalyst for Jews to return to Israel. America cooperated with God's agenda for Israel, and assistance continued until 1991. That year was the turning point when the United States began to directly interfere with God's prophetic plan.

The first phase in God's plan was restoring Israel to the covenant area of land. The second phase involved judging the nations for unbelief and rejecting God's covenant. The third phase will usher in the second coming of the Lord Jesus. Connected with the third phase is the nation of Israel turning to the Lord Jesus for salvation. Jerusalem is the central location of His second coming when, as the Bible shows, He will stand on the Mount of Olives. The second and third phases are examined in subsequent chapters.

> *I will gather all nations against Jerusalem to battle....Then shall the* L*ORD* *go forth, and fight against those nations, as when he fought in the day of battle. And his feet shall stand in that day upon the mount of Olives, which is before Jerusalem on the east.* (Zechariah 14:2–4)

The restoration of the nation under the first phase includes Jerusalem, Gaza, Judea, Samaria, the Mountains of Israel, the Golan Heights, and other areas. The prophets were very clear in their writings that when the nation of Israel is reborn it contains specific land areas. We will examine a few of these passages.

The prophet Obadiah wrote about the time period just prior to the day of the Lord, or the second coming of Jesus Christ. Obadiah said that fierce fighting will erupt between Jews and Arabs over the land but the Jewish people will prevail. The fighting will reach the point where the Israelis drive all the Arabs from the land. In the following verse, Jews are the houses of Jacob and Joseph, while the Arabs are the house of Esau:

> *The house of Jacob shall be a fire, and the house of Joseph a flame, and the house of Esau for stubble, and they shall kindle in them, and devour them; and there shall not be any remaining of the house of Esau; for the* L*ORD* *hath spoken it.*
>
> (Obadiah 1:18)

The prophet then wrote that Jews will possess the Plain of the Philistines (modern Gaza) and Ephraim and Samaria (most of the West Bank). The land of Israel also comprises Gilead, which is the western section of Jordan. The land of the Canaanites and Jerusalem includes the rest of modern Israel.

> *They of the south shall possess the mount of Esau; and they of the plain the Philistines: and they shall possess the fields of Ephraim, and the fields of Samaria: and Benjamin shall possess Gilead. And the captivity of this host of the children of Israel shall possess that of the Canaanites, even unto Zarephath; and the captivity of Jerusalem, which is in Sepharad, shall possess the cities of the south.* (Obadiah 1:19–20)

The prophet Ezekiel penned a very detailed description of a geographic location he identified as the Mountains of Israel. This mountain chain runs north-south, straight down the center of Israel. These mountains start about fifty miles north of Jerusalem and run south until Hebron. Jerusalem is located in this mountain range. The prophet wrote that when the Jewish people return, they will inhabit these mountains and God will bless them. The control of this mountain chain by the Israelis is extremely important in biblical prophecy. Today, the Mountains of Israel are located in the West Bank and control is in dispute between the Arabs and Israelis.

> *I will bring them out from the people, and gather them from the countries, and will bring them to their own land, and feed them upon the mountains of Israel by the rivers, and in all the inhabited places of the country.* (Ezekiel 34:13)

> *I will take you from among the heathen, and gather you out of all countries, and will bring you into your own land.*
> (Ezekiel 36:24)

The prophet Zechariah stated that God brings the Jewish people from all over the world back to Jerusalem. The city is restored as Israel's capital—a restoration important in both phase one and two of God's prophetic plan.

> *Thus saith the* Lord *of hosts; Behold, I will save my people from the east country, and from the west country; and I will bring them, and they shall dwell in the midst of Jerusalem.*
> (Zechariah 8:7–8)

> *It shall come to pass in that day, that I will seek to destroy all the nations that come against Jerusalem.* (Zechariah 12:9)

In 1991, President George H. W. Bush led America to victory over Iraq in Operation Desert Storm. Following the war, President Bush took upon himself the creation of a comprehensive peace plan for the Middle East. In October 1991, he convened the Madrid Peace Process. The heart of this peace plan involved Israel and the covenant land. The President used the power of the United States to pressure Israel into this peace process with the Palestinians, Syrians, and Egyptians.

The term "peace plan" was a code word that meant Israel must surrender covenant land. The "negotiable" area was a part of the land grant God gave to Abraham, Isaac, Jacob, and their descendants. It was the land that Obadiah, Ezekiel, and Zechariah wrote about so clearly, that God restored to the reborn nation of Israel. President Bush brought the United States into a direct confrontation with God. The prophets wrote that this land was not negotiable, as it was part of restored Israel. President Bush said it was negotiable, and that it must be surrendered for the sake of peace. The President placed the United States in a position diametrically opposed to God's word.

In 1993 the Madrid Peace Plan evolved into the Oslo Accords, which set a timetable for Israel's withdrawal from parts of the covenant land. The Oslo Accords also focused on the issue of Jerusalem. By 1998, seven years after the peace process started, the heart of the land issue centered on Jerusalem. The United States became the prime force in this peace process.

The prophet Joel stated that God judges nations that are involved in parting the land of Israel. Jerusalem is God's anvil for any nation that tries to divide the city, and the United States is no exception. The United States challenged God's word regarding Jerusalem. In November 1991, President Bush Sr. started the peace process. President Bill Clinton continued it, and President George W. Bush followed through. President Clinton pressured Israel to give away large sections of the land, and he made Jerusalem negotiable. He condemned Israel for building apartments in East Jerusalem. Presidents Bush Sr. and Clinton brought America into a confrontation with God over Jerusalem and Israel, but President George W. Bush went even further.

President George W. Bush committed the United States to recognizing a Palestinian state. He first announced this during his speech to the United Nations on November 10, 2001. This was the first time a United States president used the words "Palestinian state." This speech was an historic event. The two-state idea was later reinforced when, after the President's speech, Secretary of State Colin Powell met with Yasser Arafat. A section of the President's speech follows:

> The American government also stands by its commitment to a just peace in the Middle East. We are working toward a day when two states, Israel and Palestine, live peacefully together within secure and recognized borders as called for by the Security Council resolutions. We will do all in our power to bring both parties back into negotiations.[1]

President Bush then made a major policy speech on June 24, 2002. In this speech, he expanded upon his UN speech and called for two states, Israel and Palestine, living side by side. He totally committed the United States to the creation of a Palestinian state.

Bush directed Secretary of State Powell to work with international leaders to fulfill his vision of a Palestinian state. The President continued by stating that the Israeli occupation of Palestinian land since 1967 needed to end, and United Nations Resolutions 242 and 338 are the documents for settling Israel's borders. This meant Israel was required to withdraw from huge sections of the covenant land, including East Jerusalem. He referred to his plan as the "Road Map to Peace." Part of the President's speech of June 24 follows:

> This means that the Israeli occupation that began in 1967 will be ended through a settlement negotiated between the parties, based on UN Resolutions 242 and 338, with Israeli withdrawal to secure and recognized borders.[2]

The President remained focused on his "Road Map to Peace" and the two-state position. Time and again since June 24, 2002, he reaffirmed his agenda. Thus this became a fixed American policy, which started in October 1991 with President George Bush Sr. Since November 1991, God warned America that the nation was on a collision course with Him over Jerusalem and the covenant land. As America pressured Israel to surrender land, warning judgments hit the nation.

These warning judgments occurred through all three presidencies, regardless of party affiliation, and resulted in some of the greatest natural disasters in the nation's history. These include Hurricane Andrew, the Northridge earthquake, and Hurricane Katrina. These disasters occurred on the very days the United States government pressured Israel to divide the land.

America is no longer cooperating with God's agenda, but is actually hindering it. Presidents Bush Sr., Clinton, and Bush Jr. did not purposely try to thwart God's Word. It appears they are doing this for political expedience; but the Word of God is clear that their actions against Israel bring judgment.

A president acting in ignorance of God's word is no excuse. The prophet Hosea warned that lacking knowledge of the Bible leads to destruction: "*My people are destroyed for lack of knowledge*" (Hosea 4:6). The presidents' personal ignorance of the Bible, when combined with the church leaders' failure to warn the presidents, has placed the United States in grave danger. Most likely the religious leaders believe replacement theology; their doctrine blinds them to the warning judgments.

America is no longer cooperating with God's agenda but is actually hindering it. Presidents Bush Sr., Clinton, and Bush Jr. did not try to thwart God's Word on purpose, but the Word of God is clear that their actions against Israel bring judgment. God always warns before judgment, and He uses people as His instruments of warning.

For example, Noah warned the people for one hundred and twenty years prior to the great flood. Before God judged the ancient Canaanites, He warned them for four hundred years. He warned Israel, with prophet after prophet, for close to two hundred years before the Babylonian captivity. He warned Israel through the New Testament apostles and prophets for forty years before the second dispersion. God is now warning America.

The Bible lists all of God's warnings, which He verifies with awesome disasters that have hit America on the very days the nation pressured Israel to divide the covenant land. For example, every time Yasser Arafat came to America an awesome disaster occurred. At some point, the warning judgments cross over to destruction judgments. The destruction judgments will break the nation and stop the interference with God's plan for Israel. There is no recovery from destruction judgments. It appears that Hurricane Katrina was the first destruction judgment.

God takes His covenant with Abraham, Isaac, and Jacob very seriously. The judgments begin after a nation hardens its heart against His word. It appears that the rebellion and unbelief in God's word has now taken America to the brink of wrath judgments. God has warned and warned, but are people making the connection?

The following is a partial list of the warning judgments that have hit America. These events all happened on the very days the nation pressured Israel to divide the land. God loves America, and He is trying to warn the nation of this collision course. God is very serious about not dividing Israel and Jerusalem. He will not allow any nation to thwart His prophetic plan.

> *I will also gather all nations, and will bring them down into the valley of Jehoshaphat, and will plead with them there for my people and for my heritage Israel, whom they have scattered among the nations,* ***and parted my land****.*
>
> (Joel 3:2, emphasis added)

October 1991

After the Gulf War ended in 1991, President George H. W. Bush began the initiative to start a Middle East Peace plan involving Israel, the Palestinians, and the countries surrounding Israel.[3] On October 30, 1991, President Bush opened the talks with a speech, in which he said, "Territorial compromise is essential for peace." (See centerfold for a picture of President Bush speaking at the Madrid Peace Conference.)

From the very start of the Madrid Peace Process, the President made it very clear that Israel was required to surrender parts of the covenant land for peace.[4] This surrender was the foundation of

Photo Credit: President George H. W. Bush library

President George H. W. Bush speaking in Madrid, October 30, 1991: the speech that altered the course of America's relationship with God.

this peace process. The following excerpt of the President's speech shows this:

> Throughout the Middle East, we seek a stable and enduring settlement. We've not defined what this means. Indeed, I make these points with no map showing where the final borders are to be drawn. Nevertheless we believe territorial compromise is essential for peace.

In their opening speeches, delegates from Egypt, Syria, and Palestine said that Israel must surrender land for peace. The Egyptian Foreign Minister, Amr Moussa, summarized the Arab position regarding the land of Israel. Jerusalem became the very heart of this conference. An excerpt of Moussa's speech follows:

> Secondly, the West Bank, Gaza and the Golan Heights are occupied territories.

> Thirdly, settlements established in territories occupied since 67, including Jerusalem are illegal, and more settlements will foreclose potential progress toward real peace and cast doubts on the credibility of the process itself.
>
> Fourthly, the holy city of Jerusalem has its special status....The occupying power should not exercise monopoly or illegal sovereignty over the holy city. It should not persist in unilateral decisions declared to annex the holy city as this lacks validity or legitimacy.

On October 30, a powerful storm developed off Nova Scotia, catching the National Weather Bureau completely by surprise. It developed suddenly from unusual weather patterns that typically only occur once each century. The National Weather Service never officially named this storm, but it reached hurricane strength. This storm was extremely rare because it traveled for one thousand miles in a westward direction. The weather pattern for the United States is eastward! Meteorologists called this storm "extra-tropical" because it did not originate in the tropics, as most hurricanes do.[5]

On October 31, this ferocious storm smashed into New England. It was a monster hundreds of miles wide, described by meteorologists as one of the most powerful ever to occur. It created ocean waves over one hundred feet high, which were among the highest ever recorded. The storm traveled down the East Coast into the Carolinas, creating millions of dollars of damage from Maine to Florida.[6]

The National Weather Service later nicknamed this hurricane "The Perfect Storm." Sebastian Junger wrote a best-selling book about this storm that became a motion picture and captured the drama of the ships caught in it.[7] *The Perfect Storm* was the title of both the book and movie.

President Bush owns a home along the East Coast in Kennebunkport, Maine, that was heavily damaged by the Perfect Storm.[8] Eyewitnesses said that waves as high as thirty feet rose from the ocean and smashed into the President's seafront home. When the President returned from Madrid, he canceled speaking engagements to inspect the damage done to his house.

This storm hit the President's home the same day he initiated the Madrid Peace Conference. What awesome timing! An extremely rare and powerful storm developed in the North Atlantic Ocean and went one thousand miles in the wrong direction. The storm then struck the President's own home on the very day he was opening the Madrid Peace Conference. The President's land was touched the day he attempted to touch the covenant land of Israel!

Photo Credit: President George H. W. Bush library

Aerial view of President Bush's home Kennebunkport, Maine. It was heavily damaged on October 30 by the "Perfect Storm."

The front-page headlines of the newspaper *USA Today* on November 1 even had the Madrid conference and the Perfect Storm next to each other! The newspaper titled one article, "One-on-one peace talks next." The article adjacent to it was titled, "East Coast hit hard by rare storm." At the beginning of a peace plan involving Israel, a rare and powerful storm smashed into the entire East Coast of the United States. On October 30, 1991, the Lord God of Israel put America on alert.

August 1992

On August 24, 1992, the Madrid Peace Conference moved to Washington, D.C. The nations involved felt the United States was a better location for continuing the negotiations. The United States representative was the Acting Secretary of State, Lawrence Eagleburger. The *New York Times* quoted Eagleburger about the opening of the talks, as follows:

> The peace talks were resuming "in the context of an Israeli Government that is prepared to be far more forth coming." He predicted that the issue of Palestinian self-rule in the Israeli-occupied territories would be the focus of discussion.

On August 24, 1992, Hurricane Andrew smashed into southern Florida, hitting Louisiana a few days later. Hurricane Andrew was the worst natural disaster, up to this time, ever to hit America. This storm left one hundred and eighty thousand homeless in Florida, and another twenty five thousand homeless in Louisiana. The hurricane caused an estimated $30 billion in damage.[9]

This was an awesome category-five hurricane with top winds recorded at over 175 miles per hour. The winds were even stronger, but the hurricane destroyed the anemometer, the wind speed device, before the eye hit. The winds may have reached 200 miles per hour or higher! The National Hurricane Center described this storm as a twenty-five-to-thirty-five mile-wide tornado!

Hurricane Andrew struck just a few hours before the Madrid peace conference met in Washington, D.C. There was no mistaking that the purpose of this conference was to divide the land of Israel. On August 24, the front-page headlines of the *USA Today* newspaper contained several articles that made a visual link between the hurricane and the Madrid Peace Process.[10] These headlines were:

1 Million flee Andrew
This will make Hugo look weak
Monster storm targets Florida

Mideast peace talks to resume on positive note

A few days after the hurricane on August 26, the front page of the *New York Times* contained three articles that visually linked the Madrid Peace Process with the disaster. The articles, in the order in which they appeared, were:

Bush's Gains from Convention Nearly Evaporate in the Latest Poll

Israel Offers Plan for Arabs to Rule in Occupied Lands

Thousands Homeless in Florida

The Madrid meeting article was at the top in the center of the front page, while the hurricane story was directly to the right. Directly to the left of the Madrid Peace Plan article was a story about President Bush's ratings collapsing in the polls. At this time, Bill Clinton, Bush's presidential challenger, was leading in the polls by a substantial margin.

It was just a year before, following his victory in the Iraq War, that President Bush's approval rating was a tremendous 92 percent. In October 1991, he personally initiated the Madrid Peace Process and pressured Israel into these negotiations. By August 1992, less than one year later, he crashed in the polls and was heading for a reelection defeat.

Thus, three major events converged on the same day: the Madrid Peace Process meeting for the first time on American soil; the destruction caused by Hurricane Andrew; and the collapse of support for the Presidency of George H. W. Bush. The man who initiated the plan forcing Israel to give away land was removed from office almost exactly one year after the beginning of the meetings. His political collapse was apparent, for all to see, at the exact time the Peace Process moved to America!

The timing of all this was breathtaking. The front pages of the nation's largest national newspapers once again plastered this link between dividing the land of Israel and judgment. God hid nothing.

September 1993

On September 1, 1993, the front-page headline of the *New York Times* read, "Israel and PLO Ready to Declare Joint Recognition"; the subtitle read, "Met Secretly in Europe." The article went on to say that diplomatic action was going on secretly in Europe. They reached an agreement known as the Oslo Peace Accords.

This agreement involved Israel surrendering Gaza, Jericho, and the rest of the West Bank to the Palestinians. In return, the Palestinians agreed to recognize the state of Israel and live in peace. This peace plan was to conclude seven years later, ending in September 2000. Israeli Prime Minister Yitzhak Rabin and Yasser Arafat agreed to sign this document in Washington on September 13, 1993. At this time, the agreement failed to address the issue of Jerusalem; the negotiators put it off for two years.

The *New York Times* had a second front-page headline article titled, "Hurricane Hits Outer Banks as Thousands Seek Safety Inland." Hurricane Emily had meandered across the Atlantic Ocean for five days but finally hit North Carolina the very day of this peace accord agreement! This Hurricane had 115 mile-per-hour winds. It brushed the coast of North Carolina before turning and heading out to sea. The damage caused by this hurricane was light.[11]

Hurricane Emily was the third hurricane to hit the United States on the very day Israel was planning to surrender covenant land. The pattern was firmly established. The United States interfered with God's prophetic plan, and on the first three occasions, three hurricanes hit! The judgment warnings were crystal clear.

January 1994

On January 16, 1994, President Clinton met in Geneva with Syria's dictator, President Hafez Assad.[12] They met to discuss peace between Israel and Syria. President Clinton said Syria was ready for a peace agreement with Israel; this peace agreement included Israel giving the Golan Heights to Syria. The Golan is the border between Syria and Israel, and In 1967, during war with Syria, Israel gained this territory. The Golan is part of the covenant land given to Abraham. The newspapers quoted President Clinton as saying, "Israel must make concessions that will be politically unpopular with many Israelis."

On January 17, 1994, a powerful 6.8 magnitude earthquake rocked the Los Angeles area.[13] Northridge was the center of this quake, about twenty-five miles from downtown Los Angeles. This powerful quake caused an estimated $25 billion in damage. The quake was so powerful that it caused the Santa Susanna Mountains to rise one foot and the Los Angeles basin area to shrink.

What is extremely interesting about this earthquake was that scientists failed to identify the fault that triggered the quake. Scientists also found that this earthquake appeared as two separate quakes. The first earthquake movement was a powerful upward thrust followed by a violent shaking of the earth. The upward thrust was so powerful that it lifted buildings off their foundations. Scientists described this earthquake as having a "one-two punch."

Less than twenty-four hours after President Clinton pressured Israel to give away covenant land, a unique, powerful, and damaging earthquake rocked America. What an awesome warning judgment to America!

March–April 1997

On March 1, Yasser Arafat left Israel and arrived in Washington, D.C., for a meeting with President Clinton.[14] They discussed the building of a Jewish housing project in an East Jerusalem section called Har Homa. The Palestinians claimed this section of Jerusalem, but the Israeli government had begun building sixty-five hundred housing units there. Arafat was upset and met with President Clinton to discuss this issue.

President Clinton gave Arafat a warm welcome. The *New York Times* reported the meeting with this headline article: "Welcoming Arafat, Clinton Rebukes Israel." The President rebuked Israel for building the homes in East Jerusalem, and he condemned Israel for creating mistrust.

Arafat went on a speaking tour of the United States, and many people received him warmly.[15] He also spoke to the United Nations about the situation in Jerusalem. In one speech he cited the Vatican in Rome as an example of what should happen in Jerusalem, a proposed Palestinian city within Jerusalem.

The issue of Israel building homes in Jerusalem upset the entire world. On five separate occasions between March 6 and July 15, the United Nations Security Council and the General Assembly voted to condemn Israel for building homes in East Jerusalem. The entire world was upset because the Israelis were building houses in Jerusalem!

On March 6, the Security Council voted and strongly criticized Israel. The resolution said that the housing development was a violation of international law and a threat to peace in the Middle East.[16] The United States vetoed the resolution, thus preventing it from becoming official, but outside of the United Nations the Clinton Administration condemned Israel for the building project.

On March 13, the General Assembly voted again to condemn Israel for building homes in East Jerusalem.[17] The vote was 130 to 2 condemning Israel. Only Israel and the United States voted against the resolution, and fifty-one nations abstained. The resolution stated that the housing was illegal and constituted a major obstacle to peace. This vote demonstrated the strength of the world's unified opposition to Israel taking full possession of the covenant land. Outside of the United Nations, President Clinton continued the condemnation of Israel.

On March 21, the Security Council again voted to condemn Israel, and once again the United States vetoed the resolution but continued to criticize Israel outside the United Nations for the housing project.[18] On April 25, the General Assembly demanded by a 134 to 3 vote that Israel stop the housing project in Jerusalem. The resolution also called for international action against Israel.[19] The United States voted against this resolution. On July 15, the General Assembly again voted by 131 to 3 for a resolution to condemn Israel for the housing project. This was the strongest resolution yet, as it called for an economic boycott of products made in Jewish settlements in the disputed areas of Israel, including Jerusalem.[20] The United States voted against this resolution, too.

From March 1, when Arafat arrived in America, until mid-April, Israel was under constant criticism by the Clinton administration for the housing project in Jerusalem. The United States supported Israel in the United Nations, but outside of the UN, President Clinton constantly criticized Israel.

On the same day Arafat landed in America, powerful tornadoes devastated huge sections of the nation. It was one of the worst tornado storms in the nation's history. The states of Texas, Arkansas, Tennessee, Kentucky, and Ohio suffered tremendous damage. While Arafat was on his speaking tour, these storms stalled over Ohio and caused tremendous flooding.

The tornadoes destroyed Arkadelphia, Arkansas, while the flooding destroyed Falmouth, Kentucky. The storms' damage amounted to more than one billion dollars. Also, heavy snows fell during March and April in the Northern Plains. These snows melted in April, causing the worst flooding of the Red River in over a century. The flooding hit the Dakotas hard and once again caused more than a billion dollars in damage.

The *New York Times* headlines captured this link between President Clinton's meeting with Arafat and the destructive tornadoes that devastated Arkansas. On March 4, 1997, the front-page headlines said, "In Storms Wake Grief and Shock." Directly touching this article was a picture of President Clinton with Arafat. The heading of the picture said, "President Clinton Rebukes Israel." The front page of a national newspaper actually had articles about the tornadoes' destruction and the admonition of Israel touching each other!

On March 11, the Stock Market reached an all-time high of 7,085.[21] The Market had been steadily increasing since October 1996. On March 13, the UN General Assembly voted overwhelmingly to condemn Israel, and on this day the Stock Market plunged 160 points.[22] The Market continued to plunge until April 13, when it stabilized and then resumed its upward climb.[23] Between March 13 and April 13, the Market lost 694 points.

It is interesting to note that Wall Street, the location of the Market, and the United Nations are both situated in New York City. God touched the land of America and the Stock Market at the same time the United States touched Jerusalem.

On April 7, President Clinton met with Israeli Prime Minister Benjamin Netanyahu to discuss the peace process and the building of homes in East Jerusalem.[24] This meeting coincided with the plunge in the Market. Prime Minister Netanyahu refused to stop the building of the homes. After this meeting, the attacks against Israel over Jerusalem subsided. President Clinton stopped the condemnation of Israel. Soon after this, the Stock Market stabilized.

March and April 1997 were awesome months for God dealing with America. The combination of Arafat coming to America and Clinton rebuking Israel all coincided with some of the worst tornadoes and flooding in the last century. It also coincided with the storms in the Dakotas which resulted in the worst flooding ever. America pressured Israel for building homes in East Jerusalem and suffered terribly.

January 1998

On January 21, Israeli Prime Minister Netanyahu met with President Clinton to discuss the peace plan.[25] In Israel, there was pressure on Netanyahu not to surrender land—pressure so great that politicians in Israel threatened a vote of no confidence in Netanyahu's government if he gave away the land. This would result in elections for a new Israeli government.

Clinton met with Netanyahu and received him coldly. Clinton and Secretary of State Madeleine Albright refused to have lunch with him. Shortly after the meeting ended, a sex scandal involving Clinton became headline news.[26] Clinton became totally absorbed in the scandal and was unable to devote any time to Israel. He met with Arafat the next day, but at that time there was no effort to pressure Israel into surrendering land.[27]

Netanyahu came to the meeting understanding the possibility that his government might fall. How ironic that literally right after the meeting, it was President Clinton's administration that was in trouble. The President was humiliated and faced legal action on the very same day. Netanyahu returned to Israel as a "conquering hero" because he did not surrender any land.[28]

Because of this scandal, the legal action against the President continued until he appeared before a grand jury on August 17. After his grand jury appearance, the President addressed the nation and admitted he had lied to the grand jury when he testified under oath in January. On September 9, the House of Representatives received the report to determine Clinton's possible impeachment and removal from office. On October 8, 1998, the House of Representatives voted for an impeachment inquiry. On December 11, 1998, the Judiciary Committee of the House of Representatives began deliberations. The purpose was possible articles of impeachment against President Clinton.[29] On December 12, the Committee completed the deliberation and voted to approve four Articles of Impeachment. The Committee then forwarded the articles to the House for a vote.[30]

As the Committee was voting on the four Articles of Impeachment, President Clinton landed in the Palestinian controlled section of Israel. He had agreed in October to visit Israel to ensure the Wye Agreement moved forward. The timing was such that it occurred at the exact moment the House issued Articles of

Impeachment against him! Just as he landed in Israel, the House of Representatives drew up the four articles of impeachment against him.[31]

On December 11, the headline articles of major newspapers placed the impeachment and Clinton's visit to Israel on the same front page. The radio and television news reports linked the stories back to back. The Associated Press reported that the President went to Israel "under an impeachment cloud." Every type of media tied together the Articles of Impeachment and Clinton's Mideast trip.

The news sources reported that the President was the first in United States history to visit the Palestinian-ruled territory,[32] and that his visit was giving statehood status to the Palestinians.[33] The capital of this state was to be Jerusalem! These same news sources reported that this impeachment of the President was the first in 130 years.

President Clinton returned to Washington on December 15. Just four days later, the House of Representatives voted to accept two of the Articles of Impeachment against the President.[34] The House sent the articles to the Senate for a trial. At every turn of the President's impeachment proceedings, he was pressuring Israel over the covenant land.

September 1998

On September 24, 1998, President Clinton announced a meeting with Yasser Arafat and Israeli Prime Minister Benjamin Netanyahu to discuss the stalled peace plan.[35] The President wanted Israel to surrender an additional 13 percent of its land. On this same day the headlines of the national newspapers read that Hurricane Georges was gaining strength and heading toward the Gulf of Mexico. The headlines of *USA Today* stated, "Georges gaining strength; Killer storm zeros in on Key West."[36]

On September 27, Secretary of State Madeleine Albright met with Arafat in New York City.[37] Albright was working out final arrangements for Israel to surrender 13 percent of its land. On September 27, Hurricane Georges slammed into the Gulf Coast with 110 mile-per-hour winds and gusts up to 175 miles per hour.[38] The eye of the storm struck Mississippi and did extensive damage eastward into the Florida panhandle. This hurricane hit the coast and then stalled.[39] The hurricane moved very slowly inland and dumped tremendous amounts of rain, causing severe flooding.

On September 28, President Clinton met in the White House with both Arafat and Netanyahu to finalize the division of Israeli land.[40] The three agreed to meet on October 15 and formally announce the agreement. The headlines of *USA Today* stated, "Georges lingers." The article next to it was, "Meeting puts Mideast talks back in motion." The newspapers actually had the hurricane and the Israeli peace talks next to each other on the front page! The *New York Times* also headlined the hurricane and peace talks together on the front page.[41]

On September 28, Arafat addressed the United Nations and talked about establishing an independent Palestinian state by May 1999.[42] The General Assembly gave Arafat a rousing and sustained ovation. As Arafat was speaking, Hurricane Georges was smashing the Gulf Coast and causing one billion dollars' worth of damage![43] Arafat finished his business in the UN and then left America. Hurricane Georges then dissipated.

October 1998

On October 15, 1998, Yasser Arafat and Benjamin Netanyahu met at Wye Plantation, Maryland, to continue the talks that had ended on September 28.[44] They scheduled the talks for five days, and they focused on Israel giving away 13 percent of the West Bank land.

The talks stalled, but President Clinton pressured them to continue until they reached a settlement. They agreed to extend the talks, which finally concluded on October 23. In the end, Israel agreed to surrender the land for assurances of peace by Arafat.[45]

On October 17, awesome rains and tornadoes hit eastern Texas.[46] Twenty inches of rain in one day deluged the San Antonio area! The rains caused flash floods and destroyed thousands of homes. Rivers swelled to incredible sizes. The Guadalupe River, which was normally 150 feet wide, swelled three to five miles wide. The powerful floods nearly swallowed up small towns.[47] The rains and floods continued until October 22 (the end of the Middle East talks), and then subsided. The rains and floods ravaged 25 percent of Texas and did over one billion dollars' worth of damage. On October 21, President Clinton declared this section of Texas a major disaster area and directed the Federal Emergency Management Agency (FEMA) to assist in the relief for the flood-ravaged families.[48]

For almost the entire duration of the Middle East talks, torrential rains and storms were smashing Texas. The national newspapers once again had the Middle East talks and disaster together on the front page![49] As the talks ended, the storms and flooding in Texas ended. Once again, President Clinton had to declare a section of America a disaster area at the exact time he was meeting with Arafat to divide Israel!

May 1999

On May 3, 1999, starting at 4:47 p.m. Central Time, the most powerful tornadoes ever to hit the United States fell on Oklahoma and Kansas. Meteorologists officially measured the winds at 316 miles per hour, making them the fastest ever recorded. The meteorologists nearly classified this tornado as an F-6 on the rating scale. There has never been an F-6 tornado.[50]

The storm included many F-4 and F-5 tornadoes (F-5s have winds over 260 miles per hour), which are extremely rare. There were almost fifty confirmed tornadoes with nearly two hundred warnings! One F-5 tornado was over a mile wide and traveled for four hours, covering eighty miles on the ground. It destroyed everything in its path. This twister was unprecedented in the history of tornadoes. Category F-5 tornadoes make up less than 1 percent of all tornadoes. Tornadoes are usually several hundred yards wide at the most, not over a mile, and they seldom last for more than ten to fifteen minutes, not four hours.

The damage from this storm was incredible. The headlines of the newspapers stated, "Everything gone—At least 43 dead in monstrous Plains tornadoes," "20 hours of terror," "Stark scene: Miles of devastation," and "Tornadoes shred state." The National Oceanic and Atmospheric Administration stated, "This is an outbreak of historic proportions, no doubt about it." Oklahoma Governor Frank Keating said, "This is the most calamitous storm we've ever seen, and probably one of the more calamitous that ever hit the interior of the United States."

The tornadoes destroyed more than two thousand homes in Oklahoma City alone. Small communities disappeared entirely as the winds leveled everything and destroyed thousands of vehicles. The town of Mulhall, Oklahoma, ceased to exist. The storm's destruction totaled billions of dollars. On May 4, the federal government declared large sections of Oklahoma and Kansas to be disaster areas.

The storm warnings began at 4:47 p.m. Central Time. In Israel this would have been around 1 a.m. on May 4, the date Yasser Arafat was scheduled to declare a Palestinian state with Jerusalem as its capital. At the request of President Clinton, he agreed to postpone this declaration until December 1999. President Clinton had already stated the

Palestinians should have a state and that Jerusalem was negotiable. He even refused to move the United States embassy to Jerusalem.

On May 4, the same day President Clinton declared parts of Oklahoma and Kansas disaster areas, the President sent a letter to Arafat to encourage his aspirations for his "own land," saying that the Palestinians had a right to "determine their own future on their own land" and that they deserved "to live free, today, tomorrow, and forever."[51]

What an awesome warning to America! Possibly the most powerful tornadoes ever to hit the United States fell the same day that Arafat was to proclaim a Palestinian state. The very same day Clinton encouraged Arafat about the Palestinian state, he declared parts of America a disaster area from the worst tornadoes in history.

September 1999

In late August, Hurricane Dennis began to move slowly up the coast, drenching the states of Florida, Georgia, and the Carolinas. The hurricane stopped directly east of the Outer Banks of North Carolina. Dennis then acted very strangely, moving backwards along the course it had come from. It then stalled again off the Outer Banks and began to drift eastward. Finally, on September 3, after five straight days of lingering off the coast, Dennis struck North Carolina. This was not a powerful hurricane—it was a category-two with sustained winds of 105 miles per hour—but it had tremendous rainfall and flooding occurred.[52]

On September 1, Secretary of State Madeleine Albright flew to the Middle East to meet with several Arab leaders before meeting with Yasser Arafat and Israeli Prime Minister Ehud Barak on September 3.[53] The purpose of Albright's visit was to restart the stalled Wye Agreement.

Hurricane Dennis came ashore at nearly the exact time Albright met in Israel to assist in giving away the covenant land! This hurricane was literally doing circles in the Atlantic Ocean until the meeting in Israel. On this very day, the hurricane hit the United States. Remember that although this hurricane did not do tremendous damage, it did drop enormous amounts of rain. This would prove to be extremely important when Hurricane Floyd hit just two weeks later.

On September 13, 1999, the Israeli Foreign Minister and one of Arafat's deputies met to work out arrangements for the "Final Status" of Israel giving land away.[54] This meeting was a result of Secretary Albright's trip the week before. On September 13, 1999, Hurricane Floyd strengthened into a very dangerous category-five storm with sustained winds of 155 miles per hour.[55]

The forecasters at the National Hurricane Center were astonished by how quickly Floyd grew in size and strength in one day. The actual statement was, "Floyd grew unexpectedly into a monster of a storm on Sunday." This was the very day the meeting took place in Israel to surrender the land.

On September 16, Hurricane Floyd slammed into North Carolina. Floyd's winds had diminished to 105 miles per hour, making it a category-two, but the hurricane was still huge. Hurricane force winds extended 150 miles in front of it. This hurricane caused the greatest evacuation in American history up until that time. As the storm moved up the coast, it forced millions of people to evacuate in front of it.

The destructive force of this storm was in its rains. Heavy rains of twenty inches or more fell over the entire eastern part of North Carolina. Hurricane Dennis had caused the rivers to swell greatly just two weeks before, and now Floyd destroyed the entire eastern section of the state, some eighteen thousand square miles.

Twenty-eight counties declared a state of emergency and a few were almost totally destroyed.

The destruction closed approximately four to five hundred roads. Farmers estimated the storm killed over one hundred thousand hogs, 2.47 million chickens, and over five hundred thousand turkeys, along with large numbers of horses and cattle. The floods knocked out sewage and water systems. Sewage, chemicals, and dead animals all flowed into the rivers, creating an environmental nightmare. The estimated damage to agriculture was one billion dollars. The loss to buildings, homes, and roads was in the billions. This was the greatest disaster to hit North Carolina since the Civil War.[56]

While the Israelis were meeting with the Palestinians to give away the covenant land, a monster storm ravaged almost the entire east coast of America.

The Stock Market was another telling factor during September 1999. On September 21, the Dow Jones industrial average fell 225 points to the steepest loss in four months. On September 22, the Stock Market lost 74 points, and the next day, September 23, the market fell another 205 points. The total loss for the three days was 504 points. This was the first time in the history of the Stock Market that it suffered two 200-point losses during the same week![57]

The loss coincided exactly with Arafat's visit with President Clinton. They met on September 22, the day between the two 200-point losses on the Stock Market.[58] Arafat then left Clinton and went to the United Nations, where he asked the UN to back independence for a Palestinian state. The Stock Market dropped 524 points for the week that Arafat visited.

October 1999

During the week of October 11, the Israeli government evicted Jewish settlers from fifteen West Bank hilltops. The settlers resisted this eviction and the national media reported this confrontation. On October 16, the *New York Times* ran a front-page article about this confrontation titled, "On the West Bank, a Mellow View of Eviction."[59] Amazingly, there was another article right on the front page titled, "Big Sell Off Caps Dow's Worst Week Since October '89."[60] During the week, the Market had lost 5.7 percent! While Israel was forcing the settlers off the covenant land, the Stock Market was melting down.

Hurricane Irene also hit North Carolina on October 15,[61] and a powerful 7.1 earthquake rocked the Southwest on the morning of October 16.[62] It was the fifth most powerful earthquake to hit America in the twentieth century, but it was located in the desert near a sparsely populated area. The earthquake shook three states and tore a twenty-five mile-long gash in the earth. This quake triggered small quakes near the San Andreas Fault one hundred and twenty miles away. Seismologists referred to this as "nerve-rattling conversation" between the two fault lines.

Thus, in a twelve-hour span, the Stock Market closed down 266 points, a hurricane hit the east coast, and a huge earthquake rocked the west coast. This all occurred as Jewish settlers were being evicted from the covenant land!

January–April 2000

On January 3, 2000, President Clinton met with Ehud Barak, the Israeli Prime Minister, and Farouk al-Shara, the Foreign Minister of Syria, to discuss peace between Israel and Syria.[63] This peace plan called for Israel to surrender the Golan Heights, an area critical to Israel's defense. Prior to 1967, Syria controlled the Golan Heights and used it as an artillery base to shell Israel. The talks were to last two days, January 3 and 4.

On January 4, Israel's Prime Minister agreed to transfer 5 percent of this territory to the Palestinians. They were to complete the transfer by the end of the week. The hand over of this land came from previous agreements brokered by President Clinton.

By December 31, 1999, the Stock Market had reached its all-time high for this period. On January 4, 2000, the Stock Market plummeted. Both the Dow and NASDAQ plunged. The Dow fell 359 points for the fourth worst one-day decline in history, and the NASDAQ fell 229 points for its worst drop ever. The combined losses in money for the one day were six hundred billion dollars.[64] During the exact time of the meetings, the Stock Markets was reeling with huge losses.

When the meetings were completed, the Market recovered the losses and went on to register huge gains. The *New York Times* reflected on the Stock Market activity for the week with an article titled, "Three US Stock Gauges Rally to End a Turbulent Week."[65]

By March 10, 2000, the NASDAQ had reached its all-time high of 5,048 points. The DOW Industrials had already peaked in January 2000. (The NASDAQ would soon spiral out of control, lose four trillion dollars, and never fully recover.) On this same day, March 10, after years of negotiations, Israel's Prime Minister, Ehud Barak, agreed for the first time to recognize a Palestinian state.

On April 12, President Clinton summoned Ehud Barak to Washington, D.C., for a conference regarding the peace process.[66] President Clinton wanted to get more involved in the peace process. On April 11, 12, and 13, the NASDAQ section of the Stock Market collapsed. The NASDAQ trades in technical stocks during the 1990s had grown to four trillion dollars; in this week, the NASDAQ fell 618 points for its worst week ever.[67]

At the precise time that Israel's Prime Minister was in Washington to meet with President Clinton, the Stock Market collapsed into the NASDAQ's worst week in history.

July–August 2000

Starting on July 12, 2000, President Clinton, Israeli Prime Minister Ehud Barak, and Palestinian leader Yasser Arafat met at Camp David, Maryland, to try to reach an agreement for peace.[68] The talks continued until July 26, when they collapsed over the issue of Jerusalem. President Clinton was personally involved in trying to divide Jerusalem into Muslim and Jewish sections and to give away sections of land to Palestinian control. The Israelis and Palestinians failed to reach an agreement. Arafat made statements that he was declaring a Palestinian state with or without an agreement. Tension escalated after the meeting.

As the meeting was taking place, tremendous forest fires erupted in the West.[69] The fires exploded at the end of July and burned uncontrollably during August. By the end of August, some of the worst fires of the century had burned nearly seven million acres.

The federal government declared the states of Montana and Wyoming to be disaster areas. The states called for the army and National Guard to help fight the fires. All available fire fighters in America were helping, numbering more than twenty-five thousand people. There was no hope of putting the fires out, and only the winter snows and rains could do it.

The weather conditions for the fires were the equivalent to the Perfect Storm. Agriculture Secretary Dan Glickman reported the weather patterns over the western section of America were ideal for fires, and were similar to the odd meteorological events that created the Perfect Storm. High temperatures, low humidity, lightning storms with no rain, and high winds, created a pattern that lasted for months on end.

During the month of July, the rains stopped in Texas. On July 28, Governor George Bush declared the state a disaster area for 195 counties because of the drought and fires.[70] The state also went through the entire month of August without rain. This drought lasted more than sixty days and was compared to the "Dust Bowl" of 1934.

September–December 2000

On September 28, 2000, which was Rosh Hashana, the Jewish New Year, Ariel Sharon, the famous Israeli General, went to the Temple Mount in Jerusalem. This visit sparked riots, the causes of which were attributed to the failed Camp David meetings in July 2000, in which President Clinton had pressured Israel to give away some Jewish land and sections of East Jerusalem. The sections of Jerusalem included the Temple Mount.[71] The failure of the Camp David meetings destabilized the political situation between the Israelis and Palestinians. By the end of October 2000, Prime Minister Barak's government had collapsed and Israel was without leadership.[72]

The United States held its presidential election on November 7. The election resulted in total political chaos, as neither major candidate won enough electoral votes. The state of Florida's election results were key in determining the winner of the election. The election dragged on and on until the Florida vote count went to the United States Supreme Court. On December 12, 2000, the court made a ruling that declared George W. Bush the winner. From November 7 until December 12, the United States was in disarray with no elected government.[73]

President Clinton invited Arafat to Washington for the purpose of renewing the peace talks.[74] Arafat arrived in Washington on November 9, as the United States was in the worst presidential crisis in more than one hundred years! Arafat met with President

Clinton just two days after the election, while the election process was melting down! On December 9, 2000, Barak resigned his position as Prime Minister and called for new elections, which were set for February 2001. From the end of October to December 9, Israel was in political chaos.

President Clinton's action destabilized the Israeli government. Almost during the exact time the Israeli government was in chaos, the United States government was destabilized and in chaos. On December 9, the election was set in Israel.[75] A few days later the United States Supreme Court settled the American election.[76] Both governments were in chaos at nearly the exact time! What happened to the Israeli government happened at the same time to the American government!

June 2001

On June 8 and 9, 2001, one of the greatest rainfalls in the history of the United States happened in eastern Texas. In a twenty-four-hour period, more than twenty-eight inches of rain fell in the Houston area; between June 5 and June 11, three feet of rain fell on the area.[77]

The rain was the product of Tropical Storm Allison, whose ten-day history will go down in Weather Bureau records as "weird." Allison formed within one day in the Gulf of Mexico, which was unusual. This storm then headed into Texas east of Houston and broke up as a storm system. The remnants drifted to the north of Houston and circled around the city before sliding back south to the Gulf. The storm then re-formed into a tropical storm, which began to unleash incredible torrents of rain.[78]

The destruction in Houston alone was catastrophic. The floods destroyed or damaged an estimated twenty-five thousand homes and businesses along with possibly fifty thousand automobiles and trucks. The storm closed down the city for three days. The federal government declared twenty-eight counties in Texas to be a disaster area along with fourteen parishes in Louisiana.[79] The resulting damage was close to three billion dollars in Houston and four billion dollars in the state.

The storm moved from Texas into Florida and up the east coast. The federal government declared disaster areas all the way up to Pennsylvania. Meteorologists claim that Allison was the worst tropical storm in history. In its ten-day life, this storm unleashed enough rain to last the United States for a year! Texas is President Bush's home state, and he was vacationing at his ranch in Crawford, Texas, at the time of the flooding. He declared the twenty-eight counties in Texas a federal disaster area while he was in Texas.

On June 6, President Bush sent Central Intelligence Agency (CIA) director George Tenet to Israel to try to broker a cease-fire between the Israelis and the Palestinians.[80] This was the Bush administration's first real involvement in the Middle East crisis.[81] Tenet's mission was for Israel to stop building in the settlement areas.[82] Tenet arrived in the Middle East on June 6.

On June 8, the CIA director hosted talks between senior Israeli and Palestinian security officials while Assistant Secretary of State William Burns met Palestinian President Yasser Arafat.[83] This was at the same time that Allison re-formed as a tropical storm and began dumping tremendous rain. The two events coincided exactly! This tropical storm ravaged the United States for the entire time the CIA director was in Israel.

September 11, 2001

On September 11, the greatest attack ever on American soil occurred. The hijacking of four airplanes and the attacks on the

World Trade Center (WTC) in New York City and the Pentagon in Washington, D.C., left almost three thousand people dead. More Americans died on September 11 than in the attack on Pearl Harbor. These suicide attacks by Muslim terrorists caused approximately forty billion dollars in damage and stunned the country. The attack came without any warning.

The attack on the WTC was an attack on the financial heart of the United States. The largest stock brokerage firms in the world were located in the WTC, along with many international banks. The effect of this attack on the Stock Market was devastating; the week after the attack was one of the worst ever for the Market.

Before the attacks, on August 9, 2001, a suicide bomber in Jerusalem killed nineteen people and wounded more than one hundred. Later on that day, President Bush made a speech condemning the terrorist attack. After condemning the attack, the President demanded that Israel abide by the Madrid Peace Process, the Mitchell Plan, and United Nations Resolutions 242 and 338. An excerpt of the President's speech follows:

> The United States remains committed to implementation in all its elements of the Mitchell Committee Report, which provides a path to return to peace negotiations based on United Nations Security Council Resolutions 242, 338, and the Madrid Conference. To get to Mitchell the parties need to resume effective security cooperation and work together to stop terrorism and violence.[84]

These United Nations resolutions called for Israel to retreat back to the pre-Six-Day War borders. This would mean giving up East Jerusalem and the Golan Heights and ending all settlements in the West Bank. The President was totally ignoring God's covenant with Israel, and also putting the nation in a dangerous position by telling them to retreat to indefensible borders. The President ended the speech by pressuring Israel to negotiate with the very people who had just committed a horrible terrorist attack.[85]

Exactly thirty-two days after the President's August 9 speech, the terrorists struck America. The United States came under the same type of terror that the Israelis were under. America too was now engaged in a war with Muslim terrorists. Israel was fighting for its very existence and now America was in the same battle for its existence.

Historically, America began to pressure Israel with the Madrid Peace process starting in October 1991. This process reached a climax in July 2000 with Israel offering to withdraw from East Jerusalem and most of the West Bank. This offer failed because the Palestinians rejected it. In the outbreak of fighting, confusion, and terrorist attacks that followed, Israel was politically destabilized and its economy suffered greatly. The parallel between what happened in Israel since September 2000 and what happened in America is eerily similar:

- At the same time the Israeli government was destabilized in late 2000, America was too.
- Almost a year to the day that intense terrorism began against Israel, America was attacked by the same type of terrorists.
- Israel was in a low-grade war with Muslim terrorists; America also entered into a low-grade war with similar terrorists.
- Terrorists attacked Israel's capital of Jerusalem. Terrorists also attacked America's capital of Washington, D.C.
- Israel's economy suffered because of the terrorism. The American economy fell under the same pressure.
- The tourist industry collapsed in Israel because of the terrorism. The tourism industry in America collapsed after the terrorist attacks.[86]

- Israel's economy recovered from the terrorism. America's economy recovered from the September 11 attacks.

The American policy since October 1991 was to pressure Israel to concede covenant land for peace. This resulted in America suffering in 2001 from terrorism, similarly to how Israel had suffered. America had touched the "apple of God's eye" and paid an enormous price. God's word says that what a nation does to Israel comes right back upon that nation. What happened to the United States plainly illustrates this. The pressure from God will only get worse if America continues to force Israel to divide the covenant land.

November 2001

The United Nation's General Assembly meeting on September 21 was canceled because of the terrorist attack on the WTC and was rescheduled for November 10, 2001. On that day President Bush addressed the UN and spoke mostly about terrorism. He spoke briefly about the Middle East and stated that there should be two states: an Israel and a Palestine. He called for the borders to be in accordance with Security Council resolutions 242 and 338. The part of the President's speech touching on Israel follows:

> The American government also stands by its commitment to a just peace in the Middle East. We are working toward the day when two states—Israel and Palestine—live peacefully together within secure and recognized borders as called for by the Security Council resolutions. We will do all in our power to bring both parties back into negotiations. But peace will only come when all have sworn off forever incitement, violence, and terrorism.[87]

On November 11, Yasser Arafat spoke to the United Nations General Assembly. He also spoke about a Palestinian state, saying that Palestine was not completely responsible for all the fighting since September 2000. Later on that same day, Secretary of State Colin Powell met with Arafat.[88]

On November 12, 2001, an American Airline jet crashed when taking off from JFK Airport, killing 265 people.[89] This crash was less then twenty-four hours after Arafat's speech to the United Nations. The speech was about fifteen miles from the crash scene in the very same city! Arafat's activities in the United States and a national disaster were once again headlines.

April–June 2002

By April 2002, the Israelis and Palestinians were engaged in serious fighting, leaving hundreds dead. Israel eventually quarantined Arafat in his headquarters in the city of Ramallah. On April 28, the United States pressured Israel to lift the siege of Arafat's headquarters.

On this day, a massive tornado storm ravaged the east coast of the United States from Missouri to Maryland. It was the most powerful tornado ever recorded in Maryland: a monster F-5 storm packing winds between 261 and 318 miles per hour. The storm came directly over Washington, D.C., and the tornado was just south of the city. On May 1, 2002, the President declared Maryland a disaster area.

The headlines for the *Washington Post* of April 29, 2002 read, "Israel Agrees to Lift Arafat Siege" and "Deadly Tornado Hits Southern Maryland."[90]

On June 24, the President made a major policy speech regarding Israel. He called for two states living side by side and declared that the United States was going to take the lead to ensure the two states came to pass. He turned this plan over to Secretary of State Colin Powell for implementation.

Throughout the month of June 2002, record-setting forest fires were burning in the West. The worst fire in Colorado's history burned 138,000 acres. In Arizona two fires merged into a monster that burned 550,000 acres. Only the heroic efforts of fire fighters kept it from burning cities.

Immediately after the President made the two-state policy speeches, he traveled to Arizona, declared it a disaster area, and tried to encourage the firefighters. The national newspapers' headlines captured the speech and the fires. The *Washington Post*'s headlines for June 25 read, "President Outlines Vision for Mideast" and "Everything is Just a Nightmare, Forced to Flee Western Wildfires."[91]

May 2003

On April 30, the United States, Russia, the European Union, and the United Nations drafted a Road Map for peace for Israel. This plan called for Israel to surrender parts of the covenant land for peace. On May 4, Secretary of State Colin Powell traveled to Israel and Syria to promote this plan. He stayed in the Middle East until May 11.[92]

Throughout the duration of his stay, massive tornado storms were pounding the east coast of the United States. A record total of 412 tornadoes struck, causing more than two billion dollars' worth of damage. This was the worst tornado outbreak since May 1999.[93] When Powell left Israel to return home, the tornadoes stopped.

September 2003

This month witnessed tremendous activity involving Israel. Israel weighed all options against Arafat, including his assassination. The United States condemned Israel for this. On September 12, President Bush also blocked Israel from expelling Arafat.[94] On this day, Hurricane Isabel reached category-five status and its course pointed directly at the United States.[95]

On September 16, the United States vetoed a United Nations Security Council resolution against Israel; the hurricane lessened in intensity. King Abdullah of Jordan met with the President to discuss the peace plan. Hurricane Isabel was bearing down on Washington, D.C., and caused this meeting to end early! The President left Washington as the storm approached. The hurricane hit on September 19 and caused four billion dollars in damage in the mid-Atlantic states.[96]

August–September 2004

During this six-week period, a record four hurricanes slammed into Florida. Never in such a short period of time had four major hurricanes hit one state. They did enormous destruction and the combined damages totaled about forty billion dollars. The hurricanes were named Charlie, Frances, Ivan, and Jeanne.

Starting in early August and continuing through September, the United States put enormous pressure on Israel to withdraw from twenty-one settlements in Gaza and four in Samaria.[97] The Bush administration even made a one billion dollar loan guarantee to Israel for relocating Jews from the settlements. In addition, the President wanted Israel to remove security roadblocks, limit settlement construction, and unfreeze hundreds of millions in Palestinian money. On August 7 he sent the American envoy, Elliot Abrams, to pressure Israel in these areas. The key to all this pressure was relocating Jews off the covenant land, primarily Gaza.

On August 9, a tropical depression formed in the Caribbean Sea that became Hurricane Charlie. On August 12, Hurricane Charlie was bearing down on the west coast of Florida and forced the evacuation of 1.4 million people. The hurricane intensified rapidly, and within hours the destructive winds attained category-four status. On August 13, the hurricane slammed into southwest Florida and traveled diagonally across the state. This storm did over fourteen billion dollars' worth of damage.

The United States attempted to pressure Jews to evacuate the covenant land, and then 1.4 million Americans had to evacuate their homes. Bush wanted twenty-five Jewish settlements closed, and he then declared twenty-five Florida counties disaster areas. The President wanted home construction stopped in the settlements, and this hurricane destroyed ten thousand American homes and damaged sixteen thousand others.

On September 1, Hurricane Frances was bearing down on the east-central coast of Florida. Frances was tremendous in both size and power. This hurricane was the size of Texas and reached category-four status. The approaching hurricane caused the largest evacuation in American history up to this time, as 2.8 million people fled their homes.

On September 2, President Bush gave his reelection acceptance speech while Hurricane Frances stalled off the coast of Florida. On August 30, Israeli Prime Minister Sharon had said he would speed up the evacuation of twenty-one settlements in Gaza. On September 5, Frances smashed into Florida as a category-two storm and caused ten billion dollars' worth of damage.

On September 12, tens of thousands of Israelis protested the evacuations of the settlements. On September 14, Sharon's cabinet created evacuation guidelines and the Israeli army established a command to oversee the evacuation of the settlers. On this date, President Bush requested an additional $3.1 billion in aid for hurricane damage, bringing the total to $5.1 billion.

On September 15, Hurricane Ivan slammed into Florida's panhandle. Ivan was a powerful category-three that did over twelve billion dollars' worth of damage, not only to Florida but also Alabama, Georgia, South Carolina, and other states. Hurricane Ivan caused the evacuation of two million people from its path. Amazingly, this hurricane hit on the Jewish holy day of Rosh Hashanah.

On September 20, Hurricane Jeanne was in the Atlantic Ocean, traveling on a course away from the United States. On September 20, Secretary of State Colin Powell gave a speech and said the Israeli pullout from Gaza was just the first step in peacemaking. He went on to say there should not be a long time between the Gaza withdrawal and the final two-state settlement. On September 21, the President spoke to the United Nations General Assembly. During the speech he mentioned Israel and said the following:

> Israel should impose a settlement freeze, dismantle unauthorized outposts, end the daily humiliation of the Palestinian people, and avoid any actions that prejudice final negotiations.

Following the speech, the hurricane made a complete turn and headed directly toward central Florida. September 25 was Yom Kippur, the holiest day for Judaism, and on this day Jeanne roared into central Florida as a category-three hurricane. Three million people fled before this storm, which caused $6.8 billion in damage. On September 28, the President requested $7.1 billion in additional disaster relief, for a new total of $12.2 billion!

From August 13 through September 25, the United States suffered a record four direct hits from powerful hurricanes. During this time, President Bush was pressuring to divide the covenant land.[98] America pressured Israel to evacuate Jews off the land, and the hurricanes forced nine million Americans to evacuate. The President made a one billion dollar loan guarantee to relocate Jews, and it cost the United States $12.2 billion in hurricane related damages. Hurricanes Ivan and Jeanne even hit on Jewish holy days!

January 2005

On November 11, 2004, Yasser Arafat died. In January 2005, the Palestinians elected Mahmoud Abbas to replace him. President Bush immediately sent congratulations to Abbas and said that the road map to peace would go forward. The President's "road map" meant Israel surrendering covenant land for a Palestinian state. He even invited Abbas to the White House.

Like Arafat before him, Abbas continued to call for the destruction of the state of Israel. On December 31, 2004, Abbas had called for Israel to withdraw to the 1949 borders, and claimed Jerusalem as the capital of a Palestinian state. He also declared the right of the millions of Palestinian refugees to return to Israel, and, on January 4, he declared that Israel was the "Zionist enemy."[99] In his victory speech, Abbas said that the election was "a victory for Yasser Arafat and the entire Palestinian people." He added, "The small jihad is over and the big jihad has begun."

Even with all these statements, the President still invited Abbas to the White House and claimed the road map to peace was going forward. The President said:

> The United States stands ready to help the Palestinian people realize their aspirations....We look forward to working with [Abbas] and the Palestinian people to address these challenges and to advance the cause of Middle East peace consistent with the vision I set forth on June 24, 2002, of two states, Israel and Palestine, living side by side in peace and security.

While the Palestinian elections were taking place and the President was praising Abbas, awesome storms were striking the western section of the United States.[100] National Aeronautics and Space Administration (NASA) climatologist William Patzert said the weather in the Western part of the United States was the worst in 119 years, with torrential rains resulting in killer mudslides in California, and cold weather bringing snowfalls up to nineteen feet in Nevada.

The storms were not limited to California. Along the Ohio River, hundreds of Ohio and West Virginia residents evacuated their homes. The river was nearly four feet above flood stage in Ohio and in West Virginia. Meteorologists reported the storms in the Midwest were the worst in 104 years![101] All this happened when the President merely invited Abbas to the White House.

April 2005

On April 11 and 12, President Bush met with Israeli Prime Minister Sharon to discuss the "Road Map to Peace." President Bush said that this meeting with Sharon was the result of the two-state plan he had initiated on June 24, 2002, and Sharon was now ready to take the necessary steps for peace.[102]

The heart of this meeting was the closing of twenty-five Jewish settlements. Twenty-one settlements were in Gaza, while four were in Samaria. The meeting ended with Sharon agreeing to close all twenty-five of the settlements. Delighted, the President announced that they had established a timetable to close the settlements:

> Today, the Prime Minister told me of his decision to take such a step. Israel plans to remove certain military installations and all settlements from Gaza, and certain military installations and settlements from

the West Bank. These are historic and courageous actions.

President Bush also requested that Israel not build a 3,650-home complex in the Maaleh Adumim section of East Jerusalem. The President said he "opposes any further construction, saying it threatens peace with the Palestinians and violates the 'Road Map' that calls for a settlement freeze."

During this week, the Stock Market took a huge downturn.[103] This was the worst weekly decline since March 2003. All three sections of the Stock Market, Dow Industrials, NASDAQ, and S&P 500, reached their lows for the year. The mood of investors turned sour as the effect of high oil prices over the last year finally began to hit the Stock Market.

August–September 2005

The Closing of the Twenty-Five Jewish Settlements[104]

After President Bush and Israeli Prime Minister Sharon met in April 2005, Sharon set a timetable to begin the withdrawal from the twenty-five Jewish settlements. On August 16, the Israelis began the process, and by August 23, the Israeli government completed the withdrawal by removing approximately ten thousand Jews from the covenant land.

President Bush and Secretary of State Condoleezza Rice put enormous pressure on the Israeli government to evacuate these twenty-five settlements. The United States and Israeli governments were negotiating $1.2 billion in aid to help relocate the settlers. The removal of all Jews from Gaza was the first step in President Bush's plan to establish a Palestinian state next to Israel.

In Gaza, sixteen of the twenty-one settlements were collectively known as Gush Katif. These sixteen settlements together made up a small city with a population of about eight thousand. It was one of Israel's major agriculture centers, and about 15 percent of all Israel's vegetables were grown there. This was not a primitive village but a small, modern city.

To accomplish the evacuation, the Israeli government sent forty thousand soldiers into Gaza to remove approximately ten thousand residents. The government requested the settlers to leave voluntarily, and any who refused were forced out of their homes and off the land. The army then demolished their homes and destroyed the twenty-one Gaza settlements. The demolition left only twenty-one synagogues and the huge vegetable greenhouses standing. It is against Jewish law to destroy a house of worship of any religion, so the Israelis let the synagogues remain.

The Israelis removed the last of Jewish settlers from Gaza on August 22, and the last settlers from Samaria on August 23. The removal of the settlers took a mere seven days to complete. President Bush was extremely happy and mentioned the Israeli withdrawal in speeches on August 22 and 23. In the speech on August 22, he acknowledged that the closing of the settlements caused pain but called it historic. The President's speech of August 22, in part, follows:

> This past week, Prime Minister Sharon and the Israeli people took a courageous and painful step by beginning to remove settlements in Gaza and parts of the northern West Bank. The Israeli disengagement is an historic step that reflects the bold leadership of Prime Minister Sharon.

In a speech on August 23, the President again praised Prime Minister Sharon for his "courageous decision to withdraw from Gaza and parts of the West Bank." He felt this was the beginning of the creation of the State of Palestine. The following is an excerpt from the President's speech:

> I want to congratulate Prime Minister Sharon for having made a very tough decision....The Prime Minister made a courageous decision to withdraw from Gaza....This is step one in the development of a democracy....This is a very hopeful period. Again, I applaud Prime Minister Sharon for making a decision that has really changed the dynamics on the ground, and has really provided hope for the Palestinian people. My vision, my hope is that one day we'll see two states—two democratic states living side by side in peace.

On September 12, Israel handed over the twenty-one Gaza settlements to the Palestinians. This was the largest evacuation of Jews in modern Israeli history, as never before were so many Jews forced off their covenant land.

When the Palestinians took control of the settlements, their first objective was to destroy and burn the twenty-one synagogues. Mobs then looted and burned everything in sight, including the huge greenhouses which Israel had left for them.

Hurricane Katrina[105]

> The energy, the near-record low pressure in the storm's core, and its huge dimensions add up to an inevitable disaster. That's why they're basically forecasting Armageddon when it goes inland.
>
> –Bill Read, meteorologist, tracking
> Hurricane Katrina, August 28, 2005

On August 23, just as Israel removed the last settler, tropical depression twelve formed over the Bahamas and upgraded to a tropical storm named Katrina. Katrina grew rapidly in power and on August 24 became a category-one hurricane. On August 25, Katrina hit southern Florida, doing about one billion dollars' worth of damage. Katrina weakened over Florida and was downgraded to a tropical storm.

The hurricane then moved into the Gulf of Mexico and rapidly intensified. By August 29, it was a massive category-five storm about 375 miles in diameter. It was heading directly toward New Orleans. The approaching category-five storm forced 1.5 million people to evacuate their homes and flee inland.

As Katrina approached New Orleans, the eye veered slightly eastward and missed the city by fifty miles. The storm destroyed entire parishes both east and south of New Orleans, and heavily damaged the Port of New Orleans, the fifth largest in the world.

The eye struck the Mississippi coast with a storm surge up to thirty-five feet high. This was the highest storm surge ever recorded! The storm entirely devastated the fifty-mile Mississippi coast. When the eye struck land, the barometric pressure was 27.18. This was the third lowest barometric pressure ever recorded for a hurricane making landfall in the United States. The low pressure is an indication of the storm's power. This was a catastrophic storm in every sense of the word.

The storm surge reached miles inland, destroying everything in its path. This surge totally annihilated the small city of Waveland, Mississippi. A two hundred mile stretch of the Gulf coast from Louisiana to Florida felt the hurricane's powerful surge. The storm was so powerful that hurricane-force winds struck Jackson, Mississippi, one hundred and fifty miles inland! The winds and rain damaged the entire state of Mississippi.

The direct impact of Katrina initially missed New Orleans, but the next day, August 30, several of the city's levees failed and water from the surrounding lake poured into the city. Most of the city is below sea level, and now 80 percent of New Orleans was flooded. In some places the city was sixteen feet underwater.

This was one the greatest disasters in a major city in United States history, and the only comparison to it was the destruction of San Francisco in 1906 by a powerful earthquake and fire. The only comparison to the overall destruction was the Great Hurricane of 1938. The federal government declared a ninety thousand square mile area of land, an area nearly the size of Great Britain, to be a disaster area. New Orleans ceased to function as a city.

City officials estimated that entire neighborhoods were destroyed, and that 120,000 buildings, or 70 percent of the city's structures, were unsalvageable. Peter Teanen, national Spokesman for the American Red Cross, put the disaster in perspective:

> We are looking now at a disaster above any magnitude that we've seen in the United States. We've been saying that the response is going to be the largest Red Cross response in the history of the organization.

The connection between the United States government pressuring Israel to destroy twenty-five settlements on the covenant land and Katrina's destruction is obvious. The hurricane destroyed Southern Louisiana and the Gulf Coast of Mississippi a mere six days after the completion of the Gaza evacuation of Jews off the covenant land. Just as the major southern Jewish city in Gaza was destroyed, so was a major southern city in the United States.

The *New York Times* vividly captured the connection between Gaza and Hurricane Katrina. On the editorial page for August 31, there were two articles. The first, titled "New Orleans in Peril," was about the destruction of New Orleans; the second, titled "The Battle for Israel's Future," was, in part, about the evacuation of Gaza. The following are excerpts from the two editorials to show just how Gaza and Katrina were linked, so that anyone reading the articles could put them together:

> On the day after Hurricane Katrina was declared to be not as bad as originally feared, it became clear that the effects of the storm had been, after all, beyond, devastation. Home owners in Biloxi, Miss., staggered through wrecked neighborhoods looking for their loved ones. In New Orleans, the mayor reported that rescue boats had begun pushing past dead bodies to look for the stranded living. Gas leaks began erupting into flames and looking at the city, now at 80 percent under water, it was hard not to think of last year's tsunami, or even ancient Pompeii.
>
> –from "New Orleans in Peril"

> Mr. Sharon's withdrawal of Israeli settlers from Gaza completed last week was a historic shift that should be acknowledged and extended. Now that Mr. Sharon has demonstrated that he is able to carry out a territorial compromise...he needs to extend the principle from Gaza to the crucially important West Bank. –from "The Battle for Israel's Future"

A mere twenty-one days after the eviction of the last Jew, the President of the United States was publicly humiliated. On September 13, President Bush told the nation,

> Katrina exposed serious problems in our response capability at all levels of government. And to the extent that the federal government didn't fully do its job right, I take responsibility.

The man behind the humiliation of Israel, by forcing Jews from their covenant land, was himself humiliated before the entire world.

His handling of the disaster relief directly impacted his presidency. The public's opinion of him soured and started the downward spiral of his popularity.

The Similarities

The following is a list of similarities between the destruction of Gaza and Hurricane Katrina.

- Prior to removal, the Israeli government called on Jews to evacuate their homes. The US government called on residents to evacuate their homes prior to the hurricane.
- On August 17, Israel ordered a mandatory evacuation of the settlements. On September 7, the mayor of New Orleans ordered a mandatory evacuation of the city.
- The evacuation of twelve thousand Jews was the largest in Jewish history since 1948. Several million Americans would evacuate from the path of Hurricane Katrina.
- Israel sent forty thousand troops to evacuate the settlers while the United States had to send eighty thousand soldiers to the destroyed area.
- Jews went to their roofs to try and delay the eviction, while thousands in New Orleans went to their roofs to keep from drowning.
- Gaza is located in Israel's southern coastal area. A section of America's southern coast was destroyed.
- The evacuation destroyed thousands of Jewish homes. The hurricane destroyed or damaged more than five hundred thousand American homes.
- The day Hurricane Katrina hit, Jews were digging up their dead to re-inter them in cemeteries outside Gaza. Katrina's tidal surge uncovered hundreds of bodies from Gulf coast graveyards.

- The Israeli government barred citizens of Gaza from their homes. American citizens in the destroyed areas were barred from their homes.
- Many Jewish people felt abandoned by their government. Many Americans felt abandoned by the government's failure to respond quickly to Hurricane Katrina.
- The Israelis from the settlements boarded buses and were taken to locations all over Israel. The people trapped in New Orleans were loaded on buses and taken to shelters all over the United States.
- Gush Katif was a major agricultural center. The Port of New Orleans was the major agricultural shipping center in the United States, and the midwestern states shipped much of their produce through this port.
- President Bush promised $2.2 billion for the relocation of the settlers. The early estimates were a cost upwards of $200 billion to repair the damage from the hurricane.

Hurricane Rita

While the nation was still reeling from Hurricane Katrina, a second monstrous storm, Rita, headed into the Gulf of Mexico. On September 20, Rita brushed Key West, Florida, and headed into the Gulf. Rita exploded to a category-five on September 21 with 175 mile-per-hour winds and headed directly toward Texas.

The people living along the Gulf Coast began to evacuate, and eventually nearly everyone fled Houston. Traffic jams one hundred miles long stretched out of Houston as 2.8 million people fled the coast. This would be the greatest evacuation in United States history.

As Rita headed west, the hurricane weakened and turned northward. The storm dropped to a still-powerful category-three hurricane with 125 mile-per-hour winds. On September 24, the hurricane came ashore in Texas just west of the Louisiana border. The eye hit a sparsely populated area of Texas, devastating the cities of Beaumont and Port Arthur. The coastal area of western Louisiana was also devastated, and many small cities were totally destroyed. The hurricane's storm surge reached all the way to New Orleans, flooding the city for the second time in a month. The total damage inflicted by Hurricane Rita was more than ten billion dollars.

The Israel Connection

Hurricane Rita also had a connection with Israel. The destruction of New Orleans occurred just seven days after the removal of the last Jew from Gaza. On September 12, the Israelis gave control of the twenty-one settlements in Gaza to the Palestinians. On September 21, Israel completed its pullout from the four settlements in Samaria.

When Israel completed the pullout, the Palestinians poured in and destroyed the settlements, just as in Gaza. The Palestinians overran the settlements and burned everything, including the trees. They then looted everything possible. At the very time Israel transferred the final four settlements to the Palestinians, Hurricane Rita exploded into a category-five storm with sustained winds of 175 miles per hour!

On the day Israel surrendered Gaza, New Orleans and huge sections of the Gulf Coast lay in ruins. On the day Israel turned over the Samaria settlements to the Palestinians, a category-five hurricane bore down on the United States. It seems that Katrina was for Gaza while Rita was for Samaria. Within a very short time, Rita tore through the oil rigs in the Gulf, heading toward some of the major refineries in Texas, and destroyed several small towns along the Texas and Louisiana coasts.

Summary

God's "Perfect Storm Warnings"

The destruction of Houston and east Texas by Tropical Storm Allison was the third time since the Madrid Peace Process began in 1991 that a sitting president's state was the location of a powerful and damaging storm. Presidents George H. W. Bush, Bill Clinton, and George W. Bush were all personally touched by a disaster at the exact time they were forcing Israel to divide the covenant land. God gave each president what appears to be a "Perfect Storm Warning."

All three of these storms were ferocious and record-breaking. Presidents George W. Bush and Bill Clinton both declared disaster areas in their own states at the very time they were dealing with Israel. God made the connection between Israel and disasters for them. All three presidents made disaster declarations at the very time they were involved in touching "the apple of God's eye." God personally warned each president; a clear pattern of warnings developed.

The Results of Dealing with Yasser Arafat

- September 1, 1993: President Clinton announces he will meet Arafat and Rabin on September 13 in Washington, D.C., to begin the Oslo Peace Accords. After nearly a week of meandering in the Atlantic Ocean, Hurricane Emily hits North Carolina on this day.
- March 2, 1997: Arafat meets with President Clinton in Washington, D.C. The same day, awesome tornado storms unleash tremendous damage in Arkansas and flooding in Kentucky and Ohio. Arkansas and Kentucky are declared disaster areas.
- January 21, 1998: President Clinton is waiting to meet with

Arafat at the White House. At this exact time the President's sex scandal breaks.

- September 27, 1998: Arafat is meeting with the President in Washington. Hurricane Georges hits Alabama and stalls. The hurricane stalls until Arafat leaves, and then it dissipates. Parts of Alabama are declared disaster areas.
- October 17, 1998: Arafat comes to the Wye Plantation meeting. Incredible rains fall on Texas, causing record flooding. FEMA declares parts of Texas disaster areas.
- November 23, 1998: Arafat comes to America. He meets with President Clinton, who is raising funds for the Palestinian state. On this day the Stock Market fell 216 points.
- December 12, 1998: The US House of Representatives votes to impeach President Clinton. At the very time of the impeachment, the President is meeting with Arafat in Gaza over the peace process.
- March 23, 1999: Arafat meets with Clinton in Washington, D.C. Stock Market falls 219 points.
- September 3, 1999: Secretary of State Albright meets with Arafat in Israel. Hurricane Dennis comes ashore after weeks of changing course in the Atlantic Ocean.
- September 22, 1999: Arafat meets with Clinton in Washington, D.C. The Stock Market falls more than two hundred points each day both before and after the meeting, for a total loss of 524 points in the week – a historic record.
- June 16, 2000: Arafat meets with President Clinton. The Stock Market falls 265 points.
- July 12–26, 2000: Arafat attends the Camp David meetings. Powerful droughts spread across the country. Forest fires explode into uncontrolled fires. By the end of August, fire has burned seven million acres.

- November 9, 2000: Arafat meets with President Clinton at the White House to try to salvage the peace process. This was just two days after the presidential election. The nation was just entering into the worst election crisis in more than one hundred years.
- November 11, 2001: Arafat speaks at the UN General Assembly and condemns Israel. He later meets with Secretary of State Colin Powell. Within twenty-four hours of meeting with Powell, an airplane crashes in New York City, killing 265 people. The crash was fifteen miles from where Arafat spoke.
- May 1, 2002: Under pressure from the US, Israel releases siege of Arafat's headquarters. There is a massive tornado storm in the eastern US, with an F-5 tornado coming very close to White House.

Federal Emergency Management Agency (FEMA)

FEMA is the federal agency that coordinates disaster relief and releases federal funds to help disaster victims. This agency keeps a list of its top ten natural disasters ranked by the amount of relief costs. This list is just the funds allotted by FEMA and is not the total cost of damages.

Of the ten disasters, the top nine relate directly to the United States pressuring Israel to divide the covenant land. The funds paid by FEMA for these nine disasters total $25.91 billion. The tenth disaster, Hurricane Hugo in 1989, was connected directly to abortion, and is not listed. The other FEMA disasters follow, along with the cost of FEMA funding (in billions):

- Hurricane Katrina (2005)
  Alabama, Louisiana, Mississippi – $7.20
- Northridge Earthquake (1994)
  California – $6.96

- Hurricane Georges (1998)
  Alabama, Florida, Louisiana, Mississippi – $2.25
- Hurricane Ivan (2004)
  Alabama, Florida, Georgia, Mississippi, others – $1.95
- Hurricane Andrew (1992)
  Florida, Louisiana – $1.81
- Hurricane Charley (2004)
  Florida, South Carolina – $1.56
- Hurricane Frances (2004)
  Florida, Georgia, North Carolina, South Carolina – $1.43
- Hurricane Jeanne (2004)
  Delaware, Florida, Virginia – $1.41
- Tropical Storm Allison (2001)
  Florida, Louisiana, Mississippi, Texas – $1.34

(The above list is for the period ending June 2006.)

Billion-Dollar Disasters

The National Oceanic and Atmospheric Administration (NOAA) monitors billion-dollar disasters. NOAA identified forty-seven such disasters starting in 1992. Several of these disasters were droughts over a long period of time and thus could not be associated directly with dividing the land of Israel. Several others connect to abortion and homosexual events and thus are not reported in this book. Nevertheless, America pressuring Israel over the covenant land is directly linked to twenty of these disasters, and most are identified in this chapter. These twenty totaled $334.8 billion in damages! The billion-dollar disasters follow:

- Hurricane Rita, September 2005 – $5.0
- Hurricane Katrina, September 2005 – $200.0
- Hurricane Jeanne, September 2004 – $6.5
- Hurricane Ivan, September 2004 – $12.0

- Hurricane Frances, September 2004 – $9.0
- Hurricane Charlie, August 2004 – $14.0
- Hurricane Isabel, September 2003 – $5.0
- Tornado storms, May 2003 – $3.4
- Western fires, July 2002 – $2.0
- National drought, March 2002 – $10.0
- Tropical Storm Allison, June 2001 – $5.0
- Severe Drought West, July 2000 – $4.2
- Western Fires, July 2000 – $2.1
- Hurricane Floyd, September 1999 – $6.5
- Oklahoma tornadoes, May 1999 – $1.7
- Texas Flooding, October 1998 – $1.1
- Hurricane Georges, September 1998 – $6.5
- North Plains flooding, April 1997 – $4.1
- Arkansas tornadoes, March 1997 – $1.1
- Hurricane Andrew, August 1992 – $35.6

(The above list is for the period ending June 2006.)

The American Dichotomy

The Madrid Peace Plan and the subsequent two-state policy of Israel and Palestine has placed the United States in a dichotomy over Israel. The dichotomy involves the United States pressuring Israel to divide the land on one hand, while supporting and helping Israel in every way on the other hand.

The official United States policy as first formulated by President Bush Sr. is that Israel must surrender covenant land for peace. Under George Bush Jr., this has officially become a two-state policy for Israel and Palestine. This policy is diametrically opposed to God's prophetic plan and brings America under judgment. Yet America still remains close and friendly to Israel; it is Israel's greatest friend in the world. This brings a blessing to America.

This dichotomy is seen in the words of President George Bush Sr. In October 1991, he initiated the Madrid Peace Process, which pressured Israel to surrender sections of the covenant land. Then, on August 11, 1992, the President met with Israel's Prime Minister, Yitzhak Rabin. In a speech during this meeting, President Bush articulated the special relationship that existed between Israel and the United States.

Photo Credit: President George H.W. Bush Library

Bush-Rabin Meeting, August 11, 1992

What the President said is unique among all the countries of the world. The leader of no other country would dare say his nation had a special relationship with Israel. The President claimed that this special relationship started in 1948, but he was just highlighting a special relationship that dates back to the time of President George Washington.

The following are excerpts from two of President Bush Sr.'s speeches, which plainly demonstrate this dichotomy. The first is from his speech of August 11, 1992, which illustrates the blessing. The second is from his speech of October 30, 1991, initiating the opening of the Madrid Peace process, which illustrates the curse.

The blessing:

> I want to take this opportunity to say a few things about the relationship between the United States and

> Israel. This is a relationship that goes back more than four decades to Israel's birth in 1948. This is a relationship that's been tested in times of peace and war, one capable not only of weathering differences but of accomplishing great things. This is a relationship based on a shared commitment to democracy and to common values, as well as the solid commitment to Israel's security, including its qualitative military edge. **This is a special relationship. It is one that is built to endure.**[106] (emphasis added)

The curse:

> What we envision is a process of direct negotiations proceeding along two tracks: one between Israel and the Arab States; the other between Israel and the Palestinians. Negotiations are to be conducted on the basis of UN Security Council Resolutions 242 and 338. Throughout the Middle East, we seek a stable and enduring settlement. We've not defined what this means. Indeed, I make these points with no map showing where the final borders are to be drawn. **Nevertheless, we believe territorial compromise is essential for peace.** (emphasis added)

This same dichotomy is seen in the policy of President George Bush Jr. This President initiated his "Road Map for Peace" in 2002, which called for dividing the land into two separate states. Yet when the Iranian President Mahmoud Ahmadinejad threatened to destroy Israel with nuclear weapons, President Bush rushed to Israel's defense.

In a speech on March 20, 2006, President Bush said that Israel is an ally, and the United States will use military might to defend Israel from Iran. There is no other country in the world that so boldly declared its allegiance with Israel. What other country would come to Israel's aid should it be attacked? A section of the President's March 20 speech follows:

> But now that I'm on Iran...the threat from Iran is, of course, their stated objective to destroy our strong ally Israel. That's a threat, a serious threat. It's a threat to world peace; it's a threat, in essence, to a strong alliance. I made it clear, I'll make it clear again, that we will use military might to protect our ally, Israel.[107]

Even the United States government is divided over Jerusalem. Congress passed The Jerusalem Embassy Act of 1995, a law recognizing Jerusalem as the capital of Israel. This act also called for the relocation of the American Embassy from Tel Aviv to Jerusalem by

Photo Credit: DemoCast TV

Thousands of Christians gather in Washington, D.C. to show support for Israel, July 19, 2006

1999.[108] Yet Presidents Bill Clinton and George Bush Jr. have thwarted this law and failed to relocate the American Embassy. Very few nations recognize Jerusalem as Israel's capital, but America is one of them. This further shows the special relationship between the United States and Israel.

For the most part, the American people respect and want good relations with Israel. President George Washington's benevolent attitude toward the Jewish people is still the position of most Americans. In America, the Jews are not subject to anti-Semitism as they traditionally were in Europe but live in peace. America still is a great blessing to the Jewish people and the nation of Israel.

This dichotomy also creates an enigma. As the United States government continues to interfere with God's prophetic plan, how long can the benevolence towards Israel and the Jewish people hold back total judgment? Hurricane Katrina is an example of how close total judgment might be.

Part Two:
Israel's Future

CHAPTER TEN

The Day of the Lord

> *For yourselves know perfectly that the day of the LORD so cometh as a thief in the night....But ye, brethren, are not in darkness, that that day should overtake you as a thief.*
>
> (1 Thessalonians 5:2, 4)

The Bible does not conclude with the rebirth of the nation of Israel but goes into great detail about what happens after the nation is reborn. The Bible shows that the nations of the world reject reborn Israel. The wars that Israel has suffered since its rebirth, together with the rejection of the nation by nearly all religious, political, and economic organizations, fit biblical prophecy perfectly.

The wars involving Israel in 1948, 1956, 1967, and 1973 are minor compared to the future battles described in the Bible. The continuing warfare against God's covenant people does not persist forever. These wars come to an abrupt end when God supernaturally saves Israel at the second coming of the Lord Jesus. God's intervention occurs during what the Bible calls the day of the Lord.

What Is the Day of the Lord?

The "*day of the Lord*" is an expression referring to a long period of time that begins with God's judgment on the world for rejecting Him and the everlasting covenant with Abraham. It is the time when God interferes directly in the affairs of man. This is God's last attempt to reach man before the second coming of the Lord Jesus. It includes His one-thousand-year reign from Jerusalem as King Messiah, also known as the kingdom age.

The phrase "*day of the Lord*" is one of the major prophetic themes of the Bible. For example, a major portion of the book of Revelation deals with the day of the Lord. The prophets Isaiah, Ezekiel, Joel, Obadiah, Zephaniah, Zechariah, and others describe in great detail the events taking place during the day of the Lord. By looking at these prophets, a clear picture develops of the events leading up to and including the day of the Lord.

The world's political and religious rejection of Israel will eventually result in a worldwide military attack on the nation. The Bible describes at least three future wars which go beyond anything the world has witnessed before. Each war becomes progressively greater and greater until the last, known as Armageddon, which will involve all the nations of the world. This last battle will occur during the day of the Lord.

The wars involving Israel are greater in magnitude than World War II. These future wars will be cataclysmic and will result in the annihilation of huge armies, together with the destruction of entire nations. The destruction will be so extensive that these lands will become uninhabitable. The Bible says that the last war will kill one-third of mankind. With today's world population of over six billion, that would equal two billion casualties!

There is a progression to these wars. The first war involves the Arab nations immediately surrounding Israel. The Bible's description of this war indicates that these nations are destroyed with weapons of mass destruction. The second war involves additional nations, including the rest of the Islamic countries. God uses natural disasters with supernatural timing to destroy this huge army. The final war includes the nations of the world attacking Israel with a massive army of hundreds of millions. Jesus Christ supernaturally ends this war at His second coming.

The judgment aspect of the approaching day of the Lord involves two phases. The first phase involves the incredible wars, which are compressed into a short time period of seven to ten years and culminate in the battle of Armageddon. The prophet Zechariah went into detail about this war, which begins in the day of the Lord. This final war centers around Jerusalem and involves all the nations of the world.

> *Behold, the day of the LORD cometh, and thy spoil shall be divided in the midst of thee. For I will gather all nations against Jerusalem to battle.* (Zechariah 14:1–2)

The second phase involves natural disasters that affect the entire world. These disasters include earthquakes, fires, famines, and pestilence. The earthquakes during this period are so massive that they level all the cities of the world. The judgment part of the day of the Lord is a short but intense period of time.

> *Behold, the day of the LORD cometh, cruel both with wrath and fierce anger, to lay the land desolate: and he shall destroy the sinners thereof out of it. For the stars of heaven and the constellations thereof shall not give their light: the sun shall be darkened in his going forth, and the moon shall not cause her light to shine.* (Isaiah 13:9–10)

In the future, these wars and natural disasters will happen simultaneously in this short time period. Even today, the breathtaking timing of the natural disasters that struck America serves as a warning of things to come. The judgment phase of the day of the Lord climaxes with both the greatest war and greatest earthquake in history.

The war:

> *They are the spirits of devils, working miracles, which go forth unto the kings of the earth and of the whole world, to gather them to the battle of that great day of God Almighty....And he gathered them together into a place called in the Hebrew tongue Armageddon.* (Revelation 16:14, 16)

The earthquake:

> *The seventh angel poured out his vial into the air; and there came a great voice out of the temple of heaven, from the throne, saying, It is done. And there were voices, and thunders, and lightnings; and there was a great earthquake, such as was not since men were upon the earth, so mighty an earthquake, and so great.* (Revelation 16:17–18)

The day of the Lord is the time when God holds people on earth accountable for rejecting Him and following false gods and religions. It is a time when God deals with the pride and rebellion of man. God lets man's evil heart have its way for a brief time, then brings judgment on those actions. Through it all, God always has the way of salvation open to men. Many will turn to Jesus Christ and repent when they find that there is no hope outside of trusting God. God uses this time to bring man to his senses. Everything that can be shaken will be shaken, and only that which is of God will stand.

> *The lofty looks of man shall be humbled, and the haughtiness of men shall be bowed down, and the LORD alone shall be exalted in that day. For the day of the LORD of hosts shall be upon every*

> *one that is proud and lofty, and upon every one that is lifted up; and he shall be brought low.* (Isaiah 2:11–12)

It appears that the worldwide war phase involving the day of the Lord, as described by the ancient prophets, is now coming together with rapid speed. Nation after nation is armed with weapons of mass destruction. The United States, Russia, China, and Israel all have huge arsenals of these fearful weapons. Both India and Pakistan have developed nuclear weapons and threaten to use them against each other. Nations such as Iran and Syria have biological and chemical weapons and may soon have nuclear weapons as well. The Iranian government has stated publicly that when it possesses these weapons, it will use them against Israel.

Could the world be on the verge of the day of the Lord? Let us look at what the Bible describes as the day of the Lord, and the events that are now transpiring.

Key Indicators that the Day of the Lord Is at Hand

There are certain general indicators in the Bible that must be in place for the day of Lord to occur. Remember, the day of the Lord includes the second coming of the Lord Jesus Christ. These indicators are now falling into place.

Some of these indicators are the rebirth of Israel, the return of Jewish people to Israel from a worldwide dispersion, the restoration of Jerusalem as capital, Israel emerging as a great military power, the nations of the world rejecting Israel, Israel being targeted by horrific wars, Russia rising as a major military power, Russia aligning with Iran and other Islamic nations, Asia fielding an army of two hundred million, and one worldwide system of government being in place.

In addition to the general indicators, the Bible gives specific key indicators that the day of Lord is near. The first of these is the total destruction of Iraq. The Babylonian Empire of twenty-six hundred years ago was located in what today is Iraq. The ancient name for Iraq was Babylon.

The prophet Isaiah zeroed in on Iraq as the one of the key indicators to watch. He wrote that as the day of the Lord nears, God brings a nation from the "*end of heaven*" to completely destroy the area of ancient Babylon. This particular nation possesses fierce weapons that can totally destroy Iraq, rendering it uninhabitable. The geographical center of the Bible is Israel, so the expression "*end of heaven*" means as far away as possible from Israel.

It appears from the way Isaiah described this nation that it did not exist in Isaiah's day, but it does exist just prior to the day of the Lord. At the time just before the day of the Lord, the entire world is upset with Iraq. It is the focus of world attention, but one unnamed nation that is as far away as possible from Israel destroys the land that encompasses ancient Babylon.

> *The burden of Babylon, which Isaiah the son of Amoz did see.... The noise of a multitude in the mountains, like as of a great people; a tumultuous noise of the kingdoms of nations gathered together: the* LORD *of hosts mustereth the host of the battle. They come from a far country, from the end of heaven, even the* LORD, *and the weapons of his indignation, to destroy the whole land.* (Isaiah 13:1, 4–5)

Babylon is destroyed as were Sodom and Gomorrah and becomes uninhabitable. These Scriptures about Babylon were never completely fulfilled. God never judged ancient Babylon with awesome devastation. The city of Babylon and the empire fell in 539 BC to the Persians, but Babylon remained a great city. This total destruction, described in the Bible, occurs far in the future from 539 BC. The destruction takes place just prior to the day of the Lord.

> *Babylon, the glory of kingdoms, the beauty of the Chaldees' excellency, shall be as when God overthrew Sodom and Gomorrah. It shall never be inhabited, neither shall it be dwelt in from generation to generation: neither shall the Arabian pitch tent there; neither shall the shepherds make their fold there.* (Isaiah 13:19–20)

The prophet Isaiah, writing in 700 BC, reported that the total destruction of Babylon by a nation from the "*end of heaven*" is the sign for all to see that the day of the Lord is at hand. Let us look at this verse:

> *Howl ye; for the day of the* Lord *is at hand; it shall come as a destruction from the Almighty.* (Isaiah 13:6)

America fits perfectly into this biblical scenario because it is a nation from "*the end of heaven*" and possesses fearful weapons which could completely destroy Iraq; thus, it is possible that Isaiah 13 will soon be fulfilled and that America is the very nation that Isaiah described!

In 1991, America entered into a war with Iraq. In 2003, the United States again engaged Iraq in war. A nation from the "*end of heaven*" with awesome weapons of indignation came to "*Babylon.*" It appears that the two wars with Iraq are leading to a third, which could result in the destruction of the entire nation. This destruction is so horrific that everyone has to flee and the land becomes uninhabitable.

This complete and utter destruction has not occurred, but the circumstances for this possibility are now in place. Watch for the total destruction of Iraq, and then know the day of the Lord is at hand. At this point, the world has run out of time with the holy God of Israel. The terrible day of the Lord is about to begin. The awesome second coming of Jesus Christ is near.

> *Howl ye; for the day of the LORD is at hand; it shall come as a destruction from the Almighty. Therefore shall all hands be faint, and every man's heart shall melt....Behold, the day of the LORD cometh, cruel both with wrath and fierce anger, to lay the land desolate: and he shall destroy the sinners thereof out of it....And I will punish the world for their evil, and the wicked for their iniquity; and I will cause the arrogancy of the proud to cease, and will lay low the haughtiness of the terrible.* (Isaiah 13:6–7, 9, 11)

The First War

> *For it is the day of the LORD's vengeance, and the year of recompenses for the controversy of Zion.* (Isaiah 34:8)

As the day of the Lord nears, the Bible describes three different battles. Each battle gets progressively larger in scope. The first battle involves the destruction of Iraq and the nations bordering Israel. The second battle is led by Russia with the rest of the Islamic nations, and the third is the battle of Armageddon, which involves Asia with an army of two hundred million.

The destruction of Iraq is the opening salvo of the wars, but other nations are destroyed along with Iraq. It appears the people facing judgment with Iraq are the Palestinians, Jordanians, Egyptians, Syrians, and possibly Saudi Arabians. God judges these nations when they attempt to annihilate Israel. With the weapons of mass destruction that the nations have acquired, this war could eclipse all previous wars in horror. A major war in the Middle East would soon destabilize the entire world, as even the hint of a disruption of the oil flow would send the world economy crashing. Let us look at what the prophets said about the nations involved in this coming first war.

Palestinians: Philistines, House of Esau

The final battle over Jerusalem may have begun on September 28, 2000. The conflict over the Temple Mount started on this day and has not truly subsided since. The major trigger point is Jerusalem and the Temple Mount. Any disturbance on the Temple Mount or destruction of the Al-Aksa Mosque or the Dome of the Rock could instantaneously ignite an all-out war in Israel. Jerusalem is the flash point for a war of no return.

The Bible speaks directly to the current Israeli-Palestinian conflict. The Palestinians have fought Israel at every turn since 1920. Many Palestinians participated in the attacks on Israel in 1948 and 1967. They formed terrorist groups and attacked Israel nonstop. In January of 2006, the Palestinians in Gaza elected the terrorist group Hamas to head their government.

The Bible says that as the day of the Lord nears, the Jews will drive the Palestinians completely from the land of Israel. The complete removal of the Palestinians is another key sign of the approaching the day of the Lord. It is very easy to follow the explosive situation between the Palestinians and Israelis to an all out war. The prophet Obadiah, writing in 600 BC, spoke to us about this situation. The prophet tied this conflict to the coming day of the Lord:

> *The day of the Lord is near upon all the heathen: as thou hast done* [to Israel], *it shall be done unto thee: thy reward shall return upon thine own head....And the house of Jacob shall be a fire, and the house of Joseph a flame, and the house of Esau for stubble, and they shall kindle in them, and devour them; and there shall not be any remaining of the house of Esau; for the Lord hath spoken it. And they of the south shall possess the mount of Esau; and they of the plain the Philistines: and they*

> *shall possess the fields of Ephraim, and the fields of Samaria: and Benjamin shall possess Gilead.* (Obadiah 1:15, 18–19)

The prophet Obadiah stated that as the day of the Lord draws near, a horrific war erupts between the Jews, the "*House of Jacob*," and the Palestinians, the "*House of Esau*." This war results in all the Palestinians being driven from the covenant land. The prophet stated that Israel will possess the Plain of the Philistines, which is Gaza. Ephraim and Samaria, located in the West Bank, are brought under Israeli control, along with Gilead. Gilead is the East Bank of the Jordan River.

Hamas means strength and bravery, and this Palestinian terrorist organization refers to itself as the Islamic Resistance Movement. Hamas formed in the 1980s, and on August 18, 1988, it officially declared its objectives. In the Preamble, Hamas declared, "Israel will exist and will continue to exist until Islam will obliterate it, just as it obliterated others before it." Hamas does not recognize the right of Israel to exist as a nation. Article 11 contains this doctrine:

> The Islamic Resistance Movement believes that the land of Palestine is an Islamic Waqf consecrated for future Muslim generations until Judgment Day. It, or any part of it, should not be squandered: it, or any part of it, should not be given up.

The Hamas covenant leaves no room for negotiations with Israel; it calls for the total destruction of Israel.[1] It calls for no negotiations with Israel but continual Jihad until Israel is destroyed. Let's look at Article Thirteen:

> There is no solution for the Palestinian question except through Jihad. Initiatives, proposals and international conferences are all a waste of time and vain endeavors. The Palestinian people know better

than to consent to having their future, rights and fate toyed with.

With Hamas now in control of the Palestinians, it is just a matter of time before an all-out war erupts. The circumstances for this happening and leading to the day of the Lord are certainly plausible, as even now the battle rages in Israel. This fighting cannot go on forever.

Syria and Lebanon

Syria is Israel's longtime worst enemy. Israel fought Syria in 1948, 1967, and 1973. Syria is the base for several organizations like Hamas. Syria also controls Lebanon and uses this country as a front to attack Israel. With the support of Syria, many groups such as Hezbollah have attacked Israel, even up to July 2006 when fighting once again erupted. The word *Hezbollah* means "the party of God."

The relationship between Hezbollah and Syria is complicated. Syria controls Lebanon, but Hezbollah is religiously aligned with Iran. Hezbollah was first formed in Iran during the revolution started by Ayatollah Khomeini, before being transplanted to Lebanon. Both Syria and Iran supply Hezbollah with weapons to attack Israel. These weapons include thousands of missiles that can reach deep into Israel.

Hezbollah formed in 1982 to fight against Israel and now controls most of Lebanon's southern border with Israel. In 1983, it was responsible for the explosion that killed 281 United States Marines. It has evolved beyond a military organization and now wields political power along with providing social services. Hezbollah is well entrenched in Lebanon.

It also has grown into an international organization with agents all over the world, including the United States. Hezbollah uses illegal tactics to raise millions of dollars in the United States. Hezbollah is extremely well-organized, supplied, and trained by both Iran and Syria. This is a formidable fighting force.

Hezbollah's two main goals are to conquer the world through the spread of Islam and to destroy both Israel and the United States. The destruction of Israel is the main driving force behind Hezbollah. Hezbollah views Israel as organized terrorism supported by the United States, and therefore will use terrorism against Israel. The following is a quote from a June 20, 1997, broadcast from Manar TV, Beirut, stating Hezbollah's views and concepts:

> Hezbollah views the Zionist Jews' occupation of Palestine, displacing its people and establishing the entity of Israel on its usurped land as the living materialization of the most hideous kinds of aggression and organized terrorism that is supported by the USA, the sponsor of international terrorism, and some other states that claim to be democratic and protecting human rights whilst they support Israel that was founded on invasion, killing and bloodshed, besides its daily violations of human rights in Lebanon and Palestine.

Israel's borders with both Syria and Lebanon are now a flash point for a horrifying war. During the Six-Day War in 1967, Syria lost the Golan Heights and wants it back; Hezbollah wants the total annihilation of Israel. An all-out war between Israel and the Palestinians would certainly bring Syria and Hezbollah right into this conflict. As with Hamas, there cannot be a negotiated peace with Hezbollah. Hezbollah completely rejects Israel. An all-out war cannot be too far into the future.

The prophet Isaiah spoke of a war that crushes Syria but also weakens Israel. This first war totally destroys Damascus, and the nation of Syria ceases to exist. The destruction of Damascus is so great the city is never rebuilt. This war begins a chain reaction to the battle of Armageddon. When Israel totally destroys Syria, this is another key indicator that the day of the Lord is near.

> *The burden of Damascus. Behold, Damascus is taken away from being a city, and it shall be a ruinous heap....The fortress also shall cease from Ephraim, and the kingdom from Damascus, and the remnant of Syria: they shall be as the glory of the children of Israel, saith the LORD of hosts. And in that day it shall come to pass, that the glory of Jacob shall be made thin, and the fatness of his flesh shall wax lean.* (Isaiah 17:1, 3–4)

During this war, the fortress (military power) ceases from Ephraim (a name for Israel). Syria also ceases from being a nation. Israel becomes thin, or loses a large percentage of its population. Israel is presently a mighty military power, and this means the war is horrific. The destruction of Syria is the signal that the day of the Lord is extremely close and the battle of Armageddon is imminent.

> *Woe to the multitude of many people, which make a noise like the noise of the seas; and to the rushing of nations, that make a rushing like the rushing of mighty waters! The nations shall rush like the rushing of many waters: but God shall rebuke them, and they shall flee far off, and shall be chased as the chaff of the mountains before the wind, and like a rolling thing before the whirlwind. And behold at eveningtide trouble; and before the morning he is not. This is the portion of them that spoil us, and the lot of them that rob us.* (Isaiah 17:12–14)

Iran and the Mahdi

Iran's final confrontation with Israel is found in the second battle, but it does have an important place in the first battle. Iran is an extremely important player in the wars leading up to the day of lord and therefore requires special attention.

On August 3, 2005, Mahmoud Ahmadinejad became the president of the Islamic Republic of Iran. His election sent powerful forces in the Middle East rushing toward a climax in a cataclysmic war with Israel. With both Ahmadinejad rising to power, and a few months later Hamas, the die was cast for a huge confrontation with Israel.

It is important to understand Ahmadinejad's theology in order to realize the depth of his hatred for Israel and the confrontation course he is on with the United States. He follows Shiite Islam and believes in the coming of the Mahdi.[2] The Mahdi is central to his beliefs and motivates his agenda. As time goes on, the term Mahdi will become more and more common.

The *Mahdi* is Arabic for "rightly guided one." He is a special ruler who ranks just below the Prophet Mohammed. The Mahdi is the restorer of Islam and justice who will rule just before the end of the world. He is a military figure who leads the Islamic armies in conquering the entire world. Under the generalship of the Mahdi, the entire world becomes Islamic. Those who fail to submit to Islam must die. This is the Islamic theology of the Mahdi.

The background of the Mahdi is very unusual. Ahmadinejad believes that the Mahdi is the twelfth Imam, Mohammed ibn Hasan, who was a direct descendant of Mohammed. Ibn Hasan lived in the ninth century. When he was five years old, he fell into a well. He went into a state of concealment that will last until the end of time, when he emerges as the Mahdi. Ahmadinejad believes this is the end of time, and that the Mahdi is soon to be revealed.

Ahmadinejad is then a *mahdaviat*, which means "the belief in and efforts to prepare for the Mahdi." This was evident when he spoke before the United Nations in September 2005. During his speech, he offered a prayer for the hastening of the Mahdi to bring "justice and peace." This prayer follows:

> O mighty Lord, I pray to you to hasten the emergence of your last repository, the Promised One, that perfect and pure human being, the one that will fill this world with justice and peace.

Because Ahmadinejad is a mahdaviat, he has no fear of war with the United States or Israel. To him, a war with Israel might immediately reveal his Mahdi and begin the Islamic world conquest. Not since the days of Adolf Hitler's Aryanism has the world seen someone with this religiously driven concept of world conquest.

Iran is building both nuclear weapons and long range missiles to deliver these weapons of mass destruction. There is no doubt that if Iran develops these weapons, it will use them against Israel and possibly against the United States. Iran is on a course for Islamic world conquest, and both Israel and the United States are viewed as obstacles. The fanatical mahdaviats refer to the United States as the "Great Satan" while Israel is the "Little Satan."

According to the Bible, Persia (Iran) is destroyed during the second battle. During this battle, Persia is aligned with Russia and is part of the huge land army that invades Israel. The fact that Iran is part of the second battle means it survived the first battle. It appears that during the first war, Iran's weapons of mass destruction, along with its long-range capability to attack Israel, are eliminated. Iran survives only to be destroyed in the second war.

With Iran, Hezbollah, and Hamas united against Israel, the picture has become very clear that terrible wars are on the horizon. This first war is not far in the future; it is staring right now at Israel and the United States. Iran wants this war and is providing the means to start it. The Lord God of Israel is going to finish it.

Egypt

The fighting draws Egypt into this first battle, where Egypt is completely destroyed. It appears that the fighting between the Israelis and Palestinians spills over to Egypt. Egypt attacks Israel to its own doom. The destruction of Egypt is so complete that the survivors flee into the nations of the world. The Nile River stops flowing. Prophet after prophet describes the terrible destruction coming to Egypt—prophecies about the destruction of Egypt that have yet to be fulfilled. They await fulfillment when the day of the Lord is near.

> *Egypt shall be a desolation, and Edom shall be a desolate wilderness, for the violence against the children of Judah, because they have shed innocent blood in their land.*
>
> (Joel 3:19)

> *The land of Egypt shall be desolate and waste; and they shall know that I am the* Lord*: because he hath said, The river is mine, and I have made it. Behold, therefore I am against thee, and against thy rivers, and I will make the land of Egypt utterly waste and desolate, from the tower of Syene even unto the border of Ethiopia. No foot of man shall pass through it, nor foot of beast shall pass through it, neither shall it be inhabited forty years. And I will make the land of Egypt desolate in the midst of the countries that are desolate, and her cities among the cities that are laid waste shall be desolate forty years: and I will scatter the Egyptians among the nations, and will disperse them through the countries.*
>
> (Ezekiel 29:9–12)

Jordan – Saudi Arabia

In the Bible, the modern nation of Jordan comprises three small nations: Ammon, Moab, and Edom. Ammon is the northern section of Jordan, Moab is the central section, and Edom is the southern section. The prophet Zephaniah spoke about the day of Lord and the total destruction of Ammon and Moab—destruction has not yet happened and awaits future fulfillment.

Jordan faces the same dire fate as the other nations; it ceases to exist because of its confrontations with Israel. The three nations that make up modern Jordan have a long history in the Bible of warring against Israel. Jordan was the first nation to attack Israel in 1948. In fact, King Abdullah of Jordan led the attack. Jordan attacked Israel in 1967 and was defeated.

Jordan has been at peace with Israel for several years, and it is one of the few Muslim nations to have recognized Israel. Jordan's population is about 60 percent Palestinian. It appears the conflict with the Palestinians drags Jordan into the battle and the war destroys this nation. This destruction is a prelude to the day of the Lord. The prophet Zephaniah mentioned the total destruction of Moab and Ammon with the day of the Lord. He did not mention Edom.

> *The great day of the LORD is near, it is near, and hasteth greatly, even the voice of the day of the LORD: the mighty man shall cry there bitterly.* (Zephaniah 1:14)

The destruction is so great that it turns parts of Jordan into Sodom and Gomorrah.

> *I have heard the reproach of Moab, and the revilings of the children of Ammon, whereby they have reproached my people, and magnified themselves against their border. Therefore as I live, saith the LORD of hosts, the God of Israel, Surely Moab shall be as Sodom, and the children of Ammon as Gomorrah, even the*

> *breeding of nettles, and saltpits, and a perpetual desolation: the residue of my people shall spoil them, and the remnant of my people shall possess them.* (Zephaniah 2:8–9)

The prophet Isaiah described the awesome judgment on Edom, also referred to as Idumea. The region of Idumea includes southern Jordan and the northwest corner of Saudi Arabia. The fact that Idumea includes part of modern-day Saudi Arabia is important. Isaiah said that during the day of the Lord, this area will burn with pitch or oil. The very nation known for oil is going to be on fire with oil! The oil-producing region of Saudi Arabia is near the Persian Gulf, not near Israel, but the Bible is clear that in the future, sections of Saudi Arabia near Israel will be on fire because of burning oil.

Isaiah called the time of judgment on Idumea "*the year of* [God's] *recompenses*" for what this nation did to Israel. God's judgment falls directly on Jordan and Saudi Arabia.

> *It is the day of the* LORD*'s vengeance, and the year of recompenses for the controversy of Zion.* (Isaiah 34:8)

> *My sword shall be bathed in heaven: behold, it shall come down upon Idumea, and upon the people of my curse, to judgment.* (Isaiah 34:5)

This area burns so intensely that no one can pass through it.

> *The streams thereof shall be turned into pitch, and the dust thereof into brimstone, and the land thereof shall become burning pitch. It shall not be quenched night nor day; the smoke thereof shall go up for ever: from generation to generation it shall lie waste; none shall pass through it for ever and ever.* (Isaiah 34:9–10)

Thus the Bible shows that the Palestinians' hostility toward Israel erupts into an awesome war that destroys entire nations. The conflict draws in Egypt, Syria, Jordan, and Lebanon. It appears that weapons of mass destruction are used and that entire nations cease to exist. The combined population of Egypt, Syria, Iraq, Jordan, and Lebanon is approximately 120 million.

How long can the tensions with Israel continue? How long before a war erupts and quickly turns into the use of weapons of mass destruction? The Muslim hatred for Israel is so strong that it seems they would risk annihilation in an attempt to destroy God's covenant nation. These nations fail and face total destruction.

Ring of Fire around Israel

This first war results in an impassible ring of destroyed countries to the south and east of Israel. The nations of Egypt, Jordan, Iraq, and part of Saudi Arabia are totally destroyed. According to the Bible, they become like Sodom and Gomorrah.

This area of land becomes completely impassable because of the use of nuclear, chemical, or biological weapons. The soil of the destroyed nations is so poisoned that it is impossible to pass through. The area of Idumea is on fire, much like Kuwait was after the 1991 Gulf War. The approaches to Israel from the south and east are blocked, leaving only the north as an avenue to attack Israel.

In the two wars that follow, the only avenue to Israel will be through Lebanon and part of Syria. The Mediterranean Sea blocks a land invasion from the west. This blockage results in huge numbers of soldiers compressed into a very narrow area of land focused in the Mountains of Israel. It is as if the huge armies are funneled into a gigantic killing field as they rush to take Jerusalem. These armies are destroyed during the second battle and Armageddon.

God has set the nation of Israel like a trap, and Jerusalem is the bait. As the nations reject the everlasting covenant and attack Israel, they are destroyed. God's posture is defensive in these wars. If the nations do not attack, God does not destroy them. The nations are destroyed as they attempt to invade the covenant land, not before. Israel then becomes an anvil for God's judgment of the nations.

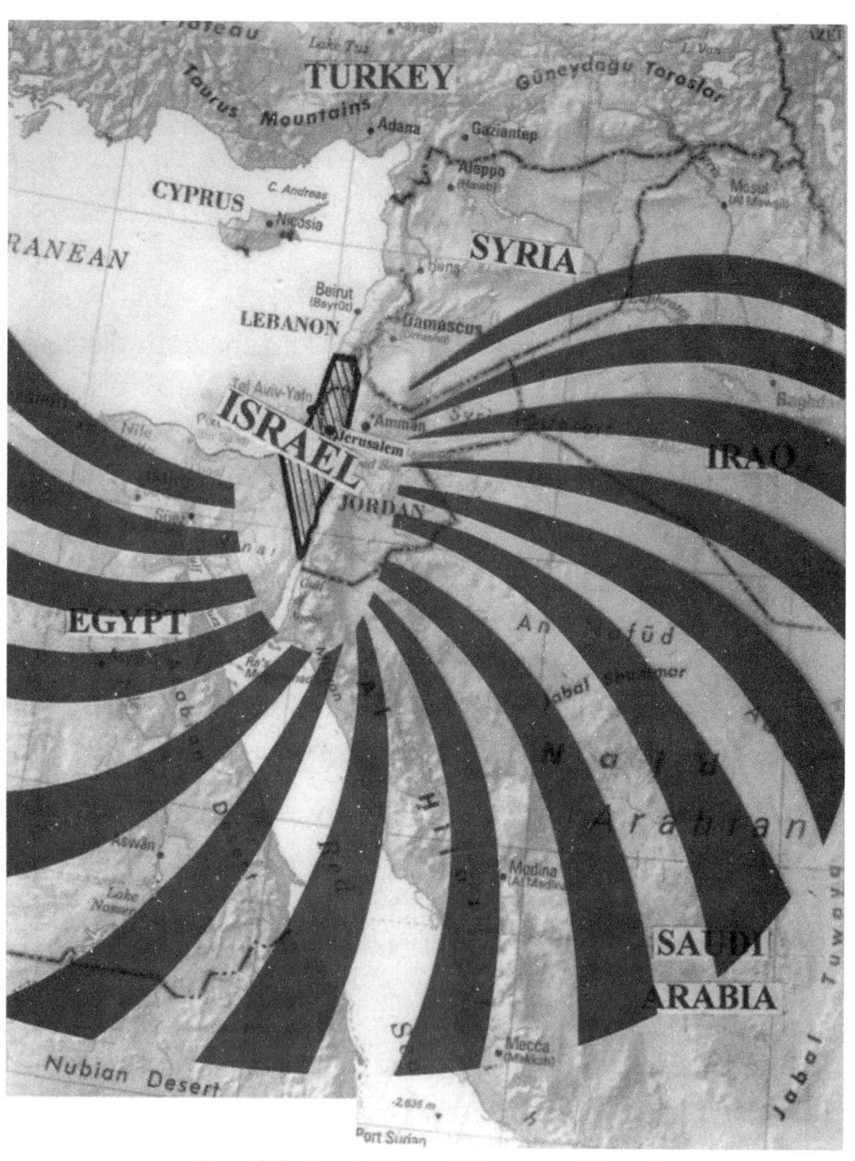

Day of the Lord: Ring of Fire around Israel

This dreadful confrontation between Israel and the surrounding nations is the key sign of the approaching day of the Lord. These signs cannot be missed. All the alarms, bells, whistles, and warnings are going forth that the awesome day of the Lord is near. Only unbelief prevents a person from seeing these signs.

The Second War

> *Thou shalt come up against my people of Israel, as a cloud to cover the land; it shall be in the latter days.* (Ezekiel 38:16)

The prophet Ezekiel wrote twenty-six hundred years ago, but still speaks directly to us today. He described a huge battle that takes place after the nation of Israel is reborn. This war is the second of the three. With great detail, Ezekiel foretold of the rebirth of Israel in chapters 36–37. In chapters 40–48, the prophet then described the rule of the Lord Jesus from His magnificent temple in Jerusalem.

Between the rebirth of Israel and the kingdom age, Ezekiel described a horrific battle in chapters 38 and 39. The war is often referred to as the battle of Gog and Magog. This is the second battle connected to the approaching day of the Lord.

Ezekiel listed a confederacy of nations united in this attack against Israel. Russia leads these nations, which include Turkey, Iran, Libya, Ethiopia, parts of Eastern Europe, and many other unnamed nations. Something strange appears immediately when you look at this list. The prophet fails to mention the nations directly bordering Israel! These countries are Egypt, Iraq, Jordan, Lebanon, Palestine, and Syria. The reason these nations are not mentioned that they were all destroyed in the first battle.

Ezekiel set the time frame of this battle as taking place after the Jews return to Israel from a worldwide dispersion. He identified this period as the "*latter years.*" Jews were scattered into all the nations for nearly two thousand years, but in Ezekiel 38 they are home again.

> *In the latter years thou shalt come into the land that is brought back from the sword, and is gathered out of many people, against the mountains of Israel, which have been always waste: but it is brought forth out of the nations, and they shall dwell safely all of them.* (Ezekiel 38:8)

This second war increases in scope and destruction. As in the first battle, this one involves many Islamic nations. The destruction of the countries of the first war may be one reason for this second battle. The time period between the first and this war is unknown.

Russia: The Land of Magog

The prophet Ezekiel identified Russia as the chief antagonist against Israel in this coming battle. Russia has a long history of hating and persecuting Jewish people. With the pogroms starting in 1881, untold numbers of Jews died at the hands of the Russians. Russian Jews were the first to return to Israel in the 1880s, leaving Russia because of persecution.

It is ironic that Russian hatred drove the Jews to Israel, and then God, in the future, will destroy Russia in a devastating war with Israel! This is divine retribution for all the Russian persecution of Jews. Let's take a close look at Ezekiel's prophecy.

> *The word of the LORD came unto me, saying, Son of man, set thy face against Gog, the land of Magog, the chief prince of Meshech and Tubal, and prophesy against him, And say, Thus saith the LORD GOD; Behold, I am against thee, O Gog, the chief prince of Meshech and Tubal.* (Ezekiel 38:1–3)

Gog is a title, such as chief prince or president. The nation is the land of Magog, Meshech, and Tubal. This war is often referred to as the battle of Gog and Magog. The names Magog, Meshech, and Tubal identify the modern nation of Russia.

Magog was the name of a people at the time of Ezekiel. The first century Jewish historian Flavius Josephus identified the Magogites. In his book *Antiquities of the Jews*, Josephus wrote, "Magog founded those that were from him named Magogites, but who are by the Greeks called Scythians."[3] The ancient Greek historian Herodotus wrote of the Scythians, saying they controlled the land between the Danube and Don rivers, and from the Black Sea north for several hundred miles.[4] Today this area is located in the nation of Russia.

Russia is the nation identified as Magog. The names Meshech and Tubal sound similar to the Russian cities of Moscow and Tubalsk. Ezekiel also identified Magog as coming from the north. Moscow is directly north of Jerusalem, "*And thou shalt come from thy place out of the north parts*" (Ezekiel 38:15). Russia has a substantial Muslim population, which fits right in with a major attack on Israel. The combination of historical Russian hatred of Jews and its Muslim population could prove to be the catalyst for attacking Israel. Thus both geographical location and history identify Russia as leading this second war against Israel.

Ezekiel then identified the confederation of nations that will join to attack Israel. Persia is modern-day Iran, having changed its name in 1935. Iran has declared publicly that it wants the complete destruction of Israel. Russia is Iran's main supplier of weapons. Iran and Russia become a perfect match for the attack on Israel.

The Bible refers to Ethiopia as the land south of Egypt. Today this would include the nations of the Sudan, Ethiopia, and Somalia. The Sudan and Somalia are both Islamic nations. The Sudan is identified as a terrorist state and hates Israel. Ethiopia has a large Muslim population of about 30 percent. Sudan and Somalia are a natural fit with Russia in a confederated attack.

In the Bible, Libya encompasses all the land west of Egypt. This would include the nations of Libya, Tunisia, Algeria, and Morocco. All these nations are Islamic and could easily fit into the confederation against Israel. Russia is once again Libya's major supplier of weapons. Algeria is in the midst of a civil war that started in 1995 and has killed more than one hundred thousand people. Muslim fundamentalists are trying to take over the country, and such a takeover would make Algeria ready for war with Israel.

Ezekiel identified Togarmah as a country north of Israel. This is Turkey, which is nearly 100 percent Muslim. Turkey is a part of the North Atlantic Treaty Organization (NATO) and has a military treaty with Israel. For this battle to happen, Turkey must line up with Russia. When Turkey aligns with Russia, it means the day of this battle is drawing near.

The identity of Gomer is not as clear as the other nations. It is possible that Gomer is Germany or some eastern European countries. Russia is going to be a guard, or a weapons supplier, to these nations. The confederation of nations follows:

> *Persia, Ethiopia, and Libya with them; all of them with shield and helmet: Gomer, and all his bands; the house of Togarmah of the north quarters, and all his bands: and many people with thee. Be thou prepared, and prepare for thyself, thou, and all thy company that are assembled unto thee, and be thou a guard unto them.* (Ezekiel 38:5–7)

The United States is currently preventing this battle from taking place. For this battle to happen, the United States has to be weakened or eliminated from the Middle East. NATO has to be weakened by Turkey forming an alliance with Russia. Russia becomes the dominant force at this time, not America. For this war to happen, something disastrous needs to happen in the future to the United States.

Even though the Soviet Union has collapsed, the Russian army is still large and well equipped. With the right leadership and motivation, the Russian army could be formidable. The Russian bear is far from being dead.

> *I will bring thee forth, and all thine army, horses and horsemen, all of them clothed with all sorts of armour, even a great company with bucklers and shields, all of them handling swords.*
> (Ezekiel 38:4)

The confederation led by Russia is enormous, for the army will cover the land like a cloud. Perhaps all the remaining Islamic nations not mentioned by the prophet Ezekiel join in this attack.

> *Thou shalt ascend and come like a storm, thou shalt be like a cloud to cover the land, thou, and all thy bands, and many people with thee....And thou shalt come from thy place out of the north parts, thou, and many people with thee, all of them riding upon horses, a great company, and a mighty arm.*
> (Ezekiel 38:9, 15)

It seems that after the destruction of Iraq and Egypt that Israel enters into a short period of peace. It is during this time that the confederation comes against Israel. God emphasizes for the second time that the army led by Russia is coming against Israel in the "*latter days*." God is allowing this army to come against Israel so that the entire world can see His mighty power.

> *Therefore, son of man, prophesy and say unto Gog, Thus saith the Lord God; In that day when my people of Israel dwelleth safely, shalt thou not know it? And thou shalt come from thy place out of the north parts, thou, and many people with thee, all of them riding upon horses, a great company, and a mighty army.* (Ezekiel 38:14–15)

When God destroys Russia and its Islamic allies, there is no doubt that this accomplishment will be from the hand of the Holy God of Israel. The nation of Israel is unable to defend itself against this army. God defends His everlasting covenant with Abraham, Isaac, Jacob, and His people Israel.

> *Thou shalt come up against my people of Israel, as a cloud to cover the land; it shall be in the latter days, and I will bring thee against my land, that the heathen may know me, when I shall be sanctified in thee, O Gog, before their eyes.* (Ezekiel 38:16)

God reacts with intense anger to this attack. All the centuries these nations spend rejecting God will climax in this cataclysmic confrontation between the huge army and the living God. God uses natural disasters with supernatural timing to destroy this army.

> *It shall come to pass at the same time when Gog shall come against the land of Israel, saith the* LORD GOD, *that my fury shall come up in my face. For in my jealousy and in the fire of my wrath have I spoken, Surely in that day there shall be a great shaking in the land of Israel....And I will plead against him with pestilence and with blood; and I will rain upon him, and upon his bands, and upon the many people that are with him, an overflowing rain, and great hailstones, fire, and brimstone.* (Ezekiel 38:18–19, 22)

The Mountains of Israel

> *But ye, O mountains of Israel, ye shall shoot forth your branches, and yield your fruit to my people of Israel; for they are at hand to come.* (Ezekiel 36:8)

In chapter 36, Ezekiel recorded a tremendous prophecy regarding the Mountains of Israel. The mountains run north-south like a spine down the middle of Israel. They start about fifty miles north of Jerusalem and run about thirty miles south. The city of Jerusalem sits on the Mountains of Israel.

> *Also, thou son of man, prophesy unto the mountains of Israel, and say, Ye mountains of Israel, hear the word of the Lord.*
> (Ezekiel 36:1)

Ezekiel set the background for this prophecy by describing the desolation of the Mountains of Israel. This desolation was the result of God judging the nation for rebellion against Him. The Jews were also scattered throughout all the nations. They were driven from the land, and non-Jews then populated the mountains. The information that the nation was destroyed and the mountains made desolate sets the stage for Ezekiel's prophecy.

> *Therefore, ye mountains of Israel, hear the word of the Lord God; Thus saith the Lord God to the mountains, and to the hills, to the rivers, and to the valleys, to the desolate wastes, and to the cities that are forsaken, which became a prey and derision to the residue of the heathen that are round about.*
> (Ezekiel 36:4)

> *I scattered them among the heathen, and they were dispersed through the countries: according to their way and according to their doings I judged them.* (Ezekiel 36:19)

The prophet then issued a prophecy regarding the Mountains of Israel that God would one day bring the people back. The desolation and destruction were not permanent. God would bless these mountains with abundant rain and crops, and people would return to rebuild the cities.

> *But ye, O mountains of Israel, ye shall shoot forth your branches, and yield your fruit to my people of Israel; for they are at hand to come. For, behold, I am for you, and I will turn unto you, and ye shall be tilled and sown: And I will multiply*

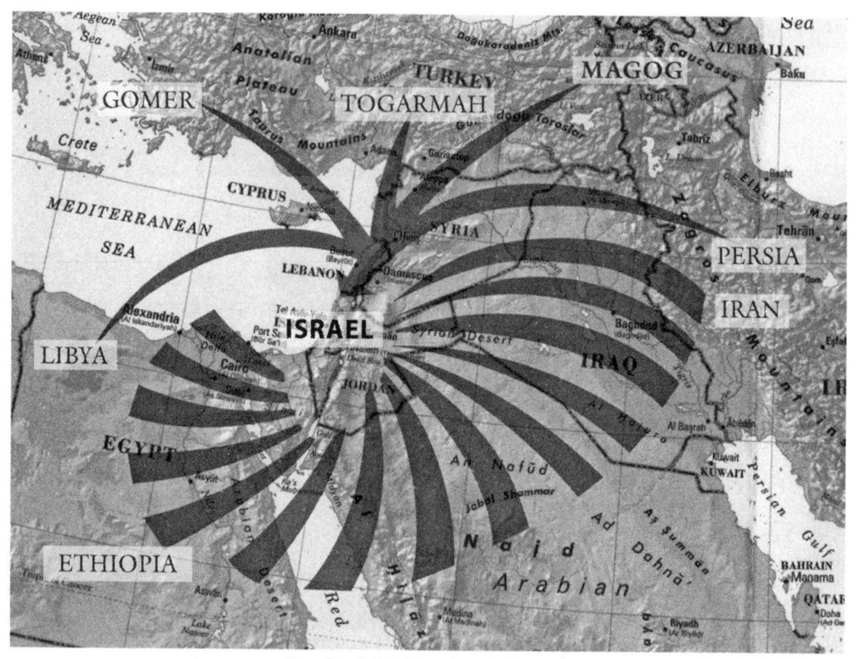

Ezekiel 38 Route of Attack

> *men upon you, all the house of Israel, even all of it: and the cities shall be inhabited, and the wastes shall be builded.*
>
> (Ezekiel 36:8–10)

God's prophetic word hovers over the Mountains of Israel. The prophet declared God would bless these mountains when He brought the Jewish people back from the nations. The people would rebuild the cities and farm the land.

The ring of fire creates a funnel pointed at the Mountains of Israel. The invading army led by Russia swarms over the Mountains of Israel. God does not judge this army hundreds of miles away, but when they cross into the covenant land and start to overrun the Mountains of Israel, this invading army runs headlong into God's prophetic word. The invasion stops in its tracks and the army is destroyed. This awesome destruction takes place directly on the Mountains of Israel.

I will turn thee back, and leave but the sixth part of thee, and will cause thee to come up from the north parts, and will bring thee upon the mountains of Israel....Thou shalt fall upon the mountains of Israel, thou, and all thy bands, and the people that is with thee: I will give thee unto the ravenous birds of every sort, and to the beasts of the field to be devoured.

(Ezekiel 39:2, 4)

The judgments God sends include a massive earthquake that shakes the entire earth, pestilence, great hailstones, fire, and brimstone. The armies turn against each other and begin killing one another. The entire army is destroyed, and then God judges the nations involved in this attack. Russia meets its doom on the Mountains of Israel, as God applies Obadiah 1:15 to the Russians. God destroys perhaps the greatest Jew-hating nation as it attempts to destroy Israel:

I will call for a sword against him throughout all my mountains, saith the LORD GOD: every man's sword shall be against his brother. And I will plead against him with pestilence and with blood; and I will rain upon him, and upon his bands, and upon the many people that are with him, an overflowing rain, and great hailstones, fire, and brimstone.

(Ezekiel 38:21–22)

The defeat of Russia and the last of the Islamic armies opens the eyes of Israel to their God. Although they do not yet recognize the Lord Jesus as their Messiah, this starts Jewish people turning to God and His Messiah. They are in awe of what God did. For two thousand years Israel wandered from nation to nation. Now the times of the Gentiles, which the Lord Jesus spoke about, draw to a close. God is once again dealing directly with His people Israel. This battle opens the spiritual eyes of many people throughout the world, and breaks the hold of Islam. Muslims who survive realize that the

God of Israel is the true God. The destruction of this army causes many to turn to God through the Lord Jesus.

> *Thus will I magnify myself, and sanctify myself; and I will be known in the eyes of many nations, and they shall know that I am the Lord.* (Ezekiel 38:23)

> *So will I make my holy name known in the midst of my people Israel; and I will not let them pollute my holy name any more: and the heathen shall know that I am the Lord, the Holy One in Israel.* (Ezekiel 39:7)

The two outstanding events that lead to the day of the Lord, massive wars and incredible natural disasters, coincide at this time. The prelude to what is coming upon the earth can be seen in the timing of the major disasters hitting the United States when pressuring Israel over the covenant land!

The Third War: Armageddon

> *He gathered them together into a place called in the Hebrew tongue Armageddon.* (Revelation 16:16)

Armageddon is one word from the Bible that almost everyone has heard. This is the final battle between God and evil. Armageddon is not a battle between good nations and evil nations; it is the battle where God Himself directly intervenes and destroys the largest army in history. This battle ends man's corrupt rule over the nations. Armageddon is the third and final attempt to destroy Israel and take Jerusalem.

Armageddon means Mount Megiddo, which is about seventy miles north of Jerusalem. Mount Megiddo is at the southern edge of the Esdraelon Valley, also called the Plain of Megiddo. This is a huge valley that runs from southeast to the northwest, right at Mount

Megiddo. This valley is the center of the final battle. The Mountains of Israel start at the southern edge of this valley.

Jerusalem is the objective of the final war. After the defeat of Russia and its confederation, the remaining nations converge on Israel. God uses Jerusalem as a lure, and the people in rebellion against Him literally come by the hundreds of millions. The prophet Zechariah showed that this final battle, before the second coming of the Lord Jesus, is over Jerusalem.

> *Behold, the day of the Lord cometh, and thy spoil shall be divided in the midst of thee. For I will gather all nations against Jerusalem to battle.* (Zechariah 14:1–2)

All of man's rebellion against God culminates in this battle over Jerusalem. During the previous battles, there is no indication from Scripture that the armies overrun Jerusalem. In this final battle, a vast army invades the Middle East from Asia. All of Asia is at this battle, along with the other nations of the world. The apostle John states in the book of Revelation that this army numbers two hundred million.

> *The four angels were loosed, which were prepared for an hour, and a day, and a month, and a year, for to slay the third part of men. And the number of the army of the horsemen were two hundred thousand thousand* [two hundred million]: *and I heard the number of them.* (Revelation 9:15–16)

The Euphrates River is the traditional dividing line between the Middle East and Asia. This army is going to cross the Euphrates River and pour into the Middle East. On the way to the Euphrates River, this army is going to spread into other nations and kill a third of mankind. The Bible says that the unified kings of the East lead this army.

> *And the sixth angel poured out his vial upon the great river Euphrates; and the water thereof was dried up, that the way*

> *of the kings of the east might be prepared...to gather them to the battle of that great day of God Almighty....And he gathered them together into a place called in the Hebrew tongue Armageddon.* (Revelation 16:12, 14, 16)

Like the previous battle of Magog, this army meets its doom on the Mountains of Israel. The ring of fire is still around Israel, and the only way to attack is from the north. This massive army fills the Valley of Megiddo and then reaches all the way to Jerusalem. Remember, Jerusalem is located in the Mountains of Israel. This army is about to destroy Israel and Jerusalem, and God stops it when it reaches Jerusalem.

The Lord Jesus Christ's direct intervention stops this army. This attempted destruction of Jerusalem triggers His awesome second coming. He personally destroys the armies gathered for Armageddon and defends His covenant land and people. This is not a battle between the nations of the world; it is a battle where God directly intervenes through Jesus Christ.

According to the prophet Zechariah, the Lord Jesus stands in Jerusalem on the Mount of Olives. There is an enormous earthquake that splits this mountain. He is in His full glory. It is the presence of Jesus Christ in His glory that destroys this invading army. The radiating glory of Jesus Christ at His second coming totally annihilates Israel's enemies. God's glory affects human flesh like a neutron bomb. The prophet describes the destruction of this army.

> *This shall be the plague wherewith the* Lord *will smite all the people that have fought against Jerusalem; their flesh shall consume away while they stand upon their feet, and their eyes shall consume away in their holes, and their tongue shall consume away in their mouth.* (Zechariah 14:12)

The day of the Lord has arrived, and Israel now realizes that Jesus of Nazareth was the Messiah of Israel. They see Him standing on the Mount of Olives and understand He is their Messiah. The entire nation of Israel turns to Him, and then goes into deep mourning with true repentance. Israel is finally reunited with the Lord Jesus.

> *And it shall come to pass in that day, that I will seek to destroy all the nations that come against Jerusalem. And I will pour upon the house of David, and upon the inhabitants of Jerusalem, the spirit of grace and of supplications: and they shall look upon me whom they have pierced, and they shall mourn for him, as one mourneth for his only son, and shall be in bitterness for him, as one that is in bitterness for his firstborn. In that day shall there be a great mourning in Jerusalem, as the mourning of Hadadrimmon in the valley of Megiddon.*
>
> (Zechariah 12:9–11)

The day of the Lord then continues through the building of a magnificent the temple, in which the Lord Jesus reigns for one thousand years. A wonderful future awaits the nation of Israel. After coming under the kingship of Jesus Christ, Israel enters the kingdom age, during which God fulfills all the prophecies in the Old Testament about Israel being blessed.

God is not finished with Israel. The day is coming soon when Israel is blessed above all nations: the day of the Lord. For a detailed study of the events that follow the second coming of Jesus Christ, see my book *Only Jesus of Nazareth Can Sit on the Throne of David.*

The Future of America

For the fulfillment of biblical prophecy about the war of Gog-Magog and Armageddon, something has to have happened to the United States' world power and influence. American military power and NATO would block any attempt by Russia to form a coalition and invade Israel. For this to happen, America can no longer be a world power. There has to be a tremendous shift of power away from America towards Russia.

For the countries of Asia to unite in a massive army, something also has to happen to American power in Asia. At the present time, the United States is blocking this from happening. Taiwan will have to be reunited with China, and North Korea has to overcome South Korea.

According to biblical prophecy, the future for the United States does not appear good. God has given America warning judgments over and over again. American foreign policy has destabilized Israel, God's covenant nation. The American government has done much to trigger God's judgment. It appears that God is going to remove America from being a world power because of national sin and rebellion against Him.

If the events we are witnessing are the start of the approach to the day of the Lord, then America's time as a superpower is very short. God in His mercy has warned of the coming judgment, but the church has failed to recognize the warnings and has not led the nation in repentance before God. It appears that worldliness and false doctrines neutralize the church, and America falls under the judgment of God. America's interference with God's prophetic plan for Israel brings this judgment.

Although America ceases to exist as a world power, repentance could preserve the nation from total destruction. The integrity of the United States is in the hands of the true church. God is about to end the religious game many Americans are playing.

> *The day of the* L*ORD is near upon all the heathen: as thou hast done* [to Israel], *it shall be done unto thee: thy reward shall return upon thine own head.* (Obadiah 1:15)

Chapter Eleven

The Clouds of Heaven

> *Jesus saith unto him, Thou hast said: nevertheless I say unto you, Hereafter shall ye see the Son of man sitting on the right hand of power,* ***and coming in the clouds of heaven.***
>
> (Matthew 26:64, emphasis added)

The heart of the day of the Lord is the second coming of Jesus Christ. All current world events are lining up and pointing to His second coming. The wars described in the Bible are awesome, but they pale in comparison to the coming of Jesus Christ. He returns during the day of the Lord to save Israel from total destruction. When the Lord Jesus returns, it is not to Washington or London or Mecca, but to Jerusalem.

The prophet Zechariah described the second coming. He saw the Lord Jesus standing in Jerusalem on the Mount of Olives. A tremendous earthquake coincides with His coming. Jesus Christ then destroys the forces of evil gathered around Jerusalem.

> *Behold, the day of the LORD cometh....For I will gather all nations against Jerusalem to battle....Then shall the LORD go forth, and fight against those nations, as when he fought in*

> *the day of battle. And his feet shall stand in that day upon the mount of Olives, which is before Jerusalem on the east, and the mount of Olives shall cleave in the midst thereof.*
>
> (Zechariah 14:1–4)

The Lord Jesus comes directly from heaven to set up His universal, everlasting kingdom. No world organization elects Him, nor is He appointed. He will not head any political organization like the United Nations. It is God's supernatural power that establishes His kingdom on the earth. The Bible describes His coming as flaming fire in great glory.

> *To you who are troubled rest with us, when the Lord Jesus shall be revealed from heaven with his mighty angels, in flaming fire.* (2 Thessalonians 1:7–8)

When Jesus Christ returns to defend Jerusalem, a massive number of believers accompany Him. Zechariah described the effect of the incredible earthquake, and then stated that the Lord Jesus is returning with all His saints. These saints are not on earth at Jesus' second coming, but this huge throng accompanies Him from heaven. In the day of the Lord, Jesus Christ returns with a vast array of people. Zechariah identified them as saints: "*The Lord my God shall come, and all the saints with thee*" (Zechariah 14:5).

Throughout the Bible, a massive number of believers are described as returning with the Lord Jesus Christ. The usual phrase describing this throng is the "*clouds of heaven.*" The New Testament uses the phrase "*clouds of heaven*" several times, but it actually originated in the Old Testament.

The prophet Daniel first used this phrase, and he identified exactly what the clouds of heaven are. Daniel gave a rare glimpse into heaven in the Old Testament when he saw events taking place before the very throne of God. He referred to the holy God of Israel as the Ancient of Days. He saw God on His throne and used fire to describe everything about God's appearance, including the surroundings of His throne.

Daniel also saw a countless number of believers around the throne. The prophet recorded the number of believers as a thousand times thousands, and ten thousand times ten thousand. This huge number is beyond calculation. The clouds of heaven, then, are the innumerable believers who are in heaven with the Lord Jesus and who return with Him. These are the saints that Zechariah stated were coming with Jesus Christ. The following verses show God's throne and this huge number of believers around it:

> *The Ancient of days did sit, whose garment was white as snow, and the hair of his head like the pure wool: his throne was like the fiery flame, and his wheels as burning fire. A fiery stream issued and came forth from before him: thousand thousands ministered unto him, and ten thousand times ten thousand stood before him.* (Daniel 7:9–10)

The clouds of heaven represent an enormous number of believers who surround the throne of God. It appears that the Bible uses the term "*clouds of heaven*" because this huge throng of believers, from a distance, appears as a massive cloud. From other Scriptures, the Bible reveals that the believers are dressed in pure white. The Lord leads this massive white cloud. They return with Him and are present when He establishes His kingdom on earth. The following verses from Daniel 7 show the Son of Man, the Lord Jesus, returning with the clouds of heaven to set up His kingdom on earth.

> *I saw in the night visions, and, behold, one like the Son of man came with the clouds of heaven, and came to the Ancient of days, and they brought him near before him. And there was given him dominion, and glory, and a kingdom,*

> *that all people, nations, and languages, should serve him: his dominion is an everlasting dominion, which shall not pass away, and his kingdom that which shall not be destroyed.*
> (Daniel 7:13–14)

At His trial when the Lord Jesus was questioned by the high priest concerning His claim of being the Son of God, He answered by joining two Scriptures together. He used Daniel 7:13 and Psalm 110:1, and referred them to His second coming. The Lord Jesus stated He was returning with the clouds of heaven. The high priest fully understood that Jesus was quoting the prophet Daniel, and he knew the meaning of this verse. He used this statement to condemn Jesus to death for blasphemy, because this phrase related to the coming of Israel's King Messiah.

> *Jesus saith unto him, Thou hast said: nevertheless I say unto you, Hereafter shall ye see the Son of man sitting on the right hand of power, **and coming in the clouds of heaven**.*
> (Matthew 26:64, emphasis added)

The Blessed Hope: The Coming of Jesus Christ with the Clouds of Heaven

> *Looking for that blessed hope, and the glorious appearing of the great God and our Saviour Jesus Christ.* (Titus 2:13)

With this foundation, let's now look at the New Testament and the coming of the Lord Jesus with the clouds of heaven. When Jesus' disciples asked what the sign of His coming was, He listed several events. These events included both awesome wars and natural disasters. Then, when all is fulfilled, the people of earth will see Him coming with power and great glory. When He returns in great glory, the clouds of heaven are with Him. Jesus directly linked His coming with the clouds of heaven. All the Gospel writers link the second coming with the clouds of heaven. The verses from the Gospels follow:

> *Then shall appear the sign of the Son of man in heaven: and then shall all the tribes of the earth mourn, **and they shall see the Son of man coming in the clouds of heaven with power and great glory**.* (Matthew 24:30, emphasis added)

> *Then shall they see the Son of man coming **in the clouds** with great power and glory.* (Mark 13:26, emphasis added)

> *Then shall they see the Son of man coming **in a cloud** with power and great glory.* (Luke 21:27, emphasis added)

The apostle John also made the link between the second coming and the Lord returning with the clouds of heaven. In the book of Revelation, John saw the Lord's return with the clouds, and all the people of the earth mourning.

> *Behold, he cometh **with clouds**; and every eye shall see him, and they also which pierced him: and all kindreds of the earth shall wail because of him. Even so, Amen.*
> (Revelation 1:7, emphasis added)

John identified the clouds of heaven as the church. These are the true believers in the Lord Jesus who are in heaven and then return with Him. This is not just the dead in Christ but the entire church. It is the Lord's completed church that returns with Him.

> *Saviours shall come up on mount Zion to judge the mount of Esau; and the kingdom shall be the LORD's.* (Obadiah 1:21)

John described a scene in heaven where the entire church is at the marriage supper of the Lamb. There are innumerable people with Jesus—a number, just like Daniel witnessed, that were before the throne of God. There can be no doubt that this event is taking place in heaven.

> *After these things I heard a great voice of much people* ***in heaven****, saying, Alleluia; Salvation, and glory, and honour, and power, unto the* L*ORD our God....And I heard as it were the voice of a great multitude, and as the voice of many waters, and as the voice of mighty thunderings, saying, Alleluia: for the* L*ORD God omnipotent reigneth.*
>
> (Revelation 19:1, 6, emphasis added)

After John identified the location, he went on to describe what is taking place. He identified what is occurring in heaven as the marriage supper of the Lamb. The Lamb is a title for Jesus Christ, and His bride is the church.

> *Let us be glad and rejoice, and give honour to him: for the marriage of the Lamb is come, and his wife hath made herself ready. And to her was granted that she should be arrayed in fine linen, clean and white: for the fine linen is the righteousness of saints. And he saith unto me, Write, Blessed are they which are called unto the marriage supper of the Lamb.*
>
> (Revelation 19:7–9)

After the marriage supper is finished, the Lord Jesus has work to do on earth. John saw Heaven open and Jesus returning to earth. He is returning as a mighty man of war. He then executes the fierceness of God's wrath towards the nations in rebellion against Him. He finally judges the nations at the battle of Armageddon.

> *Out of his mouth goeth a sharp sword, that with it he should smite the nations: and he shall rule them with a rod of iron: and he treadeth the winepress of the fierceness and wrath of Almighty God.* (Revelation 19:15)

When the Lord Jesus returns, He will destroy the armies surrounding Jerusalem, as the prophet Zechariah stated. Jesus' return in Revelation 19, with His feet standing on the Mount of Olives in

Zechariah 14, tie directly together. The Old Testament clearly maps this out, and the events of Revelation in the New Testament tie in.

John saw more than just the Lord Jesus returning; he saw the church returning with Him. He referred to the church not as the clouds of heaven, but "the armies in heaven." This army returns with Him clothed in pure white linen. This "army in heaven" that John wrote about is the clouds of heaven that Daniel saw in his vision. Jesus is coming back with His bride, the church. What a sight to witness: the Son of God returning in His power and glory with the clouds of heaven!

> *And* ***the armies which were in heaven*** *followed him upon white horses, clothed in fine linen, white and clean.*
> (Revelation 19:14, emphasis added)

God is setting an incredible backdrop to the second coming of Jesus Christ. The sky is totally darkened through either natural events or man-made actions. Suddenly there is an explosion of light as the glory of Jesus Christ lights the sky. Directly behind Him are the clouds of heaven, dressed in pure white.

Imagine being on earth and seeing this happening. The entire sky filled from one end to the other with this massive white cloud, and at the head is the Lord Jesus in flaming fire, manifesting His glory! What Daniel actually witnessed was the church returning with King Messiah, the Lord Jesus. The verses to show this follow:

> *Immediately after the tribulation of those days shall the sun be darkened, and the moon shall not give her light....And then shall appear the sign of the Son of man in heaven...and they shall see the Son of man coming in the clouds of heaven with power and great glory.* (Matthew 24:29–30)

The church returns with the Lord Jesus at His second coming. Since the church is in heaven enjoying the marriage supper of the Lamb, how and when did it get there? Jesus summons the church to heaven before He returns to save Israel at the battle of Armageddon.

It happens, as the apostle Paul said, in the twinkling of an eye. Not everyone is going to die, but those who are alive at the Lord's summons for the believing church are immediately changed. They receive eternal life and incorruptible bodies. God raises from the dead the people who believed in Jesus, and He then joins them with those who are still alive.

> *Behold, I show you a mystery; We shall not all sleep, but we shall all be changed, in a moment, in the twinkling of an eye, at the last trump: for the trumpet shall sound, and the dead shall be raised incorruptible, and we shall be changed.*
> (1 Corinthians 15:51–52)

This will happen when the Lord Jesus comes for His bride, the church. He will descend from heaven with a tremendous shout and the blast of the trumpet. The dead in Christ shall arise first, and then the believers that are alive at the time shall receive resurrected bodies. God takes the entire church to heaven, where they will be with the Lord Jesus forever. The church goes with Him to the marriage supper of the Lamb.

> *This we say unto you by the word of the Lord, that we which are alive and remain unto the coming of the Lord shall not prevent them which are asleep. For the Lord himself shall descend from heaven with a shout, with the voice of the archangel, and with the trump of God: and the dead in Christ shall rise first: Then we which are alive and remain shall be caught up together with them in the clouds, to meet the Lord in the air: and so shall we ever be with the Lord. Wherefore comfort one another with these words.* (1 Thessalonians 4:15–18)

The idea of the Lord's coming for the church is so powerful that the Bible tells us to comfort one another with this in our times of sorrow over the loss of a loved one. The loss is only temporary, as there will be a uniting with the loved ones when the Lord comes for the believers. This is truly the blessed hope: the coming of the Lord for the church and being with Him forever.

> *Looking for that blessed hope, and the glorious appearing of the great God and our Saviour Jesus Christ.* (Titus 2:13)

Looking for the coming of the Lord Jesus is the blessed hope. It is not just a hope, but a blessed hope. Immediately following the church's gathering with the Lord is the marriage supper of the Lamb.

There is a double blessing for those who are waiting for the Lord's return. There is the blessed hope, and then the blessing of anticipating the marriage supper of the Lamb. All believers should be living with the blessed hope and the excitement of the marriage supper. If these two hopes are not motivating a believer, there is something radically wrong with that person's faith. Living with the blessed hope is one of the true signs of a believer. Jesus is only returning for those who are waiting for Him.

> *Christ was once offered to bear the sins of many; and unto them that look for him shall he appear the Second time without sin unto salvation.* (Hebrews 9:28)

The second coming is not just a doctrine but a living reality in the believer's life. If this reality is not in a person's heart, it is a sign something is drastically wrong. Sin and the love of the world kill the blessed hope. Wrong doctrine about the blessed hope also deadens the reality of the Lord's coming for the church and the marriage supper of the Lamb.

The two comings of the Lord—first for His church, and then to defend Israel—can be viewed as the two comings identified in the

Old Testament. The Bible in the Old Testament does not say directly that the King Messiah is coming twice. But when you study the Old Testament, the teaching of the two comings is there.

In one coming, the King Messiah is lowly on a donkey, while in the other, He is coming in power and great glory with the "*clouds of heaven.*" These two comings can appear irreconcilable until you realize that they are actually two distinct appearances. With the proper understanding of two comings, the Scriptures fit together beautifully. The following Scriptures show the two comings:

> *Rejoice greatly, O daughter of Zion; shout, O daughter of Jerusalem: behold, thy King cometh unto thee: he is just, and having salvation; lowly, and riding upon an ass* [donkey], *and upon a colt, the foal of an ass.* (Zechariah 9:9)

> *I saw in the night visions, and, behold, one like the Son of man came with the clouds of heaven, and came to the Ancient of days, and they brought him near before him.* (Daniel 7:13)

The same pattern in Scripture holds true for the second of the two comings, and it is called "the Lord's second coming." This coming is in two stages or phases. During the first stage, He comes for the church, followed by the marriage supper of the Lamb in heaven. The second stage begins at the completion of the marriage supper, when the Jesus Christ returns with the clouds of heaven to Jerusalem. The Lord's feet will then stand on the Mount of Olives. Jesus Christ meets His church in the air at the first stage. His feet stand on the Mount of Olives during the second stage. The verses to show this follow:

> *Then we which are alive and remain shall be caught up together with them in the clouds, to meet the Lord in the air: and so shall we ever be with the Lord.* (1 Thessalonians 4:17)

> *His feet shall stand in that day upon the mount of Olives, which is before Jerusalem on the east, and the mount of Olives shall cleave in the midst thereof toward the east and toward the west... and the* Lord *my God shall come, and all the saints with thee.* (Zechariah 14:4–5)

The Coming of the Lord Draweth Nigh

> *Every man that hath this hope in him purifieth himself, even as he is pure.* (1 John 3:3)

The reality of the blessed hope has an awesome effect on the believer. It is not just the doctrine of the blessed hope, but it is the living reality that affects lives. This reality causes tremendous spiritual growth.

In Paul's letter to Titus, the Bible lists eight effects the blessed hope has on a believer's heart. When a person lives with the anticipation of the second coming, the results include victory over ungodliness and worldly lusts, sober mindedness, righteousness, godly living, victory over iniquity, purity, and a zealousness for good works. Many Christians are weak because they lack the blessed hope in their hearts. The Bible verses that show the effect of the blessed hope follow:

> *The grace of God that bringeth salvation hath appeared to all men, teaching us that, denying ungodliness and worldly lusts, we should live soberly, righteously, and godly, in this present world; looking for that blessed hope, and the glorious appearing of the great God and our Saviour Jesus Christ; who gave himself for us, that he might redeem us from all iniquity, and purify unto himself a peculiar people, zealous of good works.* (Titus 2:11–14)

The blessed hope is spiritual life to a believer, and without it worldliness sets in and chokes the word of God in a person's life. Notice in Titus 2:11–14 that the blessed hope is in the very middle of the admonition to live a godly life. This verse was placed there to show how important the blessed hope is to our spiritual life. False doctrines that do not teach the reality of the blessed hope rob believers of spiritual power.

The Bible even draws a connection between the blessed hope and being zealous for good works. If one believes in the blessed hope, it will motivate that person to work for God and not just relax in this world. This is not a time for coasting but a time to live holy lives and do great things in the name of the Lord Jesus. (See Titus 2:14 above.)

The Bible tells us we are to wait with patience for the return of the Lord Jesus. Just as a farmer plants his crops and waits patiently until the crops mature, so we are to wait for the coming of the Lord. The Bible also tells us to establish the blessed hope in our hearts so that holiness will naturally flow. The Bible leaves no doubt that we are to focus on the blessed hope and live every day patiently as if the Lord might return for His church. The Scriptures to show this follow:

> *Be patient therefore, brethren, unto the coming of the Lord. Behold, the husbandman waiteth for the precious fruit of the earth, and hath long patience for it, until he receive the early and latter rain. Be ye also patient; stablish your hearts: for the coming of the Lord draweth nigh.* (James 5:7–8)

> *To the end he may stablish your hearts unblameable in holiness before God, even our Father, at the coming of our Lord Jesus Christ with all his saints.* (1 Thessalonians 3:13)

The blessed hope is an anchor for our souls. This is the hope that God has set before us. He requires that we keep the blessed hope with full assurance until He returns or until we pass away, whichever comes first. This hope steadies us during the storms of life. We are to lay hold of this hope and let nothing or no one take it from us. The Bible verses to show this follow:

> *We desire that every one of you do show the same diligence to the full assurance of hope unto the end....That by two immutable things, in which it was impossible for God to lie, we might have a strong consolation, who have fled for refuge to lay hold upon the hope set before us: Which hope we have as an anchor of the soul, both sure and stedfast, and which entereth into that within the veil.* (Hebrews 6:11, 18–19)

The Bible places nothing in the way of the Lord's coming for His church. There is no event that is required to take place before He descends from heaven with a shout for His bride. We are to be aware of world events in the light of biblical prophecy, but our anticipation should be for the blessed hope. Focusing on world events rather than the blessed hope can hinder one's faith and often create fear. No matter what happens in the world, we are to stay focused on the Lord Jesus' second coming. This is the anchor for your soul in the time of trouble.

> *To wait for his Son from heaven, whom he raised from the dead, even Jesus, which delivered us from the wrath to come.*
> (1 Thessalonians 1:10)

Faithful or Evil Servant

Jesus told a parable identifying who is God's faithful servant and who is an evil servant. The key to understanding these two servants is the differences in how they prepared for the second coming. The faithful servant lived by the blessed hope. He watched and waited for the second coming of Jesus Christ. Not only did God call this servant faithful, but He also called him wise. Living with the blessed hope makes a person both faithful and wise. Living one's life anticipating the return of the Lord Jesus is not a hard or difficult task. A person can easily be a faithful servant by living in the blessed hope.

> *Watch therefore: for ye know not what hour your LORD doth come....Who then is a faithful and wise servant....Blessed is that servant, whom his LORD when he cometh shall find so doing.*
> (Matthew 24:42, 45, 46)

Jesus also identified the evil servant, who said that the second coming of the Lord Jesus was delayed, and thus lived without the blessed hope. Failing to focus his life on God, he focused instead on the world. He even hated the faithful servant who was living in the blessed hope. When Jesus Christ returns, He will cast this evil servant from His presence, sending him to hell with the hypocrites. A person who claims to believe in Jesus Christ but lives without the blessed hope is a hypocrite. Living in the blessed hope is one of the hallmarks of Christianity. Just tampering with the second coming by saying it is delayed until sometime in the future, and becoming aggressive towards those who live in the blessed hope, makes one a hypocrite, as the following verses show:

> *If that evil servant shall say in his heart, My LORD delayeth his coming; and shall begin to smite his fellowservants, and to eat and drink with the drunken; the LORD of that servant shall come in a day when he looketh not for him.... And shall cut him asunder, and appoint him his portion with the hypocrites: there shall be weeping and gnashing of teeth.* (Matthew 24:48–51)

Thus, we are to wait for the Lord Jesus with patience. The waiting should intensify the anticipation for His second coming and not weaken it. As we wait for His return, God works in us to fulfill all eight characteristics: victory over ungodliness and worldly lusts, sober-mindedness, righteousness, godly living, victory over iniquity, purity, and zealousness for good works.

If you have not been living with the blessed hope in your life, now is the time to confess it to God. Ask Him to place the reality of the second coming of the Lord Jesus in your heart. For more information on how to obtain the reality of the blessed hope, see Addendum E.

> *I have fought a good fight, I have finished my course, I have kept the faith: Henceforth there is laid up for me a crown of righteousness, which the* LORD*, the righteous judge, shall give me at that day: and not to me only, but unto all them also that love his appearing.* (2 Timothy 4:7–8)

CHAPTER TWELVE

Until the Times of the Gentiles Be Fulfilled

Jerusalem shall be trodden down of the Gentiles, until the times of the Gentiles be fulfilled. (Luke 21:24)

America has a tremendous track record of supporting God's plan for the Jewish people. God raised up America as a world power at the exact time He was restoring His people to the covenant land. America played a major part in this restoration. The United States has blessed the Jews. When the tyrants of Europe were slaughtering them, the people of America opened their arms and took them in. The church was the main force behind America's support for the Jewish people.

President George Washington's vision for the Jewish people was for America to resemble the messianic kingdom; in a sense, it has. He set the example and laid the foundation for America to bless the Jewish people. President Abraham Lincoln followed his example and personally protected the Jews when they were the victims of discrimination during the Civil War. There were some rough spots in American history for the Jewish people, but overall America has blessed them greatly.

The American church in the late 1800s seized the spiritual opportunity to support the Jews and focus on the restoration of Israel. The church lined up with God's everlasting covenant for the land of Israel. Throughout America, believers were praying for the Jewish people and for the restoration of Israel. Just six years after the Blackstone Memorial, the modern Zionist movement was born. God continued to answer the prayers and intercession of the church. Just twenty-six years after the Memorial, the Turks lost control of the covenant land. Modern Israel was reborn in 1948, and God's prophetic plan was moving again. The American Church was the primary spiritual force behind this.

During the late 1800s and early 1900s, the church also focused on the second coming. The church was highly motivated by the blessed hope of Christ's second coming. These two dynamics—praying for the nation of Israel and focusing on Christ's second coming—generated a tremendous response from God. Focusing on the Lord Jesus' second coming saved the American church from destruction. The great power generated by preaching the Lord's return carried down through the decades to today.

In the 1800s, the European church failed to focus on Christ's coming and grew steadily "worldly" and cold. Being worldly means focusing on things other than God and His Word. For generation after generation, the European church grew colder further away from the Bible and God until today, where the church in Europe is almost nonexistent. There are more Muslims in Europe today than true believers in Jesus Christ. The church has little impact on Europe and now Islam is filling this void. The Europeans had the opportunity, as did the American church, but they failed to seize the moment.

Europe has a long history of hating the Jewish people. The European church failed to stand with the Jews when tsarist Russia was persecuting them. Millions of Russian Jews left "Christian" Europe and traveled thousands of miles to America. The combination of failing to preach the Lord Jesus' second coming and failing to stand with God's covenant people has left Europe spiritually bankrupt.

America took a different road than Europe. The great evangelists, preachers, and seminaries of America continued to proclaim the second coming. The church continued to stand with the Jewish people and later the restored nation of Israel. The church in America remained vibrant and alive while the church in Europe died a slow death.

The American church still enjoys great blessings from the revivals that swept America from the late 1800s into the early 1900s. Nevertheless, powerful forces are eating away at the strength of the American church. False doctrines such as preterism, dominion, and replacement theology, which affect a person's view of Israel and the second coming, are drawing away large numbers of Christians.

The church is also focusing largely on wealth and materialism, a focus that drains power from believers. There are huge numbers of people focused completely on material gain and not the second coming of the Lord Jesus. This focus on materialism is called the "prosperity message." Christians are to focus on Christ's second coming and not on material wealth. Focusing on wealth starts the process that leads a person directly away from Christ. Each succeeding generation departs further from the blessed hope.

> *Take heed to yourselves, lest at any time your hearts be overcharged with surfeiting* [eating], *and drunkenness, and cares of this life, and so that day* [of the Lord] *come upon you unawares.* (Luke 21:34)

In the church, there is a widespread lack of preaching and teaching about the awesome second coming of the Lord Jesus Christ. The combination of all these factors has resulted in huge numbers of believers becoming dead to God's prophetic plan for the hour in which we live. In fact, they are heading down the same road as the Europeans. False doctrine is deadly to the church. God has not hid His prophetic plan—it is on page after page in the Bible. God is not hiding the coming day of the Lord. It is visible to all who focus on the second coming and understand God's covenant nation Israel.

The entire Christian church, and the American church in particular, has to choose which road to travel. God's road is to focus on the second coming of Jesus Christ and His prophetic plan for Israel. Any other road leads directly towards spiritual decay. The true road is getting back to focusing on the second coming and lining up with God's prophetic plan for Israel. The church in America did this one hundred and twenty years ago, and it shook the world.

As the day of the Lord approaches, the integrity of the United States depends upon believers. America has already interfered with God's prophetic plan and suffered great consequences. God has clearly warned America of the coming judgment. Entire nations will disappear during the day of the Lord, and the United States could be one of them. The coming wars indicate America will cease to be a great power. Yet if the church repents and rises up, God might spare America from total destruction. Then the nation might survive to the second coming and enter Jesus' kingdom reign.

America has a great spiritual heritage. Let us not lose it over materialism and false doctrine. As our predecessors did, let us once again, as a church, focus on the second coming and stand with the Jewish people. On God's prophetic timetable, we are now on the other side of the rebirth of Israel. The "*times of the Gentiles*" are drawing to a close. God's prophetic clock is accelerating. If the "*times of the Gentiles*" are drawing to a close, then how much sooner is the awesome coming of Jesus Christ for His church!

The Wise Shall Understand

> *The wicked shall do wickedly: and none of the wicked shall understand; but the wise shall understand.* (Daniel 12:10)

The context of the above Bible verse is the day of the Lord. The prophet Daniel stated that as the day of the Lord approached, none of the unbelievers would recognize that the time was drawing near, but those who were wise in God's Word would understand the events of the hour. The prophet Daniel used the word "*understand*" twice. The Hebrew word "understand" means "to be separate or distinguish mentally." In modern terminology, we might say it means to "put two and two together." The word "wise" means "to act circumspectly, and therefore intelligently."

As the day of the Lord nears, the people anchored in the Bible and correct doctrine can see it approaching. They are able to think things through, put two and two together, and see God's prophetic plan clearly. They act intelligently and align their life according to this plan. The wicked, however—those in rebellion against God—are unable to see the reality of God's prophetic plan. Almost daily, this plan is played out on the front pages of the newspapers. The wicked face eternal judgment from the holy God of Israel.

The true church lines up with God's prophetic plan as outlined in the Bible. The true church blesses the Jewish people. The true church is the faithful and wise servant, living in the blessed hope, patiently waiting for the coming of the Lord Jesus and the marriage supper of the Lamb.

In the hour in which we live, the difference between the faithful and evil servants is clearly manifested for all to see. Are you a faithful and wise servant? Are you living in the blessed hope? Will you be one in the clouds of heaven?

> *Hereafter shall ye see the Son of man sitting on the right hand of power, and coming in the clouds of heaven.*
>
> (Matthew 26:64)

ADDENDA

ADDENDUM A

The Major Text of George Washington's 1789 Letter to the Hebrew Congregation of Savannah, Georgia

Gentlemen: I thank you with great sincerity for your congratulations on my appointment to the office which I have the honor to hold by the unanimous choice of my fellow citizens, and especially the expressions you are pleased to use in testifying the confidence that is reposed in me by your congregation.

I rejoice that a spirit of liberality and philanthropy is much more prevalent than it formerly was among the enlightened nations of the earth, and that your brethren will benefit thereby in proportion as it shall become still more extensive; happily the people of the United States have in many instances exhibited examples worthy of imitation, the salutary influence of which will doubtless extend much farther if gratefully enjoying those blessings of peace which (under the favor of heaven) have been attained by fortitude in war, they shall conduct themselves with reverence to the Deity and charity toward their fellow-creatures.

May the same wonder-working Deity, who long since delivered the Hebrews from their Egyptian oppressors, planted them in a promised land, whose providential agency has lately been conspicuous in establishing these United States as an independent nation, still continue to water them with the dews of heaven and make the inhabitants of every denomination participate in the temporal and spiritual blessings of that people whose God is Jehovah.

ADDENDUM B

The Full Text of George Washington's 1790 Letter to the Hebrew Congregation of Newport, Rhode Island

While I received with much satisfaction your address replete with expressions of esteem, I rejoice in the opportunity of assuring you that I shall always retain grateful remembrance of the cordial welcome I experienced on my visit to Newport from all classes of citizens.

The reflection on the days of difficulty and danger which are past is rendered the more sweet from a consciousness that they are succeeded by days of uncommon prosperity and security.

If we have wisdom to make the best use of the advantages with which we are now favored, we cannot fail, under the just administration of a good government, to become a great and happy people.

The Citizens of the United States of America have a right to applaud themselves for giving to Mankind examples of an enlarged and liberal policy: a policy worthy of imitation. All possess alike liberty of conscience and immunities of citizenship. It is now no more that toleration is spoken of, as if it was by the indulgence of one class of people that another enjoyed the exercise of their inherent natural rights. For happily the Government of the United States, which gives to bigotry no sanction, to persecution no assistance, requires only that they who live under its protection, should demean themselves as good citizens.

May the Children of the Stock of Abraham, who dwell in this land, continue to merit and enjoy the good will of the other Inhabitants; while every one shall sit under his own vine and fig tree, and there shall be none to make him afraid.

May the father of all mercies scatter light and not darkness in our paths, and make us all in our several vocations useful here, and in his own due time and way everlastingly happy.

Addendum C

Jewish Messenger, April 26, 1861: Editorial by Samuel Mayer Isaacs entitled, "Stand By the Flag"

It is almost a work of supererogation for us to call upon our readers to be loyal to the Union, which protects them. It is needless for us to say anything to induce them to proclaim their devotion to the land in which they live. But we desire our voice, too, to be heard at this time, joining in the hearty and spontaneous shout ascending from the whole American people, to stand by the stars and stripes!

Already we hear of many of our young friends taking up arms in defense of their country, pledging themselves to assist in maintaining inviolate its integrity, and ready to respond, if need be, with their lives, to the call of the constituted authorities, in the cause of law and order.

The time is past for forbearance and temporizing. We are now to act, and sure we are, that those whom these words may reach, will not be backward in realizing the duty that is incumbent upon them—to rally as one man for the Union and the Constitution. The Union—which binds together, by so many sacred ties, millions of free men—which extends its hearty invitation to the oppressed of all nations, to come and be sheltered beneath its protecting wings—shall it be severed, destroyed, or even impaired? Shall those, whom we once called our brethren, be permitted to overthrow the fabric reared by the noble patriots of the revolution, and cemented with their blood?

And the Constitution—guaranteeing to all, the free exercise of their religious opinions—extending to all, liberty, justice, and equality—the pride of Americans, the admiration of the world—shall that Constitution be subverted, and anarchy usurp the place of a sound, safe and stable government, deriving its authority from the consent of the American People?

The voice of millions yet unborn, cried out, "Forbid it, Heaven!" The voice of the American people declares in tones not to be misunderstood: "It shall not be!"

Then stand by the Flag! What death can be as glorious as that of the patriot, surrendering his life in defense of his country—pouring forth his blood on the battlefield—to live forever in the hearts of a grateful people. Whether native or foreign born, Gentile or Israelite, stand by it, and you are doing your duty, and acting well your part on the side of liberty and justice!

We know full well that our young men, who have left their homes to respond to the call of their country, will, on their return, render a good account of themselves. We have no fears for their bravery and patriotism. Our prayers are with them. God speed them on the work which they have volunteered to perform!

And if they fall—if, fighting in defense of that flag, they meet a glorious and honorable death, their last moments will be cheered by the consciousness that they have done their duty, and grateful America will not forget her sons, who have yielded up their spirit in her behalf.

And as for us, who do not accompany them on their noble journey, our duty too, is plain. We are to pray to Heaven that He may restore them soon again to our midst, after having assisted in vindicating the honor and integrity of the flag they have sworn to defend; and we are to pledge ourselves to assume for them, should they fall in their country's cause, the obligation of supporting those whom their departure leaves unprotected. Such is our duty. Let them, and all of us, renew our solemn oath that, whatever may betide, we will be true to the Union and the Constitution, and Stand By The Flag.

ADDENDUM D

The Blackstone Memorial, March 1891: Presented to the President of the United States in favor of the restoration of Palestine to the Jews

What shall be done for the Russian Jews? It is both unwise and useless to undertake to dictate to Russia concerning her internal affairs. The Jews have lived as foreigners in her dominions for centuries and she fully believes that they are a burden upon her resources and prejudicial to the welfare of her peasant population, and will not allow them to remain. She is determined that they must go. Hence, like the Sephardim of Spain, these Ashkenazim must emigrate. But where shall 2,000,000 of such poor people go? Europe is crowded and has no room for more peasant population. Shall they come to America? This will be a tremendous expense, and require years.

Why not give Palestine back to them again? According to God's distribution of nations it is their home, an inalienable possession from which they were expelled by force. Under their cultivation it was a remarkably fruitful land sustaining millions of Israelites who industrially tilled its hillsides and valleys. They were agriculturists and producers as well as a nation of great commercial importance—the center of civilization and religion.

Why shall not the powers which under the treaty of Berlin, in 1878, gave Bulgaria to the Bulgarians and Servia to the Servians now give Palestine back to the Jews? These provinces, as well as Roumania, Montenegro and Greece, were wrested from the Turks and given to their natural owners. Does not Palestine as rightfully belong to the Jews? It is said that rains are increasing and there are evidences that the land is recovering its ancient fertility. If they could have autonomy in government the Jews of the world would rally to transport and establish their suffering brethren in their time-honored habitation. For over seventeen centuries they have patiently waited for such an opportunity. They have not become agriculturists elsewhere because they believed they were mere sojourners in the various nations, and were yet to return to Palestine and till their own land. Whatever vested rights, by possession may have accrued to Turkey can be easily compensated, possibly by the Jews assuming an equitable portion of the national debt. We believe this is an appropriate time for all nations and especially the Christian nations of Europe to show kindness to Israel. A million of exiles, by their terrible suffering, are piteously appealing to our sympathy, justice, and humanity Let us now restore to them the land of which they were so cruelly despoiled by our Roman ancestors.

To this end we respectfully petition His Excellency Benjamin Harrison, President of the United States, and the Honorable James G. Blaine, Secretary of State, to use their good offices and influence with the Governments of their Imperial Majesties.

Alexander III, Czar of Russia; Victoria, Queen of Great Britain and Empress of India; William II, Emperor of Germany; Francis Joseph, Emperor of Austro-Hungary; Abdul Hamid II, Sultan of Turkey; His Royal Majesty, Humbert, King of Italy; Her Royal Majesty Marie Christiana, Queen Regent of Spain; and the Government of the Republic of France and with the Governments of Belgium, Holland, Denmark, Sweden, Portugal, Roumainia, Servia, Bulgaria and Greece. To secure the holding at an early date, of an international conference to consider the condition of the Israelites and their claims to Palestine as their ancient home, and to promote, in all other just and proper ways, the alleviation of their suffering condition.

Addendum E

Assurance of the Blessed Hope

When a person lives in the blessed hope, it gives him the assurance of eternal life with the Lord Jesus. It also gives him the assurance of returning with the Lord Jesus Christ as one in the clouds of heaven. According to the Bible, this assurance is obtained by realizing that God loves you and that He wants you to have eternal life with Him. God personally cares about you and desires that you have eternal life with Him.

> *For God so loved the world, that he gave his only begotten Son, that whosoever believeth in him should not perish, but have everlasting life.* (John 3:16)

The way of believing in Jesus Christ as your Savior is to repent of sin and to trust Him completely as your Lord and Savior. When you trust Jesus Christ as your Savior, all your sin is forgiven by God, for Jesus paid the penalty on the cross for your sin. Without repentance of sin and the confession of Jesus Christ as Lord and Savior, it is impossible to have eternal life with God.

> *If thou shalt confess with thy mouth the Lord Jesus, and shalt believe in thine heart that God hath raised him from the dead, thou shalt be saved. For with the heart man believeth unto righteousness; and with the mouth confession is made unto salvation.* (Romans 10:9–10)

When you confess Jesus as your Lord and Savior, you are now to live with the expectation of His second coming in your heart.

This is the blessed hope: the expectation of the second coming of the Lord Jesus and being with Him forever. It is the evidence that you will be with the Lord Jesus when He returns with the clouds of heaven.

> *Looking for that blessed hope, and the glorious appearing of the great God and our Saviour Jesus Christ.* (Titus 2:13)

The Lord Jesus has paid the penalty for your sin by His blood shed on the cross. God has provided a way for you to have eternal life with Him. Right now you can turn to God by prayer through faith in Jesus Christ as your Lord and Savior. Please do not put this off, because now is the day of salvation.

ENDNOTES

Chapter One

1. Quote from Czech Premier Jan Syrovy: *New York Times*, 1 October 1938, front-page article titled, "Peace Aid Pledged."
2. Quote from Neville Chamberlain: *New York Times*, 1 October 1938, front-page article titled, "Peace With Honor Says Chamberlain."
3. British-German anti war pact: *New York Times*, 1 October 1938, front-page article titled, "Britain and German Agree."
4. President Roosevelt's second appeal: *New York Times*, 28 September 1938, page 9, article titled, "Text of President Roosevelt's Plea."
5. Herman Goering's speech on 10 September 1938: Radio Days-Munich Crisis, page 2, http://otr.com/munich.html.
6. Weather related background to hurricane: *Monthly Weather Review*, August 1939, Volume 67, Number 8, article titled, "The Meteorological History of the New England Hurricane of September 21, 1938," by Charles H. Pierce.
7. Seismograph record of the hurricane: *The National Geographic Magazine*, April 1939, page 533, article titled, "The Geography of a Hurricane," by F. Barrows Colton.
8. Destruction caused by the hurricane: *The Long Island Express – the Great Hurricane of 1938*, http://www2.sunysuffolk.edu/mandias/38hurricane/.
9. Lowest Barometric pressure at Bellport, New York: *The Long Island Express – the Great Hurricane of 1938*, http://www2.sunysuffolk.edu/mandias/38hurricane/.

10. Information about Henry Ford: http://history.hanover.edu/hhr/99/hhr99_2.html, *Power, Ignorance, and Anti-Semitism: Henry Ford and His War on the Jews*, by Jonathan R. Logsdon.

11. Henry Ford and the Jews cause war: *New York Times*, 29 October 1922, article titled, "Ford, Denying Hate, Lays War to Jews."

12. Bund Declarations of Principles: Free America – Fight Jews, Deutscher Weckruf und Beobachter, Volume 4, Number 11, pages 1–2, 8 September 1938. (This was the official publication of the Bund.)

13. Bund Amendment to Constitution: Ibid

14. Background information about Bund: *Brooklyn Daily Eagle*, "U.S. Citizens Drilled By Bund in 28 Camps," 26 March 1938, Front-page article; Longwood High School, http://www.longwood.k12.ny.us/history/index.htm

15. Adolf Hitler Street, Yaphank, NY: New York State, County of Suffolk, Town of Brookhaven, map number 129, abstract 1238, filed 5 January 1937.

16. Nazi Rallies at Camp Siegfried:

    40,000: *New York Times*, "40,000 at Nazi Camp Fete," 15 August 1938, page 13.
    30,000: *Mid-Island Mail*, "30,000 at Camp Siegfried Sunday," http://www.longwood.k12.ny.us/history/yaphank/bund14.htm.
    12,000: http://www.longwood.k12.ny.us/history/yaphank/bund6.htm.
    5,000: http://www.longwood.k12.ny.us/history/yaphank/bund3.htm.
    5,000: http://www.longwood.k12.ny.us/history/yaphank/bund2.htm.

Chapter Three

1. Quote of George Washington opening this chapter: *From the Ends of the Earth–Judaic Treasures of the Library of Congress*, Chapter To Bigotry No Sanction, page 236, Library of Congress, 1991.

2. Background information on Jews in early America: *A History of Jews in America*, Howard M. Sachar, pages 9–37.

3. Peter Stuyvesant quote: *The Jewish Week*, "Faith and Freedom in the New World," Jonathan D. Sarna, http://www.thejewishweek.com.

Endnotes: Chapter 3

4. Background information about Jews in the American Revolution: *A History of Jews in America*, pages, 21–28, Howard M. Sachar.
5. Francis Salvador information: *Jewish Virtual Library*, Francis Salvador, http://www.jewishvirtuallibray.org.
6. The Little Jew Broker: *The Grandees*, Stephen Birmingham, pages 132–142, and *Haym Salomon*, H.S. Baron.
7. George Washington's Letters: *From the Ends of the Earth: Judaic Treasures of the Library of Congress*, pages 231–239.
8. President Van Buren's quote: The Virtual Library, The American-Israeli Cooperative Enterprise, Americans React to Damascus Blood Libel, www.jewishvirtuallibrary.org.
9. Samuel Mayer Isaacs quote: *The Jewish Messenger*, Volume 8, Number 25, 28 December 1861, New York, article titled, "A Day of Prayer."
10. Samuel Mayer Isaacs quote: *The Jewish Messenger*, 28 April 1861, editorial titled, "Stand By the Flag."
11. Civil War Background: *A History of the Jews in America*, pages 72–76.
12. Jewish Generals of Civil War: *Jewish World Review*, "Lincoln's Jewish Generals," 19 February 2001, http://www.jewishworldreview.com/herb/geduld1.asp.
13. History of General Knefler: Stephen Beszedits, Frederick Knefler, Hungarian Patriot and American General, www.jewish-history.com/civil/war/knefler.
14. Jewish Sailor on *USS Monitor*: "Legacy of the USS Monitor, The Officers and Crew of the USS Monitor," http://home.att.net/-iron.clad/crew/MON_CREW.HTM.
15. Joseph Seligman: Jewish Heroes and Heroines in America, Florida Atlantic University Library, A Judaica Collection, http://www.fau.edu/library/brody/33.htm.
16. President Lincoln's note revoking General Order 11: *Jewish Virtual Library*, General Grant's Infamy, http//www.jewishvirtuallibrary.org/jsource/anti-semitism/grant.html.
17. Statements by Rabbi Wise: Ibid
18. Additional background about General Grant and General Order 11: A History of the Jews in America, pages 78–80.

19. Eulogy of President Lincoln: *From the Ends of the Earth – Judaic Treasures of the Library of Congress*, page 271.
20. Quotes from the London Jewish Chronicle: *The Jewish Messenger*, 7 March 1862, article titled, "The American Israelites."

Chapter Four

1. Background information about Russian treatment of Jews: *A History of the Jews in America*, pages 116–140.
2. May Laws: *The May Laws, 1882*, http://www.jewishgates.com/file?.asp_id=101.
3. Mary Antin quote: *A History of the Jews in America*, page 119.
4. Background of pogroms: Mazelev, Julia, *Pogroms: Late Nineteenth, Beginning of Twentieth Century*, http://econc10.bu.edu/economic_systems/nationalidentity/fsu/russia/pogroms-naional_ident.
5. Puck Magazine quote: *Puck Magazine*, 30 November 1881, Cartoon and Comments.
6. Background information about William Blackstone: Currie, William E., *God's Little Errand Boy*.
7. Blackstone Memorial: AMF International, The Blackstone Memorial, http://www.amfi.org/blackmem.htm.

Chapter Five

1. Congress began debating navy in 1881: Department of the Navy, Naval Historical Center, *War Plans and Preparations and Their Impact on U.S. Naval Operations in the Spanish-American War*, http://www.history.navy.mil/wars/spanam.htm.
2. US Navy 1880–1900: *United States Sea Power 1865–On*, http://www.history.navy.mil/wars/spanam.htm.
3. Treaty of Portsmouth: Treaty of Portsmouth, 5 September 1905, http://www.portsmouthpeacetreaty.com/treaty/text.cfm.
4. President Roosevelt Nobel Peace prize: Letter to Congressman James A. Gallvan, dated 22 August 1918, http://www.theodoreroosevelt.org/life/nobelportsmouth.htm.

5. America saves Zionist movement during WWI: Oren, Michael B., *Power, Faith, and Fantasy, America in the Middle East 1776 to the Present*, pages 340–358.

6. Quote from A. Mosier, *USS Tennessee: Service Aboard the U.S.S. Tennessee and Memphis*, http://www.delmars.com/family/mosier-a1.htm.

7. Jewish population of North Africa: Holocaust Encyclopedia, Jewish Population of French North Africa, http://www.ushmm.org/wlc/article.php?lang=en&ModuleId=10007310.

8. Jews under Vichy France: Holocaust Encyclopedia, Vichy Discrimination Against Jews in North Africa, http://www.ushmm.org/wlc/article.php?lang=en&ModuleId=10007311.

9. Nazis ready to exterminate Jews of Palestine: Findlaw Legal News and Commentary, *Historians Say Hitler Was Set to Launch Holocaust in Palestine*, 29 April 2006, http://news.findlaw.com/wash/s/20060429/20060429093914.html.

10. United Nations General Assembly Resolution 181, dated 29 November 1947, http://www.yale.edu/lawweb/avalon/un/res181.htm.

11. Background on President Truman's support of Israel: *Power, Faith, and Fantasy, America in the Middle East 1776 to the Present*, pages 483–502.

12. President Truman's recognition of the State of Israel: Truman Presidential Library, http://www.trumanlibrary.org/whistlestop/study_collections/israel/large/documents/index.php?documentdate=1948-05-14&documentid=48&collectionid=ROI&pagenumber=1.

13. General David Marcus: *David "Mickey" Marcus*, Military History Magazine, April 1998, http://www.historynet.com/magazines/military_history/3033716.html.

14. *Mickey Marcus: Israel's American General*, The American Jewish Historical Society, http://www.ajhs.org/publications/chapters/chapter.cfm?documentid=286.

Chapter Seven

1. William Blackstone, father of Zionism: Hilton Obenzinger, *In the Shadow of "God's Sun-dial,"* http://www.stanford.edu/group/SHR/5-1/text/obenzinger.html.

2. Quote of Justice Brandeis regarding William Blackstone: A Collection of Addresses and Statements by Louis D. Brandeis, World Zionist Organization, http://www.hagshamma.org.il/en/resources/view.asp?id=1642.

3. The Balfour Declaration: Balfour Declaration 1917, The Avalon Project at Yale Law School, http://www.yale.edu/lawweb/avalon/mideast/balfour.htm.

Chapter Nine

1. President Bush's U.N. speech 10 November 2001: *President Bush Speaks to United Nations*, Remarks by the President to United Nations General Assembly, U.N. Headquarters, New York, New York, the White House Web site: http://www.whitehouse.gov/news/releases/2001/11/20011110-3.html.

2. President Bush's speech 24 June 2002: *President Bush Calls for New Palestinian Leadership*, the White House Web site: http://www.whitehouse.gov/news/releases/2002/06/20020624-3.html.

October 1991

3. Opening of Madrid peace talks: *USA Today*, 31 October 1991, front-page article titled, "Delegates Bring Optimism to Table."

4. The land of Israel key issue: *USA Today*, 1 November 1997, front-page article titled, "One-on-One Peace Talks Next."

5. Rare condition create the Perfect Storm: *Associated Press*, 29 June 2000, article titled, "Perfect Storm Recalled."

6. Storm developments and results:

   New York Times, 1 November 1997, article entitled, "Nameless Storm Swamps the Shoreline."

   USA Today, 1 November 1997, front-page article entitled, "East Coast Hit Hard by Rare Storm" and article entitled, "Bob the Sequel a Smash (Maine to Florida under siege)."

7. The book, *The Perfect Storm*, by Sebastian Junger, 1997, HarperCollins Publisher. The power of the storm, pages 118–119.

Endnotes: Chapter 9

8. President Bush's home smashed by the storm: *New York Times*, 1 November 1997, article titled, "Stormy Waves Heavily Damage Bush Vacation Compound in Southern Maine."

August 1992

9. Damage done by Andrew:

   USA Today, 14 September 1992, article entitled, "Tale of the Hurricanes."
   USA Today, 18 September 1992, article entitled, "Andrew 3rd-Worst Storm."

10. Hurricane Andrew and Madrid peace plan together: *USA Today*, 24 August 1992, front-page articles titled, "1 Million Flee Andrew; Monster Storm Targets Fla.," and "Mideast Peace Talks to Resume on Positive Note."

September 1993

11. Hurricane Emily and dividing the land of Israel: *New York Times*, 1 September 1993, front-page articles titled, "Israel and PLO Ready To Declare Joint Recognition," and "Hurricane Hits the Outer Banks, As Thousands Seek Safety Inland."

January 1994

12. President Clinton and Assad meet in Geneva: *Harrisburg Patriot-News*, 17 January 1994, front-page article titled, "Clinton: Syria Set for Peace."

13. Earthquake in L.A.: *Los Angeles Times*, 18 January 1994, front-page article titled, "33 Die, Many Hurt in 6.6 Quake." (For more details of this earthquake, see chapter one, January 1994 heading.)

March–April 1997

14. Arafat arrives in America and meets with Clinton: *New York Times*, 3 March 1997, article titled, "Welcoming Arafat, Clinton Rebukes Israel."

15. Arafat on speaking tour: *New York Times*, 6 March 1997, article titled, "Arafat Lobbies U.S. Against Israel's Housing Plan."
16. Security Counsel's resolution of 6 March 1997: *New York Times*, 7 March 1997, article titled, "U.S. Vetoes U.N. Criticism of Israel's Construction Plan."
17. General Assembly resolution of 13 March 1997: *New York Times*, 14 March 1997, article titled, "Israel's Plan of Jerusalem Is Condemned by Assembly."
18. Security Counsel's resolution of 21 March 1997: *New York Times*, 22 March 1997, article titled, "U.S. Again Vetoes a Move by U.N. Condemning Israel."
19. General Assembly resolution of 25 April 1997: *New York Times*, 25 April 1997, article titled, "Israel Warned to Halt Housing for Jews."
20. General Assembly resolution of 15 July 1997: *New York Times*, 16 July 1997, article titled, "U.N. Renews Censure of New Israeli Housing in East Jerusalem."
21. Stock Market reaches all-time high: *USA Today*, 12 March 1997, article titled, "Dow Achieves Record Despite Rate Fears."
22. Stock Market falls 160 Points: *USA Today*, 14 March 1997, article titled, "Dow Plunges 160 Points on Rate Fears."
23: Stock Market stabilizes and begins rebound: *USA Today*, 15 April 1997, article titled, "Stock Market Summary."
24. Prime Minister Netanyahu meets with Clinton: *New York Times*, 8 April 1997, article titled, "Netanyahu Holds White House Talks."

January 1998

25. Clinton meets with Netanyahu: *New York Times*, 22 January 1998, article titled, "U.S. and Israel Talk Mainly of More Talks"; *USA Today*, 22 January 1998, article titled, "A Mideast Battle for Good Press."
26. Clinton's sex scandal breaks during meeting with Netanyahu: *New York Times*, 22 January 1998. Front-page article titled, "Subpoenas Sent as Clinton Denies Reports of an Affair with Aide at White House."

27. Clinton meets with Arafat: *USA Today*, 23 January 1998, article titled, "Arafat Calls Talks Encouraging."
28. Clinton coldly treats Netanyahu and Netanyahu returns as a hero: *New York Times*, 30 January 1998, article titled, "Analysis: In Clinton Crisis, Netanyahu Gains, Arafat Loses."
29. Judicial Committee votes on December 11 for three articles of impeachment: *USA Today*, 11 December 1998, front-page article titled, "Panel Sets Stage for Historic Vote on Impeachment."
30. House votes to begin impeachment of president: *Associated Press*, 8 October 1998, article titled, "House Approves Impeachment Inquiry."
31. Clinton en route to Israel while the fourth article of impeachment is being voted: *Associated Press News Service*, 12 December 1998, article titled, "Clinton Heads for Israel," and article titled, "Fourth Impeachment Article Debated."
32. Clinton is the first president to visit Palestinian-controlled area: *USA Today*, 12 December 1998, front-page article titled, "Clinton Fights for Mideast Agreement."
33. Clinton's visit gives status to a Palestinian state: *USA Today*, 12 December 1998, front-page article titled, "Peace Hits Snag Despite Vote."
34. On December 19 Clinton impeached by the House of Representatives: *Harrisburg Patriot–News*, 20 December 1998, article titled, "Impeached."

September 1998

35. Clinton to meet with Netanyahu and Arafat: *New York Times*, 25 September 1998, article titled, "Clinton to See Netanyahu and Arafat Next Week."
36. Hurricane gains strength: *USA Today*, 25 September 1998, front-page article titled, "Georges Gaining Strength: Killer Storm Zeros in on Key West."
37. Secretary of State Albright meets with Arafat in New York City: *New York Times*, 28 September 1998, article titled, "US Is Hoping to Announce Details on Israel-Palestine Talks."

38. Hurricane Georges slams into Gulf Coast: *New York Times*, 28 September 1998, front-page article titled, "Recharged Hurricane Batters Gulf Coast With 110 m.p.h. Winds."

39. Hurricane Lingers on Gulf Coast: *USA Today*, 29 September 1998, front-page article titled, "Georges Lingers."

40. President Clinton meets with Arafat and Netanyahu in White House: *USA Today*, 29 September 1998, front-page article titled, "Meeting Puts Mideast Talks Back in Motion."

41. Hurricane and Mideast peace talks together: *New York Times*, 29 September 1998, front-page articles titled, "U.S., Israel and Arafat Inch Toward Pact" and "Floods Trap Hundreds."

42. Arafat speaks at United Nations: *New York Times*, 29 September 1998, article titled, "Arafat, at U.N., Urges Backing for Statehood."

43. Hurricane causes $1 billion in damage: *USA Today*, 30 September 1998, article titled, "Hurricane Racks Up $1 Billion in Damage."

October 1998

44. Netanyahu and Arafat met in United States: *Harrisburg Patriot News*, 15 October 1998, front-page article titled, "Time Is Running Out in Mideast."

45. Israel to give away 13 percent of the land: *New York Times*, 24 October 1998, front-page article titled, "Arafat and Netanyahu in Pact on Next Steps Toward Peace; Modest Deal to Rebuild Trust."

46. Powerful storms hit Texas: *Harrisburg Patriot News*, 18 October 1998, article titled, "4 Killed as Storms, Floods, Tornado Ravage Parts of Texas."

47. Extent of the flooding and damage: *New York Times*, 20 October 1998, article titled, "Record Flooding Kills at Least 14 in Central Texas," and *USA Today*, October 22, 1998, article titled, "Hope Dwindles in Flooded Texas."

48. Texas declared a disaster area by president: News release, 21 October 1998 from FEMA. Release was titled, "President Declares Major Disaster for Texas: Twenty Counties Designated for Aid to Flood Victims."

49. This disaster and Mideast talks together on front-page of newspaper: *New York Times*, 20 October 1998, articles titled, "Clinton Keeps Up Hope of Mideast Talks" and "Knee-deep in the San Jacinto."

May 1999

50. Power and wind speed of the tornadoes: *USA Today*, 11 May 1999, article titled, "318-mph storm wind fastest ever"; *USA Today*, 5 May 1999, article titled, "Disasters declared in two states"; *Harrisburg Patriot-News*, 5 May 1999, article titled, "20 hours of terror."
51. Clinton and the Palestinian State: *Associated Press*, 4 May 1999, article titled, "Clinton Encourages Arafat."

September 1999

52. Hurricane Dennis: *Harrisburg Patriot–News*, 4 September 1999, front-page article titled, "Enough already! N.C. tires of Dennis."
53. Middle East meetings regarding Israel: *Harrisburg Patriot–News*, 4 September 1999, front-page article titled, "Talks yield reworking of Wye pact."
54. Middle East talks open: *Associated Press*, 13 September 1999, article titled, "Israel, Palestinians To Open Talks."
55. Floyd Strengthens: *Associated Press*, 13 September 1999, article titled, "Floyd Strengthens, Near Bahamas."
56. Hurricane Floyd: *Harrisburg Patriot–News*, 19 September 1999, article titled, "Floodwaters devastating N. Carolina."
57. Stock Market crash sets record: *Reuters*, 23 September 1999, article titled, "Dow, Nasdaq Take Late-Day Tumble."
58. Arafat meets with Clinton: *Associated Press*, 22 September 1999, article titled, "Clinton Hosts Arafat at White House."

October 1999

59. Eviction of Israeli settlers: *New York Times*, 16 October 1999, front-page article titled, "On the West Bank, a Mellow View of Eviction."

60. Stock Market crash: *New York Times*, 16 October 1999, front-page article titled, "Big Selloff Caps Dow's Worst Week Since October '89."

61. Hurricane Irene: *USA Today*, 18 October 1999, article titled, "Battered North Carolina suffers third hurricane in two months."

62. Earthquake: *Los Angeles Times*, 17 October 1999, front-page article titled, "7.0 Earthquake in Mojave Desert Rocks Southland."

January–April 2000

63. Meetings: *New York Times*, 4 January 2000, front-page article titled, "Israel and Syria Return to Search for a Major Accord."

64. Stock Market crash: *USA Today*, 5 January 2000, front-page article titled, "Market sell-off was overdue."

65. Turbulent stock week: *New York Times*, 8 January 2000, article titled, "The 3 Main U.S. Stock Gauges Rally to End a Turbulent Week."

66. Barak meets with Clinton: *Associated Press*, 12 April 2000, article titled, "Israel OKs US Involvement in Talks."

67. Stock Market collapse: *New York Times*, 15 April 2000, front-page article titled, "Stock Market in Step Drop as Worried Investors Flee; NASDAQ Has Its Worst Week."

July–August 2000

68. Camp David meetings: *Reuters*, 21 November 2000, article titled, "Jerusalem Sovereignty Debated in Public Amid Talks"; *Associated Press*, dated 20 July 2000, article titled, "Jerusalem at Heart of Mideast Talks."

69. Forest fires: *Associated Press*, 3 August 2000, article titled, "Fire Season Storms Into West"; *Reuters*, 27 August 2000, article titled, "U.S. Wildfires Converge in 'Perfect Storm.'"

70. Drought: *Associated Press*, 28 July 2000, article titled, "Bush Declares Texas Disaster Areas."

Endnotes: Chapter 9

September–December 2000

71. Fighting erupts at Temple Mount: *New York Times*, 30 September 2000, front-page article titled, "Battle at Jerusalem Holy Site Leaves 4 Dead and 200 Hurt."
72. Collapse of Barak's government: *Washington Post*, 10 December 2000, front-page article titled, "Israeli Prime Minister Says He Will Resign."
73. Presidential election: *New York Times*, 10 November 2000, front-page article titled, "Gore Campaign Vows Court Fight Over Vote with Florida's Outcome Still Up in the Air."
74. Arafat meets with Clinton: *New York Times*, 10 November 2000, article titled, "Arafat-Clinton Talks in Washington Yield No Progress."
75. Elections set in Israel: *New York Times*, 11 December 2000, front-page article titled, "Opening Campaign Netanyahu Invokes Will of the Nation."
76. Election resolved: *New York Times*, 11 December 2000, front-page article titled, "Bush-Gore Is Now in the Hands of the Supreme Court."

June 2001

77. Tropical Storm Allison great rainfall:

    Houston Chronicle, 10 June 2001, article entitled, "Allison rivals Claudette's 79 record."
    Houston Chronicle, 14 June 2001, article entitled, "Mayor: Storm city's biggest disaster ever."
78. Forming of Allison: *Houston Chronicle*, 6 June 2001, article titled, "Tropical surprise."
79. President Bush declares five states disaster areas: *Associated Press*, 23 June 2001, article titled, "Bush Releases $500M in Storm Aid."
80. U.S. involvement in mediation in cease fire: *Reuters*, 8 June 2001, article titled, "US Steps Up Middle East Peace Drive Amid Violence."

81. *Associated Press*, 9 June 2001 Article titled, "US Steps Up Mideast Efforts."

82. *Jerusalem Post*, 14 June 2001, article titled, "Settlers: Tenet plan amounts to our abandonment."

83. *Jerusalem Post*, 14 June 2001, article titled, "US Steps Up Mideast Peace Efforts."

September 11, 2001

84. President Bush's speech on 9 August 2001: CNN, 9 August 2001, article titled, "Bush condemns Jerusalem suicide bombing."

85. U.S. to recognize a Palestinian state:

New York Times, 2 October 2001, article entitled, "Before Attacks, US Was Ready to Say It Backed Palestinian State."
Washington Post, 2 October 2001, article entitled, "US Was Set to Support Palestinian Statehood."

86. Tourist industry hurt: Cybercast News Service, cnsnews.com, dated 15 October 2001, article titled, "Travel and Tourism Hurt by Fear of Flying."

November 2001

87. The president's speech before the U.N.: *New York Times*, 11 November 2001, front-page article titled, "All Must Join Fight Against Terror, Bush Tells UN."

88. Secretary of state meets with Arafat: *New York Times*, 12 November 2001, article titled, "Arafat Thankful for Bush Remark about 'Palestine.'"

89. Jet crash from JFK: *New York Times*, 13 November 2001, front-page article titled, "Jet with 260 Crashes in Queens; 6 to 9 Missing as 12 Homes Burn; US Doubts Link To Terrorism."

April–June 2002

90. Pressure from Bush on Israel and tornadoes: *Washington Post*, 29 April 2002, front-page articles titled, "Israel Agrees to Lift Arafat Siege" and "Deadly Tornado Hits Southern Maryland."

Endnotes: Chapter 9

91. President's two state speech: *Washington Post*, 25 June 2002, front-page articles titled, "President Outlines Vision for Mideast" and "Everything is Just a Nightmare—Forced to Flee Western Wildfires, Thousands Uncertain and Afraid."

May 2003

93. Record week for tornadoes: *Associated Press*, 11 May 2003, article titled, "Week's Barrage of Tornadoes Sets a Record.

92. Powell's trip to Mideast: *Pittsburgh Post-Gazette*, 12 May 2003, front-page articles titled, "Powell's Mideast blitz fails to make headway" and "Picking Up The Pieces" (story about tornado outbreak).

September 2003

94. US blocks Arafat expulsion: *Associated Press*, 12 September 2003, article titled, "Powell: U.S. Opposes Expulsion of Arafat."

95. Hurricane headed for DC: *Associated Press*, 18 September 2003, article titled, "D.C. prepares for direct hit."

96. Hurricane's damage: *Patriot–News*, 20 September 2003, front-page article titled, "A Trail of Misery: Property damage could surpass $4 billion."

August–September 2004

97. Bush pressured Israel to evacuate parts of covenant land and hurricanes: *Koenig's Eye View*, 23 August 2004, "Bush Administration Applies Major Pressure on Israel to Leave Covenant Land: While Hurricane Charlie and other News Intensifies," http://www.watch.org/resources/newsletter/koeing-sr-charley.html.

98. Evacuation of Gaza and hurricanes:

Miami Herald, 13 August 2004, front-page article entitled, "Nearly 1 million in path of storm told to leave."

Associated Press, 30 August 2004, article entitled, "Gaza Settlement Evacuation Plan Sped Up."

Associated Press, 10 September 2004, article entitled, "Sharon Says Gaza Pullout Still Planned."

Associated Press, 12 September 2004, article entitled, "Thousands Protest Gaza Evacuation Plan."
Jerusalem Post, 13 September 2004, article entitled, "Compensation to Gaza settlers $1b."
Washington Post, 13 September 2004, front-page article entitled, "Settlers are inciting civil war, Sharon says."
Associated Press, 14 September 2004, article entitled, "Bush Wants $3.1 Billion for Hurricane Aid."
Associated Press, 20 September 2004, article entitled, "Powell Seeks Israel's Assurance on Gaza."
Associated Press, 21 September 2004, article entitled: "Sharon Faces Critics, Vows Gaza Pullout."
Associated Press, 25 September 2004, article entitled, "Three Million told to Flee Jeanne in Fla."
Associated Press, 28 September 2004, article entitled, "Bush Seeks $7.1B More for Hurricane Relief."

January 2005

99. Abbas's statements about Israel: *Jewish World Review*, 7 January 2005, article titled, "The 'Zionist enemy' and her supporters is in denial yet again," http://www.jewishworldreview.com/0105/krauthammer-abbas.

100. Abbas invited to White House while storms rage in West:

    USA Today, 11 January 2005, front-page articles entitled, "Bush offers to meet Abbas" and "California rocked by storm."
    Associated Press, 10 January 2005, article entitled, "Bush invites Abbas to White House."

101. Storms in West: *Live Science*, 8 April 2005, article titled, "Christmas Storm in Midwest Ranked Worst in 104 Years."`

April 2005

102. Bush and Sharon meet: the White House Web site, 11 April 2005, article titled, "President and Prime Minister Sharon Discuss Economy, Middle East."

103. Stock Market down turn: *Fox News*, 15 April 2005, "Dow Down Almost 200 Pts on IBM, Data Disappointments."

Endnotes: Chapter 9

August–September 2005

104. Facts about the closing of the twenty-five settlements:

Jerusalem Post, 16 November 2005, article entitled, "US, Israel resume talks on aid."

New Yok Times, 16 August 2005, front-page article entitled, "Israeli Troops Press Settlers to Quite Gaza."

Harrisburg Patriot News, 1 August 2005, front-page article entitled, "Eviction Day."

New York Times, 18 August 2005, front-page article entitled, "Tearfully but Forcefully, Israel Removes Gaza Settlers."

New York Times, 20 August 2005, front-page article entitled, "Israeli Troops and Police Clear All But 5 Gaza Settlements."

New York Times, 23 August 2005, front-page article entitled, "Israel Completes Pullout Ahead of Schedule, Without Serious Violence."

MSNBC.com, 11 September 2005, article entitled, "Departure marks first time Palestinian have control over defined territory," http://www.msnbc.msm.com/id/9279728.

WorldNetDaily, 14 September 2005, article entitled, "Jews sickened by Palestinian desecration," http://www.worldnetdail.com/news/printer-friendly.asp?article-id=46310.

President Bush's speeches: 23 August 2005, the White House Web site, speech entitled, "President Honors Veterans of Foreign Wars at National Convention," http://www.whitehouse.gov/news/releases/2005/08.

The White House Web site, 24 August 2005, Question and answers, http://www.whitehouse.gov/news/releases/2005/08.

The White House Web site, 13 September 2005, speech entitled, "President Welcomes President Talabani of Iraq to the White House," http://www.whitehouse.gov/news/releases/2005/09.

Israelinsider Web site, 21 September 2005, article entitled, "After IDF completes pullout from in Samaria, Palestinians flood in."

Ynetnews.com, 22 September 2005, article entitled, "Hundreds of Palestinians loot Homesh."

105. Facts about Hurricane Katrina:

Wikipedia encyclopedia, History of storm, article entitled, "Hurricane Katrina."

New York Times, 29 August 2005, front-page article entitled, "Residents Flee as Strom Storm Nears Gulf Coast."

New York Times, 30 August 2005, front-page article entitled, "Hurricane Slams Into Gulf Coast Dozens are Dead."

New York Times, 1 September 2005, front-page article entitled, "Bush Sees Long Recovery For New Orleans; 30,000 Troops in Largest U.S. Relief Effort."

New York Times, 11 December 2005, editorial entitled, "Death of an American City."

Washington Post, 13 January 2006, article entitled, "2 Million Displaced by Storms."

USA Today, 29 September 2005, article entitled, "Katrina exodus reaches all states."

New York Times, 22 September 2005, front-page article entitled, "Gulf Hurricane of Top Strength Menaces Texas."

Harrisburg Patriot–News, 22 September 2005, front-page article entitled, "One million flee a growing monster."

American Dichotomy:

106. President Bush's speech, 11 August 1992: http://bushlibrary.tamu.edu/research/papers/1992/92081100.html.

107. President Bush's speech of 20 March 2006: http://www.whitehouse.gov/news/releases/2006/03/20060320-7.html.

108. Moving the embassy to Jerusalem: http://www.jewishvirtuallibrary.org/jsource/US-Israel/Jerusalem_Relocation_Act.html.

Chapter Ten

1. The Hamas Covenant, The Avalon Project at Yale Law school, http://www.yale.edu/lawweb/avalon/mideast/hamas.htm.

2. Background on Ahmadinejad and the Mahdi: Scott Petterson, *Christian Science Monitor*, "Waiting for the rapture in Iran," http://www.csmonitor.com/2005/1221/p01s04-wome.html.

3. Flavius Josephus, Magog: *Antiquities of the Jews*, Chapter Six ("How Every Nation Was Nominated From Their First Inhabitants"), http://www.earlychristianwritings.com/text/josephus/ant-1.htm.

4. Scythians: The Scythians, http://www.silk-road.com/artl/scythian.shtml.

BIBLIOGRAPHY

Books

Allen, Everett S., *A Wind to Shake the World*, Little, Brown and Company, Boston, 1976.

Arno Press, *Call to America to Build Zion*, *New York Times* Co., New York, 1977.

Baldwin, Neil, *Henry Ford and the Jews*, Public Affairs, New York, New York, 2001.

Baron, H.S., *Haym Salomon*, Bloch Publishing Co., New York, 1929.

Beszedits, Stephen, *Frederick Knefler: Hungarian Patriot and American General.* http://www.jewish-history.com/civilwar/knefler.

Birmingham, Stephen, *America Sephardic Elites the Grandees*, Harper and Row, New York, 1971.

Birnbaum, Pierre, *The Anti-Semitic Moment*, Hill and Wang, New York, 1998.

Burns, Cherie, *The Great Hurricane of 1938*, Atlantic Monthly Press, New York, 2005.

Currie, William E., *God's Little Errand Boy*, AMF anniversary booklet *100 Years of Blessing*, http://www.amfi.org/contact.htm.

Diamond, Sander A., *The Nazi Movement in the United States 1924–1941*, Disc-Us Books, www.disc-us.com, 2001.

Dye, Ira, *Uriah Levy: Reformer of the Antebellum Navy*, University Press of Florida, 2006.

Elsner, James B., *Hurricanes of the North Atlantic*, Oxford University Press, New York, 1999.

Federal Writer's Project, *New England Hurricane: A Factual Pictorial Record*, Hale, Cushman & Flint, Boston, 1938.

Gordon, Bernard L., *Hurricane in Southern New England*, The Book Shop, Watch Hill, Rhode Island, 1976.

Goudsouzian, Aram, *The Hurricane of 1938*, Commonwealth Editions, Beverly, Massachusetts, 2004.

Higham, Charles, *American Swastika*, Doubleday and Co, Garden City, New York, 1985.

Hitler, Adolf, *Mein Kampf*, Reynal and Hitchcock, New York, 1941.

Jenkins, Philip, *Hoods and Shirts*, The University of North Carolina Press, Chapel Hill, North Carolina, 1997.

Junger, Sebastian, *The Perfect Storm*, Harper Collins Press, New York, 1997.

Karp, Abraham, *From the Ends of the Earth – Judaic Treasures of the Library of Congress*, Library of Congress, Washington, D.C., 1991.

Knight, Jr., Vick, *Send for Haym Salomon*, Borden Publishing Company, Alhambra, California, 1976.

Lipset, Seymour Martin, *American Exceptionalism*, W. W. Norton and Co., New York, 1996.

Longshore, David, *Encyclopedia of Hurricanes, Typhoons, and Cyclones*, Checkmark Books, New York, 2000.

Marcus, Jacob Rader, *Early American Jewry: New York, New England, and Canada*, Vol. 1, The Jewish Publication Society of America, New York, 1951.

Marcus, Jacob Rader, *Early American Jewry: Pennsylvania and the South*, Vol. 2, The Jewish Publication Society of America, New York, 1953.

McTernan, John and Koenig, Bill, *Israel: The Blessing or the Curse*, Hearthstone Publishing, Oklahoma City, Oklahoma, 2001.

Miller, Marvin D., *Wunderlich's Salute*, Malamud-Rose Press, Smithtown, New York, 1983.

Minsinger, William E., *The 1938 Hurricane–An Historical and Pictorial Summary*, GreenHills Books, Vermont, 1988.

Obenzinger, Hilton, *In the Shadow of "God's Sun-dial,"* Stanford University, http://www.stanford.edu/group/SHR/5-1/text/obenzinger.html.

Oren, Michael B., *Power, Faith, and Fantasy: America in the Middle East 1776 to the Present*, W. W. Norton and Company, New York, 2007.

Perry, Margaret B., *The 1938 Hurricane As We Remember It*, Quogue Historical Society, Quogue, New York, 1995.

Providence Journal Co, *The Great Hurricane and Tidal Wave, Rhode Island*, Providence Journal Co. (No author, location, or date of publishing.)

Russell, Charles Edward, *Haym Salomon and the Revolution*, Cosmopolitan Book Corp., New York, 1930.

Sachar, Howard M., *A History of Jews in America*, Vintage Books, New York, 1992.

Scotti, R.A., *Sudden Sea*, Little Brown and Company, Boston, Massachusetts, 2003.

Magazines, Journals, and Miscellaneous Sources

Adolf Hitler Street, Yaphank, NY: New York State, County of Suffolk, Town of Brookhaven, map number 129, abstract 1238, filed January 5, 1937.

Ahern, John L. "Flood and Hurricane," New England Power Association, Boston, MA, 1938.

American Jewish Historical Society, "Mickey Marcus, Israel's American General." http://www.ajhs.org/publications/chapters/chapter.cfm?documentid=286.

AMF International, "The Blackstone Memorial." P.O. Box 5470, Lansing, IL 60438-5470, http://www.amfi.org/blackmem.htm.

Colton, F. Barrows, "The Geography of a Hurricane," *National Geographic Magazine*, Vol. LXXV, Number 4, National Geographic Society, Washington, D.C., April 1939.

Department of the Navy, Naval Historical Center, "War Plans and Preparations and Their Impact on U.S. Naval Operations in the Spanish-American War," http://www.history.navy.mil/wars/spanam.htm.

The Jewish Messenger, Volume 8, Number 25, 12/28/1861, article titled, "A Day of Prayer."

Jewish World Review, "Lincoln's Jewish Generals," February 16, 2001, http://www.jewishworldreview.com/herb/geduld1.asp.

Keppler, Joseph, "Cartoons and Comments," *Puck Magazine*, Volume 10, No. 247, Keppler and Schwarzmann, New York, November 30, 1881.

Legacy of the USS Monitor, "The Officers and Crew of the USS Monitor," 2001, http://home.att.net/~iron.clad/crew/MON_CREW.HTM.

Life Magazine, "Fascism in America," Time Inc, New York, Volume 6, Number 19, March 6, 1939, Page 57.

Mazelev, Julia, *Pogroms: Late Nineteenth, Beginning of Twentieth Century*, http://econc10.bu.edu/economic_systems/nationalidentity/fsu/russia/pogroms-naional_ident.

Military History Magazine, "David 'Mickey' Marcus," April 1998, http://www.historynet.com/magazines/military_history/3033716.html.

Mosier, Alvion P. Mosiers and Perraults Some Family History, *Life Abroad the USS Tennessee and Memphis*, http://www.delmars.com/family/mosier-a1.htm.

Puck Magazine, Volume 10, Number 247, November 30, 1881, New York.

Sarna, Jonathan D., *The Jewish Week*, "Faith and Freedom in the New World," http://www.thejewishweek.com/bottom/specialcontent.php3.

Truman Presidential Library, "Memo from President Truman stating that Israel's government had been finally recognized, May 14, 1948:" http://www.trumanlibrary.org/whistlestop/study_collections/israel/large/documents/index.php?documentdate=1948-05-14&documentid=48&collectionid=ROI&pagenumber=1.

United Nations, Resolution 181, November 29, 1947, The Avalon Project at Yale Law School: http://www.yale.edu/lawweb/avalon/un/res181.htm.

United States Sea Power 1865–On, Department of the Navy, Naval Historical Center, Washington, D.C. 20374, http://www.history.navy.mil/wars/spanam.htm.

The Virtual Library, *The American-Israeli Cooperative Enterprise*, "Americans React to Damascus Blood Libel," http://www.jewishvirtuallibrary.org.

Francis Salvador, Jewish Virtual Library, http://www.jewishvirtuallibray.org

Videos

Allen, Everett S. *A Wind to Shake the World – The Story of the 1938 Hurricane*, produced and directed by M. L. Baron, 1988.

Federal Works Agency, *The Shock Troops of Disaster – The Story of the New England Hurricane of September 21, 1938*, The Works Projects Administration, The Federal Work Agency.

George Bush Presidential Library, *President Bush Speaks at the Madrid Peace Conference*, October 30, 1991.

Public Education Against America: The Hidden Agenda
Marlin Maddoux

The US educational system has been hijacked! While America wasn't looking, Reading, Writing, and Arithmetic were largely replaced by Moral Relativism and Secular Humanism in our public schools and universities. Radio talk show legend Marlin Maddoux exposes the plots and methods used by the academic elite to capture the hearts, minds, and values of the next generation. Through the use of "political correctness" on college campuses, Moral Relativism in high school sex ed classes, brainwashing techniques starting in kindergarten, and much more, Maddoux reveals how public education has eroded the faith and values of American children in an ongoing effort to create a godless, humanistic society. Thoroughly researched and documented, this is one book that every taxpayer, parent, and college student must read!

ISBN: 978-0-88368-813-7 • Hardcover • 288 pages

www.whitakerhouse.com

10 Curses That Block the Blessing

Larry Huch

Have you been suffering with depression, family dysfunction, marital unhappiness, or other problems and been unable to overcome them? Within the pages of this groundbreaking book, *10 Curses That Block the Blessing,* Larry Huch shares his personal experience with a life of anger, drug addiction, crime, and violence. He shows how he broke these curses and reveals how you can recognize the signs of a curse, be set free from generational curses, and restore your health and wealth. You don't have to struggle any longer. Choose to revolutionize your life. You can reverse the curses that block your blessings!

ISBN: 978-0-88368-207-4 • Trade • 272 pages

www.whitakerhouse.com

Protection from Deception
Derek Prince

According to Scripture, supernatural signs and wonders will multiply as we approach the end times. God isn't the only one with a plan, however—Satan is plotting to deceive believers with supernatural signs and wonders of his own. With relentless deceptions, the devil tries to keep us from the divine love and protection of God. But what can we do? In *Protection from Deception*, renowned Bible scholar Derek Prince will equip you to test the source of supernatural signs and wonders, discern truth from falsehood, distinguish between the Holy Spirit and counterfeit spirits, and break free from the strongholds of Satan. You, too, can uncover the enemy's strategies, effectively engage in spiritual battles—and WIN!

ISBN: 978-0-88368-230-2 • Trade • 240 pages

www.whitakerhouse.com